on track ...

The Yardbirds

every album, every song

Andrew Darlington

sonicbondpublishing.com

Sonicbond Publishing Limited
www.sonicbondpublishing.co.uk
Email: info@sonicbondpublishing.co.uk

First Published in the United Kingdom 2025
First Published in the United States 2025

British Library Cataloguing in Publication Data:
A Catalogue record for this book is available from the British Library

ISBN 978-1-78952-362-1

Typeset in ITC Garamond Std & ITC Avant Garde Gothic
Printed and bound in England

Graphic design and typesetting: Full Moon Media

Follow us on social media:
Twitter: https://twitter.com/SonicbondP
Instagram: www.instagram.com/sonicbondpublishing_/
Facebook: www.facebook.com/SonicbondPublishing/
Linktree QR code:

Dedication
For Cathy, who didn't really like The Yardbirds very much.

on track ...
The Yardbirds

Contents

Author's Note

This book is largely about The Yardbirds, both the 1960s group and the much later version from the late 1990s and early 2000s. The band was, of course, a launching point for the careers of many other artists. The solo work of Jeff Beck, Eric Clapton and Jimmy Page is not mentioned here, although Led Zeppelin – who for a while went under the name The New Yardbirds – are mentioned in passing, as is the surprise return of 'Top' Topham. After the Yardbirds split, Keith Relf and Jim McCarty formed the first lineup of Renaissance, and their two albums are dealt with here in detail. Following Relf's death in 1976, McCarty continued that band as Illusion for two further recordings and while these are referred to, their rather more tangential relationship to the source band means that I have not covered those albums in detail.

A Most Blueswailing Introduction

Your trusty *Guinness Book Of Hit Singles* lists just five shiny top-ten hits for The Yardbirds, from Graham Gouldman's tempo-shuffling, bongo-powered 'For Your Love' in March 1965 through to the sharp Bill Haley-esque rhythms of 'Over Under Sideways Down' little over 15 months later. Two more of their vinyl 45rpms barely scratched the top 50. They only ever recorded one proper studio album – *The Yardbirds* aka *Roger The Engineer*. It sold modestly well, only peaking at number 20, although it continues to sell. Over the long decades since the group's demise, innumerable forgotten and mostly ignored names have equalled such a score and achieved far greater commercial success. Yet, there are now more CD anthologies and compilations on Amazon than there ever were during The Yardbirds' brief lifetime. Furthermore, people still write about them. Prior to Alan Clayson's well-researched history-trip *The Yardbirds* (2003, Backbeat Books), there was a 1983 *Yardbirds* (from Sidgwick & Jackson), a clippings-rich, archive-plundering volume with a wealth of memorabilia spattering its pages, produced by the band's Chris Dreja (rhythm guitar) and Jim McCarty (drums), with *Comstock Lode*'s John Platt on board for editorial assistance.

Reasons for all this continued high-profile interest are not immediately obvious. Slavering critics used to point out the group's Eric Clapton, Jeff Beck (Malcolm McLaren's 'the Paganini of the guitar') and Jimmy Page Family Tree lineage. But guitar heroes are now a devalued commodity. The New Yardbirds' transition into Led Zeppelin still has slight currency value, despite the tenuous sound continuity – Robert Plant's raunchy swagger is light-years from Keith Relf's high nervous adenoidal whine or to Clayson, 'barely the 'Mannish Boy' that Muddy Waters bragged about being.' So, a large part of their continuing appeal must be their temporal positioning as a technicolour band in a monochrome era, an exact spacetime nexus that is trapped onto legendary celluloid by that incandescent 'Stroll On' *Blow-Up* movie-clip of rock's most mutationally exciting moment, a film-clip that catches The Yardbirds at a moment of huge cultural change. After all, The Yardbirds' hits were acting directly against The Who, The Kinks and The Small Faces at their most innovative. And that's before you even get to The Beatles and The Stones. The Yardbirds were there on 'Ready Steady Go'. They were there at psychedelia's first Dayglo quivers. Peter Green told me of his awed fixation with Paul Samwell-Smith's bass while watching the Five Live Yardbirds at their most blues-wailingest at Giorgio Gomelsky's 'Crawdaddy Club'. They were cool r&b cult. They were effortless art-school class. They were a high of blissful nostalgia for mod anoraks.

Of course, as a teenager, I loved The Yardbirds for their ability to compress a 'progressive shape-of-things to come' vision – not into tediously pretentious concept albums, but with precise and enticingly strange two-and-a-half minute singles structured into immaculately segmented moments of tantalisingly evocative weirdness until 'only restrictions such as the common chord and rock instrumentation put much of their music in the realm of 'pop' at all.' Until, by the time they were recording the *Roger The Engineer* album – in less than a week on a primitive four-track machine – they were still pop in the way that Russ Conway and Thelonius Monk were both still pianists. To Alan Clayson, too, I guess. His appreciation 'mutated into a craving, an obsession, almost a religion' with an 'attic floor groaning beneath the weight of vinyl, tapes and memorabilia.' And he remained loyal to what was left of the group (Relf died aged just 33 in May 1976) through their fall-out Renaissance and Box of Frogs bands, and their continuing reformations with other 1960s remnants. Hence, his book is a 'rather personal telling' of their story, more 'an extended meditation than a strict chronological biography.'

But it's one rich with images of a young Jeff Beck struggling with chord shapes from Bert Weedon's *Play In A Day* manual. To The Yardbirds backing a bowler-hatted Sonny Boy Williamson – who could play harmonica with his nose, then chew the Benzedrine from Vick inhalers to get high. To the young Yardbirds listening to Howlin' Wolf. To them improvising extended instrumental 'rave-ups' in 'scruffy jive-hives'. Then to them teasing the visionary hit single 'Shapes Of Things' 'from nothing more than a riff' at the Chicago 2120 South Michigan Avenue's 'Chess' Studios, and the backing tracks for its B-side, 'You're A Better Man Than I', with Sam Phillips at 'Sun' in Memphis. All the way to The Yardbirds' inevitably messy end.

In his book, Alan Clayson's appendix provides a taste-sensitive day-by-day 'Yardbirds Diary' covering the period 1 June 1963 to 31 October 1968, an all-too-brief window in time that took the Yardies from 'Eel Pie Island' supporting The Cyril Davies Blues All-Stars through itemised time-fixed dates at legendary venues such as the Manchester 'Twisted Wheel' and 'The Marquee'. From the 'Ricky Tick' to the Leeds 'Majestic'. Through the Hull ABC, sharing a tour-package bill with The Kinks and The Ronettes, to manager Peter Grant negotiating the final contract with Atlantic Records in New York for what would be *Led Zeppelin 1*. You can check out exactly where they were and what they were doing on your birthday, when you lost your cherry, or perhaps to confirm the date, time and venue when your lives briefly intersected. Perhaps you actually saw them live? Or perhaps you weren't even born?

In which case, that provides all the more reason for you to buy this book, to learn just exactly what you've missed out on!

A Most Blueswailing History

As esteemed music journalist, Lillian Roxon, pointed out in her *Rock Encyclopedia* (Grosset & Dunlap, 1971) that 'in late 1963/early 1964, when the English 'scene' was having its birth pangs, The Yardbirds followed The Rolling Stones into the 'Crawdaddy Club' (by day the somewhat staid Richmond Cricket Club) as house band.' This is the root of the legend.

The Rolling Stones had been signed by Dick Rowe to Decca Records, they'd appeared on ABC-TV's *Thank Your Lucky Stars* pop show, and by September 1963, their debut single, 'Come On', had charted and climbed as high as a UK number 21. Suddenly, they were moving up and out. Suddenly, they were too big to play small venues anymore.

So, there seemed to be a natural progression, a kind of inevitability about the rise of The Yardbirds from that point on. As Roxon says, 'like the early Stones, they (The Yardbirds) used standard material – Bo Diddley, Isley Brothers, Muddy Waters, Sonny Boy Williamson – always remaining more faithful to the original than the improvisational/variation-prone Stones. This was important at a time when the concept of original material was not as overworked as it was to become in 1967-69. Also, man for man, The Yardbirds were better instrumentalists than The Stones were then.'

Although there had been school-age rock 'n' roll groups for the soon-to-be members, such as The Strollers and the Country Gentlemen, the original Yardbirds came out of a parent group called The Metropolis Blues Quartet – sometimes referred to as The Metropolitan Blues Quartet (MBQ). Keith listened to the Modern Jazz Quartet, abbreviated as the MJQ. Formed at the Kingston Art School, it featured Chris Dreja (born in Surbiton on 11 November 1945) on rhythm guitar, Paul 'Sam' Samwell-Smith (born in Brentford on 8 May 1943) on bass, Jim McCarty (born in Liverpool on 25 July 1943, but grew up in Teddington) on drums and Keith Relf (born in Richmond, Surrey, on 22 March 1943) doing vocals. They were joined by a very straight-looking crew-cut Eric Clapton, who played lead guitar, and they became The Yardbirds. At that time, the mods – or 'modernists' – followed The Who, The Action and The Small Faces, but the more discerning blues purist mods also steered their Vespa and Lambretta scooters towards the 'Crawdaddy' to catch The Yardbirds. And although The Yardbirds may well have been better musicians in the 1963-64 period, The Rolling Stones were arguably more charismatic performers, as a result of which their rival fan-factions used to fight it out, rather bitterly at times.

There was also Anthony 'Top' Topham (born on 3 July 1947 in Southall) in that formative lineup. His father had a collection of r&b records, which Chris and 'Top' were permitted to listen to. 'I went ballistic when I heard the electric sounds of Jimmy Reed,' Chris told biographer Alan Clayson, 'it wasn't regimented. It was pure emotion, feel. That was probably what shaped me forever – and partly what shaped The Yardbirds, too.' Topham became written into The Yardbirds legend by quitting – in October 1963 – before they ever got to record, returning to college, and thereby making way for Eric Clapton (born on 30 March 1945), who had been playing with a rival r&b group called The Roosters.

A feature in *The Daily Mail* on 2 March 1964 claimed the Crawdaddy 'should be called the southern equivalent of Liverpool's Cavern. The Rolling Stones started their career there, but now they've moved on to higher things. The Yardbirds will soon be whisked away on the elevator of fame. Or so they say.'

In retrospect, the British Blues Boom was a strange and unlikely phenomenon, with skinny white youths earnestly attempting to replicate the sound of old black American blues musicians, learning licks and techniques from old hoarded scratchy records, traded and shared in a kind of cult code with others of a similar ilk.

Mick Jagger met Keith Richards on 17 October 1961 on platform two of Dartford railway station. They recognised each other because they'd both gone to Wentworth Primary School before Jagger went on to study at Dartford Grammar. But more than that, Keith was carrying his guitar and Mick was carrying two albums, Chuck Berry's *Rockin' At The Hops* and *The Best Of Muddy Waters*. That was the unifying catalyst.

In much the same way, during May 1963, Anthony Topham and his secondary school friend Chris Dreja visited the Railway Hotel located at the junction of Coombe Road and Station Road close by the Norbiton Tube station and Kingston-upon-Thames, where the upstairs music lounge featured trad jazz sessions, with the option for local musicians to jam together during intermissions in the scheduled sets. It was here they happened to meet up with fellow enthusiasts Relf, McCarty and Samwell-Smith. McCarty and Samwell-Smith were still pupils at Hampton Grammar School, where they'd formed a group called The Country Gentlemen – named after a Gretsch guitar favoured by Chet Atkins. They'd even taped a song written by Paul with older brother Brian, called 'With Love', which led to a failed audition with EMI's John Schroeder during the autumn of 1961. Meanwhile, Dreja and Relf were studying at Kingston School of Art.

The new band held their first rehearsals at the Railway Hotel in Norbiton, where – as Chris recalls – the group 'became very good very quickly.' They upgraded to the South Western Hotel in Richmond, which became their regular rehearsal spot, close by the old Station Hotel, which had hosted The Rolling Stones' early Crawdaddy gigs. There were inevitable crossovers. Both bands drew material from the same pool of original r&b artists, although The Yardbirds deliberately selected songs that The Stones neglected. And where The Rolling Stones' sets were tightly structured, from their beginning, The Yardbirds featured the free-form open-ended 'Rave-up' improvisations that were always to be their speciality.

The issue of *Fabulous* magazine dated 26 September 1964 included a neat little free 52-page book called *Alan Freeman's Mini-Pop Guide*, which offered concise pen-portraits of the group members. 'Vocalist Keith Relf resembles Brian Jones of The Stones with his long fair hair and delicate features. Rhythm guitar is handled by fair-haired Chris Dreja. Paul Samwell-Smith, usually called Sam, is the bass player. Lead guitar is Eric Clapton. Eric wears American Ivy League suits and keeps his hair short, as do all The Birds except Keith. Jim McCarty is the handsome, dark-haired drummer.' Collectively, 'their way-out music has the fans hanging from the rafters.'

Oddly, the trad jazz connection is relevant. The post-war austerity years of the uptight conformist 1950s were enlivened by a boom in home-grown Dixieland or New Orleans jazz from which many of the attitudes and cult exclusivity of the blues fraternity would derive. The Chris Barber band were responsible for arranging and promoting the first UK tours for Muddy Waters, the amazing Sister Rosetta Tharpe, Big Bill Broonzy and Sonny Terry & Brownie McGhee, tours that provided British audiences with their first opportunity to see such exotic artists perform live. The Barber band also accidentally kicked off the skiffle craze when Lonnie Donegan's 'Rock Island Line' was spun off from Chris Barber's 1955 *New Orleans Joys* 10" LP (Decca LF1198). The single sent shockwaves through a music scene dominated by staid crooners and dreary balladeers, and motivated DIY amateurs across the country to hunt out Huddie 'Lead Belly' Ledbetter, Woody Guthrie and Big Bill Broonzy songs to flesh out their scanty repertoire.

The Ken Colyer band had a more hard-line Stalinist approach to what was and what wasn't 'authentic', despite many of the original American jazz musicians themselves enjoying a quite playful openness to their instrumentation and presentation. As a merchant seaman, Colyer had jumped ship in America and played in New Orleans, which granted him a degree of awed authority within trad jazz circles, and it was that quest for 'purity' that he transmitted down the genetic timeline to the young blues pretenders.

Cyril Davies and the mighty Alexis Korner both came from trad or skiffle backgrounds but gravitated towards specialising in Chicago-style blues, with Davies' harmonica technique heavily influenced by hearing Little Walter. To novelist Michael Moorcock in 2024's *The Woods Of Arcady*, they 'passed their lore down to us, the beginnings of what would become The Stones and The Yardbirds.' It was Korner and Davies who launched what they named the 'London Blues & Barrelhouse Club' that ran from 1957 to 1961 at the 'Round House' pub in Wardour Street, Soho, which soon became a meeting place for devotees who came to watch performers such as Champion Jack Dupree or Ramblin' Jack Elliott.

Then, again through Chris Barber's good graces, their Blues Incorporated band – claimed to be Britain's first amplified r&b group with Long John Baldry and Art Wood (older brother of Ronnie Wood) – as well as Korner and Davies, got to play regular spots at the 'Marquee' before relocating operations by founding the 'Ealing Club' in March 1962 as a regular 'Rhythm & Blues Night'. This rapidly became the focus for numerous embryonic wannabes inspired by their gritty example, numbering future-Animal Eric Burdon, who hitchhiked all the way south from Newcastle, Pretty Things' Dick Taylor, plus Paul Jones, Jack Bruce, Zoot Money, Rod Stewart, Graham Bond and Dick Heckstall-Smith. Jazz-literate Ginger Baker played with Blues Incorporated. The Mann-Hugg Blues Band played at the Club, and The Rolling Stones debuted there. It became a spawning ground for everything that would follow.

Long John Baldry was known to have an extensive collection of blues records, and through his natural generosity, aspiring musicians used his collection as a library from which to draw material. To McCarty, 'there were only really about two Chuck Berry albums, *Jimmy Reed At Carnegie Hall*, a Howlin' Wolf album – *Moanin' In The Moonlight* – and a Slim Harpo one. And that was about it.'

And then there was Giorgio Gomelsky. To Rod Stewart, commenting in *Rod: The Autobiography* (Arrow Books, 2013), the heavyweight Georgian émigré 'was one of the pivotal figures in British pop music – a big bloke on the scene, and a big bloke literally, with a tubby stomach, a lot of presence and a throaty eastern European accent.' Gomelsky was a sometime documentary film editor who doubled as an after-hours music promoter on the London jazz circuit: 'He had persuaded the Marquee to stage a weekly blues night in a period when there was outright hostility to the idea among the trad jazz purists.' A sometime jazz journalist turned entrepreneur, he wrote in *Jazzbeat* magazine in 1964 under the headline 'Is There A Rhythm & Blues Boom?' The answer was a fairly obvious 'yes'.

During the early months of 1963, he opportunistically took over the back room of the 'Station Hotel' in Richmond as a venue for what he named 'The Crawdaddy Club' – lifting the name from a Bo Diddley song. He installed The Dave Hunt Rhythm & Blues Band from his previous club in central London's Piccadilly as the first house band (The Kinks' Ray Davies played guitar with the band for 'about six weeks'). The Dave Hunt band were replaced as early as February by The Rolling Stones, who caused such a sensation that they were also booked for a slot at the 'Eel Pie Island' club, while the 'Crawdaddy' had to find a larger venue in order to accommodate the audience demand of mods and art-school beatnik types. Gomelsky settled on the Clubhouse of the Richmond Athletic Ground until The Rolling Stones moved up and out ... to be replaced by The Yardbirds! A Friday night set would earn the group a respectable £120.

McCarty was taken by surprise when Cyril Davies enquired what their group was called prior to their first Eel Pie gig, and Keith promptly volunteered 'The Yardbirds'. It was a title Keith claimed he'd plucked from the Beat Generation novels of Jack Kerouac, although it was a name widely venerated in jazz circles because of bebop innovator Charlie Parker. At Art School in 1960, Charlie Watts had written and illustrated a small book, *Ode To A High Flying Bird*, about Parker, which was published in January 1965 (Beat Publications). So, it was a name in insider circulation.

The Yardbirds played all-nighters with Downliners Sect at a basement club in Great Newport Street called Studio 51, and they played the Railway Hotel in Harrow after first standing in there for Cyril Davies. Jim was still working in the 'city' for stockbrokers Phillips & Drew, but once Eric Clapton joined the lineup, the group moved collectively into an old house in Kew, renting the top floor for an intense period of bonding. Keith's father, Bill, drove the group to gigs in his plumber's Ford van.

'Over in Richmond, down the way from Twickenham and placed conveniently opposite the Railway Station, was the Crawdaddy Club,' recalled Rod Stewart, 'nothing more than the back room of a pub, but a sensational place to be when it was packed with people jumping around and going nuts. It was where I saw and loved The Yardbirds. They had a guitarist called Eric Clapton, who didn't seem too shoddy. The Crawdaddy had to close eventually because it got a bit too rowdy, but everyone simply shifted over to the Richmond Athletic Club, where there was no stage, and the audience could get right in a band's face. Incredible atmosphere.'

Years later, Keith recalled to Nick Watts in *Melody Maker* that 'the best days we had were with Eric (Clapton) at the Crawdaddy, when it had not got far enough to become so serious.' He went on to point out that temperamental guitarist Eric is 'cynical, but then he always has been, right from the start with The Yardbirds. He wanted a measure of obscurity to work in.' Keith's observation was to prove prescient.

The astute Gomelsky maximised his profits by setting up complementary gigs at the Croydon 'Star Hotel' public house, with the upwardly mobile Yardbirds headlining. On 8 December 1963, at Richmond, he taped a set by visiting Bluesman Sonny Boy Williamson II with The Yardbirds playing back-up. This was part of a short tour in which The Yardbirds also played with Sonny Boy at the 'Star Hotel' and at the Birmingham Town Hall. Although unreleased at the time, those tapes would finally be released in January 1966, by which time, The Yardbirds would be considered a hot commercial property.

But all that still lay in the future. Meanwhile, acting in his capacity as their manager, 'Big Daddy Crawdaddy' Gomelsky used a demo tape to hawk his protégés around the major record labels. Wrongfooted when EMI had scooped up the Brian Epstein stable, Decca had been on a signing spree and already had more beat groups than they could handle. But EMI's Columbia took the new group on...

Right: The Yardbirds of the hits. Paul Samwell-Smith (upper left), Keith Relf, Chris Dreja, Jim McCarty, with a crouching Jeff Beck. (*Alamy*)

Below: With a grinning Eric Clapton, The Yardbirds perform for Lord Willis in 1964. (*Alamy*)

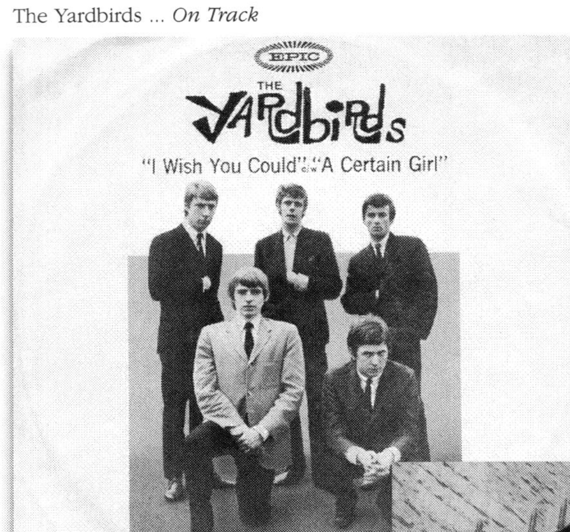

Left: Where it all began. The Yardbirds' debut American single, 'I Wish You Would'. (*Columbia/Epic*)

Right: The most blues-wailing lineup for the classic *Five Live Yardbirds* album. (*Columbia*)

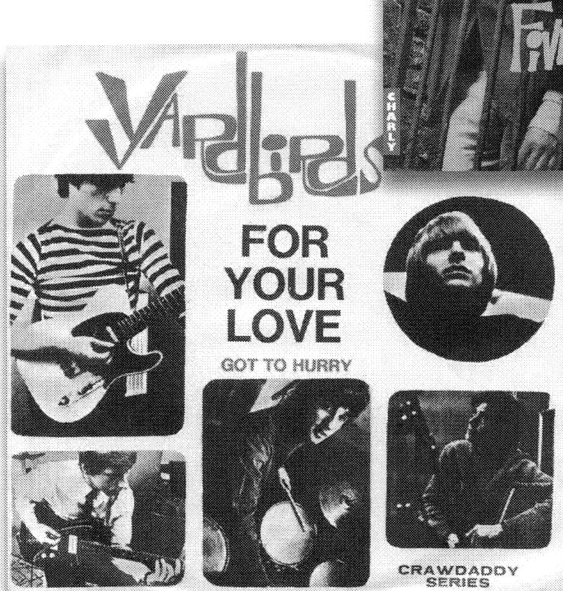

Left: The Italian edition of 'For Your Love', showing Jeff Beck, although it's Eric Clapton who plays on the single. (*Columbia/Epic/Ricordi*)

Right: The American sleeve of 'Heart Full Of Soul' shows Eric Clapton, although Jeff Beck plays on the record. (*Columbia/ Epic*)

Left: The American *For Your Love* album sleeve, with Jeff Beck pictured at the piano. (*Epic*)

Right: The highly collectable *Five Yardbirds* UK EP includes 'My Girl Sloopy'. (*Columbia*)

Above: Unmistakably, the live Yardbirds on set, with Eric Clapton. (*Mediapunch/Shutterstock*)

Below: Sometimes, even blues bands must pose for embarrassing publicity

The Dramatis Personae

Geoffrey Arnold Beck (24 June 1944 – 10 January 2023)
Eric Patrick Clapton (born on 30 March 1945)
Chris Walenty Dreja (born on 11 November 1945)
Giorgio Sergio Alessando Gomelsky (28 February 1934 – 1 January 2016)
James Stanley McCarty (born on 25 July 1943)
James Patrick Page (born on 9 January 1944)
William Keith Relf (22 March 1943 – 12 May 1976)
Paul Granville Samwell-Smith (born on 8 May 1943)
Anthony 'Top' Topham (3 July 1947 – 2 January 2023)

Early Singles

The First Yardbirds Single – 'I Wish You Would'

'I Wish You Would' (Billy Boy Arnold) 2:19 b/w **'A Certain Girl'**
(N Neville) 2:15
Personnel:
Keith Relf: lead vocals
Eric 'Slowhand' Clapton: lead guitar
Chris Dreja: rhythm guitar
Jim McCarty: drums
Paul Samwell-Smith: bass guitar
Produced by Giorgio Gomelsky at Olympic Studio during late March/early
April 1964
Released: 1 May 1964 (UK), 17 August 1964 (US)
Columbia DB7283 (UK), Epic 5-9709 (US)
No chart position

A small, bizarre, box-shaped advert on page four of *Record Mirror* on 9 May
1964 announced in the distinctively scrawled typeface that artist/photographer
Hamish Grimes had designed for them that 'Yardbirds are not very good to
eat, but they play r&b with good taste!' with the title 'I Wish You Would'
appended below. It was an attention-grabbing device designed to hook the
curious. The following issue carried an equally brain-teasing page 14 box-ad,
'Everymody Loves Yardbirds, Everymody Loves Crawdaddy, Every Yardbird
Loves Crawdaddy, Big Daddy Crawdaddy Loves Yardbirds, Everymody Loves 'I
Wish You Would', Infact, Everymody Loves Everymody!' ('mody' being code for
a mod). Poignantly, the same page carried Peter-Jones's New Faces feature
about the arrival on the scene of bluesbreaker John Mayall.

A rather fuller run-down introducing The Yardbirds followed in the 30 May
issue, claiming that 'Eric (Clapton) is one of the most fashionable dressers in
showbiz. In fact, The Yardbirds in general are regarded as the most
fashionable group, but fashion-leader Eric is often accosted by mod girls who
blandly accuse him of being 'one of the top faces'… everybody knows three
feet make a yard, but *every moddy* knows that ten feet make The Yardbirds.'

A few short years earlier, Columbia had been EMI's most important label with
a chart domination of Britain's best-selling group, The Shadows and their top
male vocalist Cliff Richard, as well as Helen Shapiro, who was the biggest
female singer of the time. The Merseybeat upsurge had capsized that cosy
arrangement. Columbia had signed Freddie & The Dreamers, The Animals and
The Dave Clark Five. But they were still in need of new blood. The Yardbirds'
record came in a uniform green sleeve – no picture sleeves yet – while the label
on the record itself was black with silver lettering, with a big 45 in the upper
right side to indicate the correct speed to play it at – as if we needed telling!

Drop the stylus into the groove, and after only the slightest surface-hiss,
there's the most blueswailing harmonica, a propulsive bassline, a repetitive,
nagging guitar riff, Keith's high nasal voice caught up in a cavernous echoey

Olympic Studios performance, with Giorgio Gomelsky taking producer credits. And it's done in virtually one live take in just ten minutes. Only the sound levels needed balancing against each other. The Yardbirds were playing safe by taking a highlight of their stage set at the time, where it was extended with lengthy improvisations suited to the mood. However, the song was severely edited and compressed down to create the group's debut 7" single, with Keith taking Billy Boy Arnold's lyric about wishing his girl would come back at a frantic beat-group pace. David Bowie would later tribute The Yardbirds by including 'I Wish You Would' on his 1973 *Pin-Ups* album.

Billy Boy Arnold would play the *American Blues Legend* UK tour during the summer of 1975 when he spoke of how it was only when The Yardbirds picked up on his 'I Wish You Would' that his name became known outside of a circle of cognoscenti: 'I got a whole lot of recognition out of that, nothing financially, but a lot of recognition.'

Now, flip the record over, drop the stylus into the B-side groove. Written under alias by New Orleans tunesmith Allen Toussaint and first recorded in October 1961 by Ernie K Doe, 'A Certain Girl' has Keith bragging about the chick he's been sweet on for a long, long time, but when the backing voices (said to include Gomelsky himself) ask 'what's her name', he responds, 'I can't tell you' – he can't repeat her name until he gets her. As with the A-side, there's wailing harmonica driven by solid rhythms, with a brief but precise Eric Clapton guitar solo. It's a quality flip making a value-for-money coupling that attracted positive radio and press attention, without actually charting.

Things were happening quickly. During February, The Yardbirds recorded three tracks during their first studio session. Then, they played on a bill at the Birmingham Town Hall as part of its first 'Rhythm & Blues' Festival with Sonny Boy Williamson on Friday 28 February. They made their TV debut for Granada in Manchester, on the same bill as American folk trio Peter, Paul & Mary, then they played the snappily titled *Discs A Go Go* for TV West & Wales in Bristol, introduced by wrestling pundit Kent Walton. But *Ready Steady Go!* was as good as it got, and they played 'I Wish You Would' live on the edition broadcast on Friday 22 May, alongside bland balladeer Mark Wynter and the self-proclaimed 'Quasar Of Rock' Little Richard, the King & Queen of Rock 'n' Roll. On Thursday 18 June 1964, The Yardbirds travelled north to play the Manchester 'Twisted Wheel' mod club, with Bill Relf driving the van, as well as the famous Liverpool Cavern Club on a bill with Jimmy Powell & The Five Dimensions, plus rocker and future-comedian Freddie Starr. Admission was just 2/6d.

There was also a bizarre 'happening' that promoted the Yardbirds name into national newspapers. Labour Party peer Lord Ted Willis – creator of the BBC's safe cop-show *Dixon Of Dock Green* and the adaptation of *The Adventures Of Black Beauty* for ITV (as well as the screenplay for Norman Wisdom's 1953 film *Trouble In Store*) – had spoken out in the House Of Lords criticising crass pop music as disposable 'candyfloss culture'. Giorgio Gomelsky's tyro

PR man Greg Tesser hatched the idea of using The Yardbirds for a retaliatory promo-stunt, which saw the five-piece turning up uninvited at Willis' grand Chislehurst, Kent home on the May Bank Holiday afternoon in order to gatecrash and play an impromptu guerrilla performance on his front lawn. From photographic evidence, the event seems to have resulted in a remarkably good-natured confrontation, with a catalyst provided by 14-year-old daughter Sally Murray (née Willis), who remembered in a letter featured in *Word* #16 in June 2004 that 'they played two or three songs and people just drifted along from neighbouring houses to see what was going on. Unfortunately, another neighbour complained, and after a few songs, they had to stop. What a great day for me and my mother, who had shown Eric round the house, (who) always says, with her tongue in her cheek, that she had Eric Clapton in her bedroom.' It was a clash of cultures that reaped healthy tabloid coverage in *The Daily Mirror*, while even the staid *Daily Telegraph* ran the story with a photo, although they insisted on referring to the group as 'The Yardsticks'!

Around the same time, the casual music-paper browser may have glanced at a 'New Names' feature in the 25 April 1964 *Record Mirror* issue noting the release of a single, 'Baja' b/w 'A Foggy Day In Vietnam' (Pye 7N15637), produced by Andrew Loog Oldham and featuring 'the bass guitarist with the Tony Meehan Group', who was 18-year-old John Paul Jones from Sidcup, Kent. Jones would play a part in The Yardbirds' story ... and in Led Zeppelin afterwards.

The Second Yardbirds Single – 'Good Morning Little Schoolgirl'
'Good Morning Little Schoolgirl' (H Demarias) 2:47 b/w **'I Ain't Got You'** (Calvin Carter) 2:01
Produced by Giorgio Gomelsky at Olympic studio between August and September 1964
Released: 30 October 1964
Columbia DB 7391. No US release
Highest chart position: UK: 44
The issue of *Fabulous* magazine, dated 14 November 1964, carried an intriguing snippet:

> Fans of The Yardbirds who have been getting more and more impatient waiting for a follow-up to the group's first disc, released five months ago, can now relax. Out this week is 'Good Morning Little Schoolgirl' (Columbia) – and I can report that the disc was worth waiting for. The reason for the delay was, in fact, because lead singer and harmonica player Keith Rolf (sic) had collapsed with a punctured lung, and it was two months before he was fit enough to be able to record.

Keith had suffered from chronic asthma all his life, almost dying during an attack at the age of three. When the girls screamed for The Yardbirds, they screamed for frail Keith, who, to Alan Clayson, 'looked as if he needed mothering.' Keith always carried an inhaler, on occasions resorting to using it on stage mid-song. But the long recuperation from his collapsed lung had not been allowed to slow the group's upward mobility. Mick O'Neill from The Authentics acted as stand-in vocalist, even for their prestigious slot at the Fourth Richmond Jazz/Blues Festival on Sunday 9 August 1964. For the benefit of readers with short attention spans, *Fabulous* added that 'The Yardbirds, you may remember, are the group who took over from The Rolling Stones at The Crawdaddy Rhythm & Blues Club in Richmond. They recently toured the country with Billy J Kramer and received a tremendous reception from audiences of all ages. 'Good Morning', a very catchy ditty, could be their first hit.'

The Billy J Kramer tour opened at the Walthamstow 'Granada' theatre on 18 September, with Cliff Bennett & The Rebel Rousers on the bill, as well as The Nashville Teens and The Yardbirds. The 'package tour' was a rite of passage for 1960s pop, which allowed upcoming acts exposure to nationwide audiences, although down-bill names were only allotted a timeslot sufficient for three or four numbers, hardly an appropriate vehicle for The Yardbirds, who specialised in a long improvisational set building to intense climaxes. Yet, it led to a one-off concert at the Brighton Hippodrome on Sunday 22 November supporting rock 'n' roll wild man Jerry Lee Lewis, alongside Popstrel Twinkle – who had a hit death-disc with 'Terry' – plus The Sack O' Woes, The Quiet Five and The Worryin' Kind.

The Yardbirds recorded the 'Good Morning Little Schoolgirl' song twice, first as a studio single, then as an in-concert track on the *Five Live Yardbirds* album. The two performances are largely similar, though the Marquee version benefits from the energy of the audience feedback. Keith's harmonica is strongly featured on both. For the flip, they selected 'I Ain't Got You', which had been recorded in 1960 by Jimmy Reed. In a tongue-in-cheek way, it stacks up all the things he has – a Maserati GT, a closet full of clothes, a tavern and a liquor store – against the one thing he doesn't have ... which is 'you'. Keith has a mojo, women to the left of him, women to the right of him ... and some cutting blasts of harmonica. It has a raw sound with little production gloss, but boasts a stinging Clapton guitar solo.

Meanwhile, in another part of town, young Rod Stewart switched from his night job with Jimmy Powell's Five Dimensions to become the second vocalist with Long John Baldry's Hoochie Coochie Men. As that group broke up, Rod took time out to cut a solo single ('Good Morning Little Schoolgirl' b/w 'I'm Gonna Move To The Outskirts Of Town' for Decca F11996, October 1964), with a young John Paul Jones playing session bass. The Yardbirds issued their own version of the same lasciviously risqué Sonny Boy Williamson blues standard at the same time, which divided sales to the extent that neither made the impact they might otherwise have done. Its visibility was further hampered by BBC radio's timidity regarding the prurient lyrical content. As a result, The Yardbirds' single limped into the chart at number 49 on 12 November, the week that Roy Orbison's 'Oh, Pretty Woman' was holding the top slot. 'Good Morning Little Schoolgirl' stayed there for a second week before dropping out. The single did marginally better on the charts published by other music magazines.

Five Live Yardbirds

Personnel:
Keith Relf: lead vocals (except on 'Good Morning Little Schoolgirl'), harmonica, maracas
Eric 'Slowhand' Clapton: lead guitar, co-vocals on 'Good Morning Little Schoolgirl'
Chris Dreja: rhythm guitar
Jim McCarty: drums
Paul Samwell-Smith: bass guitar, co-vocals on 'Good Morning Little Schoolgirl'
Recorded live at The Marquee Club on 20 March 1964
Producer: Giorgio Gomelsky, with Phillip Wood engineering
Released: 4 December 1964. No US release in this form
Columbia 33SX 1662
No chart position

On 19 December 1964, *Fabulous* magazine carried a brief blink-and-you-miss-it note in a column credited to Ken Bow: 'A real treat for fans of The Yardbirds is their first long player, *Five Live Yardbirds* (Columbia), containing ten prime examples of the kind of r&b that's building up such a reputation for the boys.'

The sleeve photo has become iconic across the years and decades since its first release, with the group shot in a stark, urban alleyway seen behind ill-repaired, chain-padlocked railings, Keith Relf to the left, with Chris partially eclipsed behind a smiling, neatly-combed Clapton, who stands to the centre, Paul Samwell-Smith to the right, with Jim McCarty crouching.

The monochrome liner photos on the reverse show Relf and Clapton looking painfully schoolboy young. The text, by Gomelsky, is headed by a large quote in the distinctive Yardbirds lettering: 'If Only We Had A…' or 'Confussion He Say: Too Much Vagueness Maketh A Song' (his spelling!). His prose style is equally impressionistic as he tells the tale of how the album was recorded, the build-up as 'mody-body' people wander about the red-&-white stripes of the so-far empty late-afternoon Marquee club. The engineer bewails the lack of some 'ortophonic, omnidirectional, inter-coaxial plugs' as 'Keith Yardbird' paints a set-list sign that reads 'Monkey-Love-Schoolgirls-Smoke-Respectable' as song-prompts.

According to Bruce Eder of Allmusic, '*Five Live Yardbirds* was the first important – indeed, essential – live album to come out of the 1960s British rock 'n' roll boom. In terms of the performance captured and the recording quality, it was also the best such live record of the entire middle of the decade. Cut at a Marquee Club show in 1964, Five Live Yardbirds was a popular album, especially once Eric Clapton's fame began to spread after leaving the band.' He goes on to point out that although the album didn't appear officially in the United States until its CD release by Rhino in the late 1980s, four of its tracks – 'Smokestack Lightning', 'Respectable', 'I'm A Man' and 'Here 'Tis' – made up one side of their classic US album *Having A Rave Up*, and the British EMI LP became a very popular import during the early 1970s as a showcase for both the band and the playing of Eric Clapton.

As indicated, this first album was recorded live at the famous Marquee Club, where The Yardbirds used to play every Friday night. The club had relocated and re-opened on Friday 13 March at the 'new' 90 Wardour Street premises with an all-star session, including Long John Baldry, The Yardbirds and Sonny Boy Williamson. Poet Joolz Denby recalls how 'the management deliberately didn't have any air con or ventilation so people would get sweaty and drink more.' Although, in 1964, they didn't yet have an alcohol license!

'It was one of the best gigs for us', recalled Keith, 'the acoustics suited us and there was a resident crowd who knew us and our material. It was like a party every time we played there … (but) it was a hard gig. We used to totally collapse after a set there, absolutely covered in sweat. Our drummer, Jim McCarty, and I used to have salt rings on our shoes from the sweat running down our legs. You had to put everything into a set there; it became like a weekly purge of the system.'

The ten tracks were fine, but to fit them all onto the album, they had to be sped up, only a fraction, but enough to make the music almost unrecognisable to hard-core Yardbirds fans (Jim McCarty denies this story; he says they simply played faster!). As Lillian Roxon pointed out, 'the tragedy was that the album *was* The Yardbirds – 'Five Long Years', 'Louise', 'Smokestack Lightning', 'I'm A Man'', as though some critics consider this to be their peak moment – the moment that most defines them. During that time, the group happened onto what they termed the 'rave-up', a long, wild instrumental break, spinning out sometimes to as long as 30 minutes, during which all the attention was focused on Clapton's guitar for a change, since Keith was the group's natural star. The rave-ups were Clapton's Opportunity Knocks moment: he took off and the audience flew with him.

This is when the 'Clapton Is God' graffiti began to appear spontaneously on London walls. His entire personality changed during those improvisational flights, and because they weren't ever as long and as frequent as he wanted them – or needed them to be – he eventually quit to join John Mayall's Blues Breakers. 'For Your Love' was supposedly the catalyst. He disliked its more pop orientation, so he sacrificed fame and wealth for blues authenticity – this is the story around which his legend was built. Mayall had been impressed by Eric's playing on 'Got To Hurry'. There was chemistry.

Mayall's first album – *John Mayall Plays John Mayall* – had also been recorded live, but at 'Klooks Kleek', a club at the 'Railway Tavern' in West Hampstead on 7 December 1964. Eric would first appear on John Mayall & The Bluesbreakers' October 1965 single 'I'm Your Witchdoctor' b/w 'Telephone Blues' (Immediate IM012), two Mayall compositions released through a one-off deal with Andrew Loog-Oldham's Indie label, produced by future-Yardbird Jimmy Page and with a distinctive, long, single-note Clapton solo! Then, Eric was lead guitarist for the *Blues Breakers* LP (22 July 1966), pictured reading a copy of *The Beano* (issue number 1242, 7 May 1966) on the cover photo! Although it was the only Mayall album Eric played on – with John McVie on bass and drummer Hughie Flint – it formed a significant step forward in British blues. Eric was replaced by Peter Green for the subsequent *A Hard Road* (17 February 1967), by which time, Clapton had formed Cream with Jack Bruce and Ginger Baker. And although the long, free-form extemporised guitar solo became the core of their massive appeal, there were also the flimsy early pop singles 'Wrapping Paper' – their debut single in October 1966 – and 'Anyone For Tennis' (May 1968), with Clapton miming playing a tennis racket in the tie-in video!

Yet, the rave-up continued as an essential part of The Yardbirds' live set. The only other group to compete in the stakes were The Animals, who also knew how to extend a song by building it into peaks of excitement. Their take on Ray Charles' 'Talkin' 'Bout You' was first issued as the 1:51 B-side of their epic 'House Of The Rising Sun' single, although later, the full unedited 7:04 version was issued on 1990's *The Complete Animals* (EMI167), hinting at their full live performance energies. Meanwhile, as Jeff Beck (born on 24 June 1944) took over the status of The Yardbirds' guitarist extraordinaire frontman, that long, generic instrumental break that The Yardbirds pioneered would start to be associated with the San Francisco psychedelic scene. By 1968 journalists were acknowledging that The Yardbirds had been the first to get into the freak-out bag. But this debut live album is where it all begins.

In an interview with Giorgio Gomelsky (from the online Tapeop com), he was asked about the decision process that went into making the group's debut a live recording. He explained:

> Very simple – in England, we didn't have the recording business that was so established and dominant as here (in the US), you know? So, bands really had to gather an audience by playing live. This was something they could do. Most English bands were very good live bands. In England, the club idea was not like here (in the US). It wasn't that there was a physical place and that was it. It was evenings run by promoters in the back of pubs who had little rooms where music happened, and people used to go and dance. The English music scene from skiffle onwards – even before that, traditional jazz and stuff – really took place in the back of pubs, and those were 'clubs'.

Meanwhile, The Yardbirds completed a successful year by playing the London Hammersmith Odeon as part of The Beatles' Christmas Show. Brian Epstein had spotted them on the Billy J Kramer tour and was impressed. For The Yardbirds, this was a step up into the big time.

Side One
'Too Much Monkey Business' (Chuck Berry) 3:51
According to Gomelsky's text, stage announcer and grossly underpaid aide Hamish Grimes proclaimed, 'and now, the most blueswailing BIRD-YEARDS

... sorry, hum, I'll start again. And now, the most yardwailing BLUEBIRDS ... sorry ... LIVE FIVE YARDBIRDS...' Whereas, on the record, he simply says, 'Good evening, welcome, and now it's time for burglarising, yarderising, in fact the most bluesworthy Yardbirds. Here they are one-by-one', and he name-checks each member in turn, leading up to Eric 'Slowhand' Clapton and Keith Relf, 'singer and harp. FIVE LIVE YARDBIRDS!' The Chuck Berry word-cascade classic rock 'n' roller is delivered with full-on high-energy live ambience, with frantic Clapton soloing and Keith doing his light blue-eyed soul voice, falling into talk-sing lines about working in a filling station. It's not a clean sound by any means; it's a dirty mix, but it is a rave-up captured in a single track. *Mojo* writer Mark Blake noted in June 2024 that 'Eric Clapton's solo shreds long before that word was in common parlance.'

'I Got Love If You Want It' (James 'Slim Harpo' Moore) 2:40
In the small world of Brit-blues, The Kinks had already featured 'Too Much Monkey Business' as well as their own laconic version of 'Got Love If You Want It' on their debut album, barely months before. The Yardbirds turn in a more high-energy performance. As Gomelsky's unique phrasing notes, 'Strangely, very strangely, the place really became alive – the band, the audience, the meters of the recording gear – and before long, the vagueness had become a 'sound' – urgent, precise, real.' In other words, this track truly becomes a Yardbirds feature when they perform it live. They closely follow the 1957 Slim Harpo original, on the Excello label, where it was relegated to the B-side of 'I'm A King Bee' – which the Stones covered on their debut album. The Rolling Stones would also artfully pun the title for a UK-only EP, *Got Live If You Want It*, subsequently spun out into an American album.

'Smokestack Lightnin'' (Howlin' Wolf, Chester Burnett) 5:35
'Smokestack Lightning' was also the opening track on the September 1964 debut LP *The Five Faces Of Manfred Mann*. Does their vocalist, Paul Jones, capture the Wolf's howling growl more authentically than Keith Relf's higher, lighter delivery? Does Manfred Mann's more jazz-literate arrangement take the song into a more sophisticated groove? Does it even matter? It's not a competition. The awesome original is there on the 1959 Chess label *Moanin' In The Moonlight* album – no-one can touch that one, not ever. Yet, The Yardbirds' bassline is a powerful throb, the harmonica wails, the guitar cuts through like an oxyacetylene torch and the track builds into a mighty climax that will be used as a template for a thousand American garage-acid bands – check out Count Five's 'Psychotic Reaction'.

'Good Morning Little Schoolgirl' (Don Level & Bob Love, original credit as Demarais) 2:42
Can it be that it was all so simple then, or has time rewritten every line? When Chuck Berry's pay-off line to his 'Memphis, Tennessee' was 'Marie is

only six years old', at the time, it was interpreted as a cute comedic turn-around, whereas we of a more cynical age would probably sniff out paedophile innuendo. Blues had always been full of knowing double entendre, and bragging sexual inference was commonplace. This is a song with a long and confused history. The 1961 Don & Bob version gave it a teen-fad twist – 'have a party at the soda shop, so we can do the twist, do the stroll, to the music of the Rock 'n' Roll' – on which The Yardbirds base their version. But Muddy Waters' leering 'good morning little schoolgirl, can I go home, can I go home with you? tell your mother and your father, I once was a schoolboy too' sounds altogether more predatory. And after The Yardbirds, there would be further versions, including one by The Grateful Dead and a more explicit take by Ten Years After.

'Respectable' (O'Kelly, Ronald & Rudolph, the Isley Brothers) 5:35
The Isley Brothers span a vague doo-wop vibe on their original 1959 RCA 45rpm single of this song, which later crossed over to become a Northern Soul dancehall favourite. It was featured on the brothers' LP *Shout* (November 1959). Brian Epstein's protégés The Fourmost recorded their own Merseybeat cover of the song as early as November 1963 (as the B-side of hit single 'I'm In Love'), while American garage band The Outsiders would score a minor upbeat hit (number 15) with it in August 1966 (Capitol 5701). But now Keith announces, 'This one now, to end the set', with the band quizzing him call-and-response style: 'Did you kiss her? Did you hug her?' as he protests 'no, no, no'. Why Keith breaks into an impromptu 'Humpty Dumpty' nursery rhyme midway is anyone's guess, but it was part of their regular interpretation, as shown by the performance on the *Live! Blueswailing July '64* album, taped around the same time but not issued until 2003.

Side Two
'Five Long Years' (Eddie Boyd) 5:18
'Still alive ... Five Live Yardbirds' announces the night's second set with a slow, intense blue-collar 12-bar blues enlivened by Keith's harmonica, and a rambling Clapton guitar solo. Keith protests that he's learned his lesson from working in the steel mill for five long years, bringing home his pay every Friday for his first wife, only for her to turn him out, 'if you've ever been mistreated, you'll know what I'm talking about'. Eddie Boyd was a piano player whose seminal recording of his own song, featuring Ernest Cotton's rasping tenor sax, was a *Billboard* r&b chart number one in 1952. It must be conceded that Boyd invests the song with a more mature authority than the youthful Yardbirds can muster.

'Pretty Girl' (Bo Diddley, aka Ellas McDaniel) 3:04
Coming from McComb, Mississippi, with 'a gun on his hip and a rose on his chest', Bo Diddley was a mighty, mighty man, his customised 'shave and a

haircut, two bits' syncopated beat was as instantly recognisable as part of the first rock 'n' roll wave as a Chuck Berry guitar run or a spine-shivering Little Richard howl. His single 'Pretty Thing' was recorded in 1955, but when reissued on the Pye International label in response to The Rolling Stones' use of his 'sound' on 'Not Fade Away' and 'Mona', it climbed into the UK chart as high as number 34 in October 1963. This is also the song from which The Pretty Things took their name.

'Pretty Girl' began as a track on Bo's 1962 LP *Bo Diddley & Company*, and when that company includes Jerome Green on maracas and the awesome 'Duchess' – Norma-Jean Wofford on guitar and support vocals – you just know it's bound to be wonderful. With group back-up vocals, Keith takes the song unadorned and with considerable authority, although he misses out on Bo's mischievously knowing humour about 'these homely girls got a marrying man jumping for joy'. As only Bo confides, 'you know you're the real McCoy'.

'Louise' (John Lee Hooker) 3:43

As a direct result of his music becoming buzz-trendy through beat-group name-dropping and covers – including The Animals' take on his enduring classic 'Boom Boom' – John Lee's 1956 track 'Dimples' was reissued on the Stateside label and climbed to number 23 on the UK chart on 2 July 1964. The Yardbirds took 'Louise', a slow walking blues, from John Lee's 1959 Chess Records *House Of The Blues* album, although it had been recorded as early as April 1951 with Eddie Kirkland on second guitar, and previously issued as a jukebox single. Keith opens the track with some virtuoso harmonica blowing before declaiming how the sweetest gal he knows made him 'walk from Chicago down to the Gulf of Mexico', which sounds less than convincing from a slender white boy in Croydon ... because he suspects that 'somebody been fishin' in my pond'. The blues has always been rife with smart, earthy innuendo!

They take the song at a faster pace than the original, with Keith dropping into his approximation of John Lee's semi-spoken passages while fired up by Clapton's strategic guitar bursts. Eric was already developing a following, but never cuts across other band members when they're in the spotlight; the group play as a unit, and Eric waits to take his turn playing lead fills where appropriate. His playing with The Yardbirds was always polite and restrained, never pushy or flashily obtrusive. He was always conflicted. As Keith observed about him: 'He wanted a measure of obscurity to work in.' He had a burning passion to play, but was a reluctant focus for adulation. With Cream, he was quite content for Jack Bruce to take vocals, just as with Blind Faith, he was equally happy for Steve Winwood to assume frontman status, and with Delaney & Bonnie, he preferred to be just one of the band.

There is a July 1964 film of The Yardbirds playing 'Louise' in a TV studio, with Keith's voice mixed more to the fore as he confesses that he has a girl called Mamie who treats him nice, but he still has Louise on his mind.

'I'm A Man' (Bo Diddley, the original album credits Pomus-Shuman) 4:33
'I'm A Man' was to become a recurring motif throughout The Yardbirds' story. There would be an American hit studio version with Jeff Beck's 'scratch-picking' guitar, and the song would remain an integral part of their set-list right through to their final Jimmy Page days as an example of their 'rave-up' style It sometimes seems that, even towards the end of their active career, the group race through the obligatory hit singles in order to get to 'I'm A Man'. The version included on the *Live Yardbirds: Featuring Jimmy Page* – recorded on 30 March 1968, but unissued until September 1971 – extends to a full 11:59.

Keith invites the pretty women to stand in line, bragging that he's a man spelt 'M-A-N', although he's just 'made twenty-one'. The propulsive bassline drives the track, with Keith's harmonica blasting in between his vocals, then he takes a lengthy solo as it accelerates. If he'd been minded to take a guitar solo, this would have been Eric's ideal opportunity. But no, it's a powerful concoction with immaculately controlled dynamics that provides evidence of just how intense it must have been at a sweaty, crowded Yardbirds gig. A 'Yardbirds Consumer Guide' published in *NME* on 7 April 1973 says that 'the interaction of Clapton, Relf and Samwell-Smith generated an excitement never heard before.' Here is the evidence!

'Here 'Tis' (Bo Diddley, McDaniel) 5:10
A song taken from Bo's 1962 *Bo Diddley's A Twister* album. There's also a version of this song by the proto-Who when they were still called the High Numbers. Although, greatly daring, The Yardbirds have the edge on them both! There's also a stereo instrumental version issued on *The Yardbirds: Train Kept A-Rollin' (The Complete Giorgio Gomelsky Productions)* (Charly Records CD LIK BOX3, 1993) that sounds like it was intended as a studio backing track. But it still carries considerable power. There's also a story that, at The Marquee on the night, this was the first track they attempted, but Clapton broke a string, so they stopped and tried it again later. It's a furiously rhythmic Diddley-beat work-out with staccato percussive effects within the drum solo, Keith at his raucous best leading an 'Oh-oh-oh-ooh' call-and-response chant, and Clapton at last breaking loose to solo, in sonic conversation with Samwell-Smith's bass. In conversation with Charles Shaar Murray for *NME* on 7 April 1973, for rock academic Roy Carr, Paul 'was, along with his contemporary Jack Bruce, the first man to liberate the bass guitarist from the confines of strict figures based on root notes.' 'Here 'Tis' forms an explosive album closer.

To Gomelsky, 'the job had been done. Something of the excitant and freshness of The Yardbirds' sound had been captured on tape. Some parts of the performance could have been better; maybe the recording itself could be improved on? Perhaps, but who knows, it could also have been much worse.'

'Very hot, very hot, but still alive, the five Yardbirds', gushes Hamish, the announcer.

Singles, EPs & Albums 1965

The First Yardbirds Hit Single – 'For Your Love'

'For Your Love' (Graham Gouldman) 2:38 b/w **'Got To Hurry'** ('O Rasputin' who is Giorgio Gomelsky) 2:29

Personnel:

Keith Relf: lead vocals

Eric Clapton: lead guitar

Chris Dreja: rhythm guitar

Jim McCarty: drums

Paul Samwell-Smith: bass guitar

Produced by Giorgio Gomelsky at IBC studio on 1 February 1965, 'Got To Hurry' at Olympic on 6 August 1964

Released: 5 March 1965 (UK), 12 April 1965 (US)

Columbia DB 7499 (UK), Epic 5-9790 (US)

Highest chart position: UK: 3, US: 6

Manfred Mann co-wrote their own first two hits, but because the second, 'Hubble Bubble (Toil And Trouble)' (number 11), did not chart as high as the first, '5,4,3,2,1' (number five), they lost their nerve and fell back on relying on a highly successful series of covers and songs by other songwriters, such as Bob Dylan, Randy Newman, Geoff Stephens or Tony Hazzard.

Andrew Loog Oldham told The Rolling Stones that there was not a limitless reservoir of old blues songs ripe for reviving, so the group needed to originate more of their own new material. Just like The Beatles did. So, the story goes, he locked Mick and Keith in a room and refused to allow them out until they'd written some hit songs. And they wrote hit songs for Chris Farlowe, Marianne Faithfull, Gene Pitney and Twice As Much, as well as chancing their own 'The Last Time' as a Stones A-side.

The Yardbirds started out as a blues band, but they had ambitions that transcended the restrictions of merely replicating what had gone before. The blues was also an evolving medium. They needed to evolve with it. Nevertheless, 'For Your Love' proved a major revelation. It was one of the first songs that 18-year-old Salford-born Graham Gouldman had written. He tried it out with his own group, The Mockingbirds, but the Columbia label – who had signed them – turned it down. It was brought to Gomelsky's attention by song publisher Ronnie Beck, and Giorgio passed it on to the group he was managing.

The unconventional song structure, with its tempo-change sequence, appealed to Relf. Clapton was less enthused. The core of the group recorded the song during a 1 February session in London's IBC Studio. In surviving TV footage, it's a seated Keith, dark shades rendering his eyes expressionless, face framed by his immaculate blonde fringe, who plays the pattering bongos lodged between his knees, although it was session musician Denny Piercy on the record itself. Paul Samwell-Smith assumes arranger and production chores, although it is Gomelsky who gets the credit on the label. A puzzled

Brian Auger was brought in to play the harpsichord ... a highly unlikely pop-rock instrument at the time, while Eric and Chris play only during the mid-section. The rhythm section was provided by Jim, with session player Ron Prentice on bowed bass. In total, there's an eerie, unsettling quality to the record that makes it immediately stand out from the pack. If it was pop, it was strangely skewed pop, in both creative and innovative ways.

As if to reassure fans, the B-side was a generic, moody, mid-tempo, guitar-led instrumental credited to Gomelsky, but likely the result of a jam session that evolved around Clapton's vicious blues riff.

The single entered the chart at number 32 on 18 March 1965 on a list headed by The Rolling Stones ('The Last Time'), with the reassuringly commercial Herman's Hermits, The Hollies and The Searchers all well placed. 'For Your Love' eventually peaked at number three on 8 April, just as Unit 4+2's 'Concrete And Clay' took over the top slot, and as The Yardbirds started out on a UK tour headlined by 'the dynamic' Kinks. Opening with two houses at the Slough 'Adelphi' on 30 April, the tour featured 'America's Fabulous' all-female group Goldie & The Gingerbreads, who scored a minor UK hit with 'Can't You Hear My Heartbeat'. Compered by Bob Bain, there was also The Riot Squad, The Micky Finn, Jeff & Jon, plus 'the delightful' Val McKenna. The tour would have provided a useful showcase for 'the exciting' Yardbirds' new chart status – as 'Hit Recorders Of 'For Your Love' – were it not for an onstage Kinks fight between Dave Davies and drummer Mick Avory that stole the headlines!

Fleetwood Mac later recorded 'For Your Love' on their 1973 *Mystery To Me* album, while Humble Pie also played their own version of the song. Don Fardon of 'Indian Reservation' fame recorded a note-for-note revival on his 1970 *I'm Alive* album (Young Blood YBL15003).

The Next Hit Single – 'Heart Full Of Soul'
'Heart Full Of Soul' (Graham Gouldman) 2:28 b/w **'Steeled Blues'** (Relf, Beck) 2:38
Personnel:
Keith Relf: lead vocals
Jeff Beck: lead guitar
Chris Dreja: rhythm guitar
Jim McCarty: drums
Paul Samwell-Smith: bass guitar
Plus:
Denny Piercy: tablas
Produced by Giorgio Gomelsky with Paul Samwell-Smith as Musical Director, recorded at Advision Studio in late April, 'Steeled Blues' on 15 March 1965
Released: 4 June 1965 (UK), 19 July 1965 (US)
Columbia DB 7594 (UK), Epic 5-9823 (US)
Highest chart position: UK: 2, US: 9

The credits beneath the B-side read 'featuring Jeff 'Steel' Beck', and yes, it's another slow blues instrumental in the 'Got To Hurry' vein, but showcasing Clapton's replacement on slide guitar, framed by Keith's wailing harmonica and underpinned by McCarty's relentless drums. Yet, the A-side played safe only in that it was another composition from Gouldman, who was by then both prolific and hitting his stride. Musically, it was nudging further into experimental sounds, with Beck's fuzz-tone guitar tuned to imitate the sitar, replicating an eastern orientalism months before The Kinks edged into similar terrain with 'See My Friends' in October, and well before The Beatles' 'Norwegian Wood'. To Alan Clayson, 'it was primarily thanks to both The Yardbirds and The Kinks that non-European sounds, if not musical theories, became more than a trace element in pop.' Samwell-Smith adds haunting harmony vocals, accelerating into the 'and I know if she had me back again, well, I would never make her sad, I've gotta h-e-a-a-a-a-rt full of soul' chorus, while Beck's brief, concise solo is a wonder of compressed invention. To hear it on the radio was a revelation, and very much on the leading edge of the new wave that was reshaping rock.

Born on 24 June 1944 in Wallington, Surrey, Geoffrey Arnold 'Jeff' Beck was struck by Les Paul (with Mary Ford)'s 'How High The Moon' when still a child. Many years later, Jeff would acknowledge that inspiration by playing the song – with Imelda May – in a 2010 Les Paul Grammy Awards tribute. He played with various bands while attending Wimbledon College of Art and recorded with Screaming Lord Sutch's Savages during 1964 – the highly collectable 'Dracula's Daughter' b/w 'Come Back Baby' (Oriole CB-1962), produced by Joe Meek at his RGM Sound studio at Islington's 304 Holloway Road. It's a novelty song about 'Vampire Mary', with Jeff's mildly fuzzed guitar contributing unmistakable fills.

After stints trying out with various short-lived groups – The Nightshift and The Rumbles – Jeff found his r&b place with The Tridents, based in Chiswick (to complicate things, bland late-fifties crooner Craig Douglas toured and recorded with a different group called The Tridents, which has led to the confused, erroneous idea that Jeff played on Craig's 1964 Chris Andrews-penned 'Come Closer' single). But, befriended by Jimmy Page, Jeff did do session work. He played on a single by the Manchester-based four-piece Fitz & Startz, 'I'm Not Running Away' b/w 'So Sweet' (Parlophone R5216). Although the vocal harmonies are weak, Jeff's guitar gives the record a rough garage-band edge. There are various semi-legal bootleg editions that collect Jeff's session-work for avid enthusiasts, with groups such as Nightshift ('That's My Story' b/w 'Stormy Monday Blues'), former Manfred Mann singer Paul Jones ('And The Sun Will Shine' b/w 'The Dog Presides'), The Smoke ('Utterly Simple') and John's Children ('But She's Mine').

It was on Page's recommendation that Jeff auditioned for The Yardbirds as Clapton's replacement. Whereas Clapton, at the time, preferred the austere form of blues purism he found with Mayall – he had yet to hear Jimi Hendrix!

– Jeff Beck brought a new openness to the group, willing to try new techniques and use whatever effect pedals he could lay his hands on. The first gig he played as a Yardbird was at the Croydon Fairfield Hall on Friday 5 March 1965. It was a Radio Caroline 'Sounds Of '65' promotion with The Moody Blues, introduced by compère Simon Dee. This was the original Moody Blues, fronted by Denny Laine, who were following up their breakthrough hit 'Go Now' with 'I Don't Want To Go On Without You'. Also on the bill were The Mark Leeman Five, Jimmy James & The Vagabonds and Barry St John.

But soon, he was enhancing the group's sound with feedback, and their stage presentation with moody theatrics. A teenage pre-Queen Brian May recalled 'seeing him put the guitar down, make it feedback and play a whole tune without even touching the fingerboard', leaving the guitar squealing up against the speaker as Jeff prowled the stage, only to retrieve the distressed instrument and slide it up and down the microphone stand to create a bottleneck effect, in defiance of electrical Health & Safety advice.

'Heart Full Of Soul' was launched by a live performance on the popular BBC Light Programme *The Ken Dodd Show*, with the tape salvaged onto the 1991 LP *The Yardbirds... On Air* (re-issued in 1999 as *The BBC Sessions*). The single entered the UK *Record Mirror/Record Retailer* chart at number 32 on 17 June, a few places above The Byrds' 'Mr Tambourine Man'. 'Heart Full Of Soul' climbed to number 20, peaking at number two below The Hollies' 'I'm Alive' on 15 July ... and it stayed there for three weeks as The Byrds replaced The Hollies at the top slot.

The Yardbirds supported The Beatles at the Paris 'Olympia' theatre on 20 June, then flew out to America, where the single was launched by a live spot on *Shindig* on 23 September, with the group neatly suited, and Keith wearing his trademark shades. Raquel Welch was also on the show, singing 'Dancing In The Street' with a cast of cavorting Go-Go Dancers.

The First American Album – For Your Love

Personnel:
Keith Relf: lead vocals
Eric Clapton: lead guitar
Jeff Beck: lead guitar
Chris Dreja: rhythm guitar
Jim McCarty: drums
Paul Samwell-Smith: bass guitar
Released: 5 July 1965 (US)
Epic LN24167/BN26167. No UK release
Highest chart position: US: 96)
This is an opportunistic re-shuffle of material designed to appeal to the American market. The sleeve art is divided into six panels, with the title in the first (with Yard-Birds hyphenated), then Chris Dreja and Jeff Beck sitting at a

keyboard – although he only plays on three tracks! – then a second row of Jim McCarty, Keith Relf and Paul Samwell-Smith.

By 1964, The Beatles had hit America, The Rolling Stones had hit America, everyone English and his brother had hit America – including some of the poorest groups England had produced. Because of that factor, The Yardbirds, like some other good, even great groups, were finding themselves lost in the shuffle. A lot of things went wrong. They were never as lucky as other, often lesser, groups. This first American package was made up of material the label thought – or were made to think – was more suitable for American ears. According to Lillian Roxon, 'the material was more modern than material they had done in England.'

There are both sides of the first three singles, with Eric Clapton playing – although he's not mentioned anywhere on the album sleeve – with three new tracks featuring Jeff Beck's guitar, plus a couple of demos that would remain unissued in the UK until the 1980s. Although concentrating attention on the guitarists alone can be a distraction, as Richard MacKay pointed out in his *Yardbirds World* fanzine, 'to my mind, The Yardbirds made names for their successive guitarists, not the other way round.'

The Yardbirds' first American trip was complicated by visa problems resulting from Gomelsky's lack of managerial experience, complicated by the Musicians' Union policy. A news item tucked away on page 31 of *Melody Maker* on 21 August 1965 was headed 'Yardbirds Fly Out For States Debut', reporting that they were 'probably' flying out on Thursday 26 and that 'they are set for two weeks of TV and promotional work with radio dee-jays', although no concerts had been finalised. They arrived in New York, played a single gig in Oklahoma, called off at Memphis 'Sun' Studios for a recording session, and eventually arrived in LA, where 'amongst the sunshine and swagger, they had a Hollywood Hills party experience that would contribute to Jeff Beck leaving the group just one year later.'

In the Beck biography, *Hot Wired Guitar*, he described the trip, saying, 'London might have been swinging, but California was sunny.' In LA, there were '18-year-old girls driving around in convertible cars. It truly was the land of milk and honey.' To celebrate his Californian freedom, Beck rented a Corvette Stingray to cruise the Sunset Strip. It was 'endless sunshine and Beach Boys songs on the radio.' Chris Dreja – who was flat-sharing at the time with Keith in a ramshackle Westbourne Grove house above a betting shop – recalled that 'It was another world, like something from a movie we'd watched at home, but now we were in it.'

The fascination was a two-way thing. Five long-haired, sharply-dressed r&b musicians on the leading trend-edge of London-cool was – as the hipsters phrased it – 'where it was at'. While in LA, Giorgio Gomelsky met a young Hollywood mover and shaker, Bob Markley, who was putting together his own group, The West Coast Pop Art Experimental Band, and was throwing a party at his oil-tycoon father's Hollywood Hills mansion.

With no proper Yardbirds gigs finalised for this visit, Gomelsky was looking for ways to get the band seen, and the party sounded like the perfect opportunity for them to become the coolest house band in the Hollywood Hills. 'Everyone turned up,' recalls Dreja, 'even Marlon Brando, Bob Dylan and Roger McGuinn of The Byrds were meant to be attending. And I'm sure they did, though sadly we never saw them as we were playing in the living room behind a sofa.'

Meanwhile, Beck's time at the party was spent trying to get the phone number of the gorgeous Mary Hughes, an actress in B-movies like *Muscle Beach Party* and *Beach Blanket Bingo*. She'd appeared in cult *Caged Fury* (1948) and the Bix Beiderbecke biopic *Young Man With A Horn* (1950), as well as TV series such as *Dragnet*, *Rawhide* and *Dennis The Menace*. She was also host Markley's girlfriend. 'Well, you can't blame Jeff for that,' reasoned Dreja, 'like the rest of us, Jeff had come from black-and-white, and Mary Hughes was all the colours of the rainbow.'

The Yardbirds did do some TV during the tour, including *Hullaballoo* with comedian Jerry Lewis, and Dick Clark's *American Bandstand*. Furthermore, Andy Warhol came to a New York Epic Records reception to seek them out.

Side One
'For Your Love' (Graham Gouldman) 2:28
If Salford-born Graham Gouldman served his rock apprenticeship as writer-for-hire, penning hits for The Hollies, Herman's Hermits and The Jeff Beck Group as well as the run of three consecutive chartbusters for The Yardbirds, he hit his musical stride as a member of 10cc, one of the 1970s' most consistent and reliable bands, operating from their own Strawberry Studios. But it was here, with 'For Your Love', that it all began. His debut solo album – *The Graham Gouldman Thing*, issued in 1968 (reissued 1992 as Demon EDCD346) – was recorded with John Paul Jones' production assistance and Clem Cattini on drums. It included his own version of 'For Your Love'.

'I'm Not Talking' (Mose Allison) 2:31
Mississippi-born white bluesman Mose Allison had jazz roots, too, which enriched his writing, which was promptly seized upon by John Mayall ('Parchment Farm') and The Who ('Young Man Blues'), through to Georgie Fame and The Clash. Mose also wrote and recorded his tribute to jazz revolutionary Charlie 'Bird' Parker – 'Yardbird Suite' – on his 1958 LP *Creek Bank* (Prestige Records). His cool piano-based 'I'm Not Talking' debuted on his strongly jazz-literate 1964 album *The Word From Mose* (Atlantic Records).

'Putty (In Your Hands)' (Big John Patton, Eddie Snyder under his 'Kay Rogers' alias) 2:11
This is a song originally and beguilingly recorded by The Shirelles in March 1962, later revived by Kim Wilde in April 1985. The Yardbirds open with a

'Money'-style groove before Keith oozes into a sweet soul vocal about him being like a hunk of clay for his woman: 'You can stretch me until I'm ten feet tall, or cut me down to the size of a rubber ball'. It's an adequate but not exceptional track, although it stands up well to comparison with other group efforts of the time. Jim McCarty suggests that this song – as well as 'Sweet Music' – was recorded to placate an increasingly dissatisfied Eric Clapton, who was unhappy with the pop direction the group were taking with 'For Your Love', and who would quit on 13 March 1965.

'I Ain't Got You' (Calvin Carter) 1:59
The B-side of the second single. The Animals do their version on their second album, *Animal Tracks* (May 1965), where a raucous Eric Burdon gets a more prominent vocal than The Yardbirds' more collective treatment of the song.

'Got To Hurry (Demo, Take 3)' ('O Rasputin' who is Giorgio Gomelsky) 2:34
There was also an 'alternate, take 4' issued later from the Gomelsky archives, although there is little to distinguish between the lazy-paced studio jams in terms of quality, and only Eric Clapton obsessives would find it worth teasing out the slight variant takes of the 'For Your Love' B-side.

'I Ain't Done Wrong' (Keith Relf) 3:37
Although credited to Keith, this song is essentially a reworking of Eddie Kirkland's 1959 single 'I Must Have Done Somebody Wrong', while taking note of Elmore James' rejig – 'Done Somebody Wrong' – from a year later. Jeff's repetitive chop and slide guitar also owes more than a little to Elmore James. The dialogue between Keith's harmonica echoing Jeff's guitar is a joy until it breaks into a hard riffing fusillade that would blueprint a raft of American psych-acid bands. The song was to be further developed by The Allman Brothers.

Side Two
'I Wish You Would' (BB Arnold) 2:18
In June 2024, *Mojo* magazine commended the version included on the album *Live In France* (Repertoire, 2020), recorded live at Paris's Palais Des Sports in June 1965, where 'I Wish You Would' 'gets a futuristic makeover from new kid Jeff Beck, with Relf howling during its dissonant mid-song breakdown – like 'Whole Lotta Love' came early.'

'A Certain Girl' ('Naomi Neville' who is Allen Toussaint) 2:16
In 1980, Warren 'Werewolves Of London' Zevon revived 'A Certain Girl' as a single issued on Asylum Records K12437. The Yardbirds were a hard act to follow, but Zevon made it work by minimising the frills and concentrating on the song's basic propulsive drive.

'Sweet Music (Stereo Demo, Take 3)' (Major Lance, Otis Leavill Cobbs, Walter Bowie) 2:29

This was produced by Manfred Mann during a November 1964 session, with a richer sound-depth than we usually associate with The Yardbirds, perhaps due to Manfred adding keyboard to the mix, while fellow Manfred's Paul Jones (backing voice), Mike Hugg (vibraphone), Mike Vickers and Tom McGuinness (both guitar) all contribute (during October 1963, McGuinness had briefly played alongside Eric Clapton as members of the Mersey-based Casey Jones & The Engineers). 'Sweet Music' was originally done in a smooth, finger-popping soul style by Major Lance as the B-side of his classic hit 'Um, Um Um, Um, Um, Um', first released in December 1963 and collected on his *Greatest Hits* album. It's a paean to music itself: 'Could it be the beat of the drum? Could it be the horns that charm?' For The Yardbirds, this track is a demo; maybe further takes would have refined the production? As it is, it makes a fine album filler, but – to be honest – Major Lance has the edge.

'Good Morning Little Schoolgirl' (HG Demarais) 2:52

This single dates from the time when their reputation was still building. Pete Townshend of The Who recalled in *Who Am I* (HarperCollins, 2012) that 'a band called The Yardbirds, with Eric Clapton playing lead, was hot, and Roger (Daltrey) had seen a rehearsal of a band called The Trident, whose guitar player he raved about – young Jeff Beck. In both cases, we had real competition right in our backyard.'

'My Girl Sloopy' (B Russell, W Farrell) 5:36

Writer Alan Clayson agrees that this is 'The Yardbirds' worst cover' and that they 'continued to get by on the 'intellectual' ticket – even though there had been nothing intellectual about 'My Girl Sloopy' or 'Questa Volta', unless regarded as Dadaist for their calculated mindlessness.'

The First EP – Five Yardbirds (EP)

Personnel:
Keith Relf: lead vocals
Jeff Beck: lead guitar
Chris Dreja: rhythm guitar
Jim McCarty: drums
Paul Samwell-Smith: bass guitar
Produced by Giorgio Gomelsky at Advision, London
Released: 11 August 1965. No US release
Columbia SEG 8421
Highest position on UK EP chart: 5

This neat little EP package featured tracks from the American *For Your Love* album unavailable in the UK. It featured the earliest Jeff Beck recording sessions with The Yardbirds – dated 15 March 1965 ('I Ain't Done Wrong') –

and two from 13 April 1965, with 'My Girl Sloopy' taking up the full first side of the EP. Paul Samwell-Smith is credited as 'unpaid' Musical Director.

The Yardbirds featured on the Friday 6 August 1965 bill of 'The Fifth National Jazz & Blues Festival' held, for the last time, at the Richmond Athletic Association Ground, alongside The Who, The Moody Blues, Georgie Fame, Manfred Mann, The Spencer Davis Group and The Mike Cotton Sound. An American camera team reporting for the *Shindig* TV show indicate that The Yardbirds' set included 'For Your Love' and 'My Girl Sloopy'. A day ticket cost 10/- (50p).

Side One
'My Girl Sloopy' (Bert Russell Berns, Wes Farrell) 5:36
The story of this song is complex. It starts out with Los Angeles soul five-piece The Vibrations, who enjoyed a 1964 US pop and r&b chart hit (number 26 and number ten, respectively) with their original Atlantic Records single of 'My Girl Sloopy'. Recorded with live audience sounds and taking advantage of the outfit's vocal range from high upper-register lead voice to deep Mr bass-man voice, the song was the co-written product of two prolific composers, Wes Farrell – who had co-written 'Boys' with Luther Dixon for The Shirelles, subsequently covered by The Beatles on their debut album, which also included 'Twist And Shout' written by Bert Berns with Philip Medley (not the Righteous Brother!).

Bertrand Russell Berns deserves a chapter in his own right. He wrote 'Piece Of My Heart' for Erma Franklin and Janis Joplin, 'Here Comes The Night' for Them (with Van Morrison) and Lulu, as well as songs for The Exciters, Solomon Burke and many others. While varying the phrasing, The Yardbirds largely follow The Vibrations' template for 'My Girl Sloopy' – not entirely convincingly. What follows is a slow build, with call-back harmonies urging on Keith, who sounds a little uncertain, while incorporating the technique of going 'a little bit quieter', then the ascending voice-sequence that The Beatles had employed so effectively on 'Twist And Shout' into another fade and another build. Keith throws in 'Mmmm, Baby, don't you know, you thrill me so' and 'love the way that you dance, give me one chance', with collective wild howling, until it closes with Keith pleading 'oh, oh, oh, I got something more to say to you, little Sloopy blue, I want to say, hang on Sloopy'.

When Bert Berns formed his own label – 'Bang Records' – he scored an immediate American number-one hit with teenage Rick Derringer's group The McCoys' revival of The Vibrations song retitled 'Hang On Sloopy', which then became the first release on Andrew Loog Oldham's 'Immediate' label in the UK where it hit number five. It must be conceded that The McCoys tighten, accelerate and repoint the song with contagious energies that The Yardbirds conspicuously lack!

To further complicate the story, The McCoys' follow-up single – 'Fever' – was flipped with 'Sorrow', which became a number-four hit in 1966 in its own right for two former members of The Merseybeats, re-naming themselves The Merseys. The drummer on The Merseys session – Clem Cattini – would also drum on The Yardbirds' 'Ten Little Indians' single, while 'Sorrow' itself would join two Yardbirds songs on David Bowie's *Pin-Ups* album. Rick Derringer went on to become an in-demand session guitarist and was long-rumoured to be the 'Ricky' in the title of Steely Dan's hit 'Rikki Don't Lose That Number', a rumour that Donald Fagen denied.

Side Two
'I'm Not Talking' (Mose Allison) 2:31
Keith meets Mose Allison's jazzy phrasing head-on and proves himself more than equal to the challenge with one of his most dextrous vocal exercises, while the band take the original record's oozing piano setting and translate it into a hard-edged garage burn driven by Keith's tambourine and Jeff's stinging lead guitar.

'I Ain't Done Wrong' (Keith Relf) 3:37
Whatever the faults of 'My Girl Sloopy', this most blueswailing track more than compensates, pitching Jeff's eloquent soloing against Keith's harmonica, building to a storming climax. In December 1993, *Vox* magazine noted that 'as this rattling hard guitar-and-drums workout verifies, The Yardbirds played louder than the recording equipment of the day could handle, making for speaker-shredding amounts of distortion!' Always most at home when playing ensemble, sparking off each other, this song became part of the group's live set through to their final American tours, where Jimmy Page's extemporised free-form passages ably demonstrate just how mesmerising an on-stage unit they could still be.

The First Canadian Album – Heart Full Of Soul
Personnel:
Keith Relf: lead vocals
Eric Clapton: lead guitar
Jeff Beck: lead guitar
Chris Dreja: rhythm guitar
Jim McCarty: drums
Paul Samwell-Smith: bass guitar
Released: 6 September 1965 (Canada). No UK release
Capitol T-6139, the 6000 series
No chart position
Another fix-up – a Canadian variant compilation of the US *For Your Love* album, also known as *Presenting The Yardbirds*. This package became collectable in that 'I Wish You Would' and 'A Certain Girl' are not sourced from the official singles, but are early-1964 demo versions recorded at the R.G. Jones Studios in Morden.

The Yardbirds never scored a number-one hit, not anywhere. 'Heart Full Of Soul' stayed in second place on the UK chart for three weeks from 15 July 1965, held off the top spot first by The Hollies' 'I'm Alive', then by The Byrds' 'Mr Tambourine Man'. That was as good as it got. But then again, The Who never had a number-one single, nor did The Pretty Things. The highest the Syd Barrett era Pink Floyd ever got was number six with 'See Emily Play'. They would have to wait until the tail-end of the 1970s, with a reconfigured lineup, for the Floyd's only chart-topping single. The Moody Blues had a number-one during their first Denny Laine period with 'Go Now', but even 'Nights In White Satin' barely scraped into the top 20 on its first release in 1967.

Conversely, there were other groups who achieved number-one hits, such as The Overlanders, whose opportunistic cover of The Beatles' 'Michelle' from *Rubber Soul* took them to the top, or The Four Pennies with 'Juliet', a chart-topper on 21 May 1964, which left no lasting trace on pop culture whatsoever.

So, unopposed at the apex of the 1960s pop pyramid were The Beatles and The Rolling Stones. A rung lower were The Kinks and The Who. Then, there was a tier of other consistent names who all made their own unique contribution to that most swinging of decades, The Animals, The Hollies, The Searchers, Manfred Mann, The Spencer Davis Group, The Small Faces ... and The Yardbirds. But as Simon Napier-Bell is quoted as saying in his autobiography, *You Don't Have To Say You Love Me* – a book that *NME*'s Penny Reel called 'a vile item of innuendo and invective' – 'there were four rock bands in the world that really counted, and The Yardbirds was one of them.'

The Yardbirds' influence extended beyond mere chart statistics; it continued and continues way beyond their active lifetime. Highly regarded and respected at the time, their mystique would only grow.

Side One

'I Wish You Would' 4:15
'A Certain Girl' 2:20
'Good Morning Little Schoolgirl' 2:46
'I Ain't Got You' 2:00
'For Your Love' 2:27
'Got To Hurry' 2:27

Side Two

'My Girl Sloopy' 5:34
'I Ain't Done Wrong' 3:39
'I'm Not Talking' 2:32
'Heart Full Of Soul' 2:27
'Steeled Blues' 2:37
'Putty (In Your Arms)' 2:18

The Double A-Side Single – 'Evil Hearted You'
'Evil Hearted You' (Graham Gouldman) 2:28 b/w **'Still I'm Sad'**
(McCarty, Samwell-Smith) 2:59
Produced by Giorgio Gomelsy at Advision Studio on 23 August 1965 'Still I'm
Sad' at Olympic Studio on 27 July 1965 and Advision in mid-August
Released: 1 October 1965
Columbia DB 7706. No US release in this form
Highest chart position: UK: 3

By 1965, the beat boom was getting seriously strange. The Who were using
feedback and distortion on 'Anyway, Anyhow, Anywhere', which reached
number ten on 1 July 1965. Bob Dylan had gone electric, and there were
further advanced ripples of American strangeness from The Byrds, Sam The
Sham & The Pharoahs and Sir Douglas Quintet ('She's About A Mover'
reached number 15 on 15 July 1965). The Kinks used oriental drone tunings
on 'See My Friends', which reached number ten on 2 September, while
market-leaders The Beatles used sitar on 'Norwegian Wood' on *Rubber Soul*
(December 1965).

But this double-sided Yardbirds hit was a game-changer in a league of its
own. At the time of its release, I remember the impact of this single as being
totally stunning, unlike anything else that had happened in pop-rock before.
Once again, it wrongfooted the rock world and tilted pop on its axis. 'Evil
Hearted You' was a third cuting for a Graham Gouldman song, very much in
the drone-spun 'Heart Full Of Soul' vein, but this time it was credited as a
double-A-side release with the group's own bizarre composition 'Still I'm Sad'
getting equal billing. Oddly, the *NME* chart listed both sides separately, with
'Evil Hearted You' peaking at number ten, and 'Still I'm Sad' one rung higher,
at number nine, on 4 November 1965 – a week in which the chart was
headed by The Rolling Stones' 'Get Off Of My Cloud' at top position, with
comedian Ken Dodd's maudlin 'Tears' conceding the top slot at number two.

Keith spits out the 'Evil Hearted You' lyric with a degree of vehemence
about the lover with the phony smile and the siren song – 'You lead me on 'til
all hope's gone, persuading, degrading, on my knees I try to please' – while
there are typically Gouldman abrupt tempo switches in the bridge and a brief
but scorching Jeff Beck solo. Some claim to hear an eastern bend to Jeff's
ringing slide guitar, and the expansive influence of Ennio Morricone's
spaghetti western soundtracks (his *A Fistful Of Dollars* from 1964 was already
a cult favourite).

… There was a kind of magic in the grooves. We were vaguely aware of the
science and technology involved in making analogue microgroove polyvinyl
chloride records; we'd seen the cut-away diagrams of how the recording
studio translates sound waves into grooved indentations pressed into the
master lacquer. And the pressing process that churns out new 7" singles. But
lift the arm, blow the fluff of dust from the diamond stylus and drop it into
the play-in groove of the new single that cost you all your pocket money or

took you a week delivering the Morning Papers to earn ... the single you bought across the counter in the local record shop and carried eagerly home, to hear that faint surface-noise crackle before the first crash of Jeff Beck's guitar. It was a kind of magic that no-one born into the YouTube-Spotify era can ever know.

For 'Still I'm Sad', bass player Paul Samwell-Smith is credited with writing the poetic lyrics, in musical collusion with Jim McCarty: 'For myself, my tears just fall into dust, day will dry them, night will find they are lost, now I find the wind is blowing time into my heart'. Giorgio Gomelsky gets the co-producer credit (with Samwell-Smith), but it's largely the group's arrangement and production, with harmony vocals creating the eerily haunting supernatural effect of a Gregorian liturgical chant, with Jeff feeding in mournfully plangent guitar and Keith throwing in oblique phrasing to the final 'how I'm sad'. If 'Still I'm Sad' could still be termed blues, it must surely be medieval blues.

Fabulous magazine – dated 23 October 1965 – reveals that 'most of The Yardbirds live with their parents' and that Jeff is 'just about the world's worst person' for getting up in the morning. There's also a fashion spread of Jeff and Jim 'of the Fab Yardbirds' shopping for clothes in a trendy Carnaby Street boutique.

The American Hit Single – 'I'm A Man'
'I'm A Man' (Ellas McDaniels aka Bo Diddley) 2:37 b/w **'Still I'm Sad'** (McCarty, Samwell-Smith) 2:59
A-side production credited to Giorgio Gomelsy, recorded at Chess Studios in Chicago on 19 September and Columbia Studio in New York on 21 September 1965
Released: 6 October 1965 (US). No UK release in this form
Epic 5-9857
Highest chart position: US: 17 (Billboard)
As we have seen, The Yardbirds had recorded a live version of 'I'm A Man' for their first UK album *Five Live Yardbirds* with Eric Clapton in 1964 (later released in the US on their 1965 Epic Records album *Having A Rave Up*). But during their first American tour in 1965, The Yardbirds – now with Jeff Beck – recorded this studio version of 'I'm A Man' on 19 September 1965, with engineer Ron Malo. Appropriately, recording took place at the legendary Chess Studios on 2120 South Michigan Avenue in Chicago, with additional recording at the Columbia Studios in New York.

Giorgio Gomelsky retained producer credit with Paul Samwell-Smith listed as Musical Director. And there are considerable differences in emphasis, in Keith's phrasing and in the intensifying guitar solo that Jeff Beck adds. Both Yardbird versions of the song feature their signature 'rave-up' arrangement, when the beat shifts into double time and the instrumentation builds to a crescendo, but this time it's raw.

The new 'I'm A Man' was released as a single – making number one on the Los Angeles regional chart, number two in Vancouver and number three in Sacramento – and was later also added to the track listing of *Having A Rave Up*. The studio version was eventually released in the UK only as late as 1976. Diddley himself praised The Yardbirds' cover as 'beautiful', while counting his royalties, and the track has been called 'a defining moment for the band.'

Having A Rave-Up With The Yardbirds

Personnel:
Keith Relf: lead vocals
Eric Clapton: lead guitar
Jeff Beck: lead guitar
Chris Dreja: rhythm guitar
Jim McCarty: drums
Paul Samwell-Smith: bass guitar
Giorgio Gomelsky is credited as producer
Released: 30 November 1965 (US), 5 January 1966 (Germany & Sweden)
Epic LN 24177/ BN26177 (US), Columbia SCXC 28 (Germany & Sweden)
No UK release
Highest chart position: US: 53

Issued just prior to, and to coincide with The Yardbirds' second American trip
– they flew into Buffalo, upstate New York, for a first gig on Christmas Eve
– this was a fix-up compilation that included four tracks lifted directly from
Five Live Yardbirds with Eric Clapton. Lillian Roxon suggested that this
'second American album seemed to be designed to correct this (the faults of
the earlier *For Your Love* set), with new material on one side – the 'Evil
Hearted You' side – but with older material – Muddy Waters and Bo Diddley
tracks from their first English album – on the other... Because they were
recorded when Clapton was still with the group, he is, naturally, featured on
them, even though he had left by the time the album was released. The
problem was, though, that this material was wildly exciting in England, where
no-one had access to the originals. Americans seemed to prefer the 'modern'
Yardbirds. With the 1968 blues revival, this was to change, but too late for the
old Yardbirds.'

During this American stint, they hung out in New York and returned to the
West Coast to play dates. 'What's a RAVE-UP?' asked the original album liner
notes before helpfully explaining that...

it's the sound of the future – The Yardbirds sound of the future! ... You'll
be treated to some inspired improvisation coloured with a healthy handful of
what can only be described as 'oriental' chords – and spice. Put all of these
ingredients into an electronic mixer and you're HAVING A RAVE-UP WITH
THE YARDBIRDS! If you still don't know what a RAVE-UP is, just listen to
The Yardbirds' exciting new album and find out!!

A 1999 Digipak CD reissue from the Repertoire Records edition (REP
4758-WY) included a bonus CD of outtakes and previously unissued
material, including 'Here 'Tis (Version For RSG)', plus two bluesy
instrumental group compositions, 'Like Jimmy Reed Again' (3:02) and
'Chris Number' (2:21).

Side One (1965, With Jeff Beck)
'You're A Better Man Than I' (Mike & Brian Hugg) 3:17

Mike Hugg was more than just the drummer with Manfred Mann, which had originally been named The Mann-Hugg Blues Band. He was also an able vibraphone player with a jazz slant. He wrote or co-wrote hits for Manfred Mann, songs for the 1968 *Up The Junction* movie, and later, the distinctive theme song for the BBC sitcom *Whatever Happened To The Likely Lads*. It was with brother Brian that he wrote the frequently covered 'You're A Better Man Than I' for The Yardbirds.

Recorded on 12 September 1965 during their first US tour in Phillips Recording Studio in Memphis – where Elvis cut his legendary 'Sun Records' sides – although Keith was so 'overwhelmed' by the occasion that his vocal was later overdubbed in New York, the track was first released by The Yardbirds on this American album, then as the British B-side of 'Shapes Of Things', although the song's liberationist theme and assertive delivery would easily have qualified it for A-side status in its own right. It catches the 'protest' mood of the time to perfection, calling out the racist prejudices of those who judge others by race, creed, religion … or the length of their hair, with the bonus of a stunning, precise Jeff Beck guitar solo. There is also a remastered version that runs to 3:58.

'Evil Hearted You' (Graham Gouldman) 2:24

See single entry

'I'm A Man' (Ellas McDaniels aka Bo Diddley) 2:37

The press advertisement announced 'Third hit in a row … and their biggest! Wild, wonderful, exciting, exuberant … danceable and different!' 'I'm A Man' had originally been written and recorded by Bo Diddley in 1955, a moderately slow blues with a stop-time figure that was inspired by an earlier blues song. It became a number one US r&b chart hit and was subsequently recorded by a wide variety of artists.

'Still I'm Sad' (Paul Samwell-Smith, Jim McCarty) 2:57

'Nothing religious about our hit', Paul Samwell-Smith told *Record Mirror* on 21 October 1965 about this track. In a bizarre spread of styles, 'Still I'm Sad' was revived by Boney M on their May 1977 *Love For Sale* album and recorded live at Nuremberg by Ritchie Blackmore's Rainbow for their July 1977 *On Stage* double-album.

'Heart Full Of Soul' (Graham Gouldman) 2:28

With Clapton out of the picture, the group were free to explore brave new sonic territory. And they wasted no time jumping back into it with 'Heart Full Of Soul', featuring one of Beck's first performances with the group, and one of his best. Adventurous in ways that Clapton was rigid, Beck tunes his guitar into a sitar by cranking up the distortion and filtering the fuzzy results into one of rock's great riffs. This was claimed to be the first recorded use of a fuzzbox.

'The Train Kept A-Rollin" (Tiny Bradshaw, Lois Mann aka Syd Nathan) 3:26
R&B bandleader Tiny Bradshaw wrote and performed the original version of 'Train Kept A-Rollin" as far back as 1951, but The Yardbirds grabbed inspiration from Johnny Burnette's rockabilly cover, one of the first songs to include guitar feedback. Beck dirties up the distortion even more, making The Yardbirds' version the definitive one. Everyone from Aerosmith to Zeppelin borrowed their arrangement.

The take on 'Stroll On', which The Yardbirds perform so effectively in the *Blow-Up* movie, was an updated version of 'Train Kept A-Rollin", with rejigged lyrics. Antonioni 'wanted us to do 'Train Kept A-Rollin", which he'd seen us perform and fitted what he wanted', explained Chris, 'In the end, we rewrote it as 'Stroll On' because there was some sort of problem with the copyright.' It was Jimmy Page who carried the song over into early Led Zeppelin gigs.

Side Two (1964, Live With Eric Clapton)
'Smokestack Lightnin" (Chester Burnett aka Howlin' Wolf) 5:35
'Respectable' (O'Kelly Isley, Ronald Isley, Rudolph Isley) 5:28
'I'm A Man' (McDaniel) 4:24
'Here 'Tis' (McDaniel) 5:04
Side two is a sequence of tracks lifted intact from the *Five Live Yardbirds* LP. Onstage, 'Here 'Tis' and 'I'm A Man' were accelerated and extended into six-minute jams. 'We really whipped up the audience,' recalled McCarty, 'people would swing from the rafters.' For *NME*'s Charles Shaar Murray, 'the closing 'Here 'Tis' on the live side is pretty damn messy and is of interest mainly for its (for Clapton's) uncharacteristically manic guitar. Keith Relf grates more than somewhat, both for his off-pitch vocals and his refusal to stop playing the goddam harp and let Clapton get it on, but it's still a joyful noise.' Lester Bangs, in *Rolling Stone* on 9 July 1970, took a different view: 'Incredible chances were taken with stunning success, as in the wild rhythmic interplay of 'Here 'Tis', where Clapton's ringing guitar fairly whooped while Paul Samwell-Smith ran double-time circles around him on bass and the percussion thundered like an African stampede.'

Above: The Yardbirds check out their latest press: Keith looks over Jim's shoulder, Chris is on the phone, while Jeff wishes he was elsewhere. (*Alamy*)

Below: The band miming on BBC's *Top Of The Pops*, with Jeff Beck, and Chris

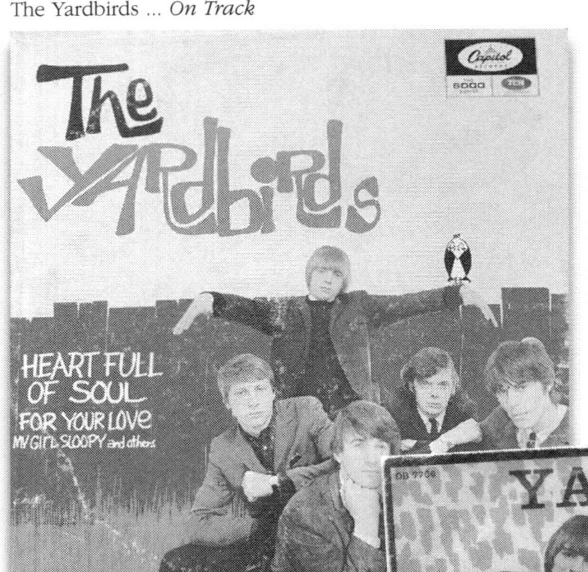

Left: The Canadian *Heart Full Of Soul* album release, for which the graphic artist takes the 'bird' a little too literally. (*Capitol*)

Right: There were – as yet – no picture sleeves supplied for UK single releases, but this sleeve for 'Evil Hearted You' is a Danish edition. (*Columbia*)

Left: The final part of the 2017 trilogy, *Midnight To Midnight*, was an edited version of Johnson's 12-hour live 2015 UK Election broadcast. (*Cineola*)

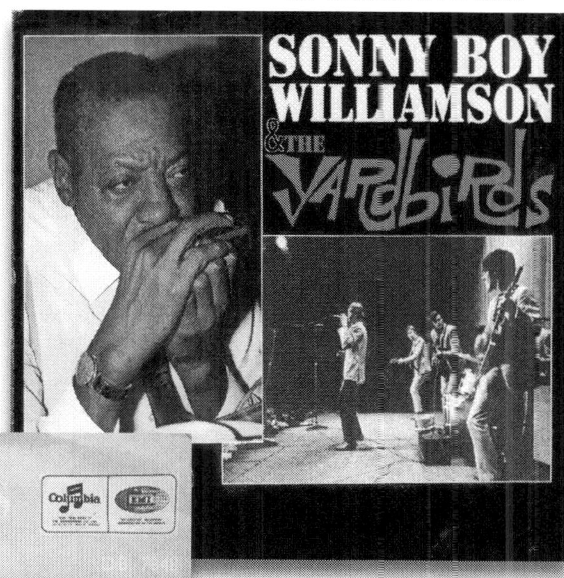

Right: UK dates providing backup for visiting Bluesman Sonny Boy Williamson proved a valuable learning experience for The Yardbirds. (*Fontana/ Mercury*)

Left: Possibly The Yardbirds' finest-ever coupling of 'A' and 'B' sides, 'Shape Of Things' is a stunning single. (*Columbia*)

Right: John Lee Hooker's 'Boom Boom' was a long-term staple of The Yardbirds' live shows but was never a UK single. This is a German release. (*CBS*)

Left: The distinctive Yardbirds lettering made their name stand out from the rest in magazine and poster advertising.

Right: Pirate broadcaster 'Radio Caroline' was a vital influencer in providing pop airtime when the only alternative was the BBC.

Live Albums & Singles 1966

Sonny Boy Williamson Meets The Yardbirds – Sonny Boy Williamson And The Yardbirds

Personnel:
Sonny Boy Williamson II: vocal, harmonica
Eric Clapton: guitar
Chris Dreja: guitar
Jim McCarty: drums
Paul Samwell-Smith: bass
Keith Relf: shouting, foot-tapping and handclapping
Released: 7 January 1966 (UK), 7 February 1966 (US)
Fontana TL5277 (UK), Mercury MG21071/SR61071 (US)
No chart position

The Yardbirds' earliest business card (yes! they had a business card!) proudly carried a quote from Sonny Boy: 'Them young gentlemen's wail the blues so well, they get me real satisfied.' They were billed from the start as 'The Most Blueswailing Yardbirds', and predating the group's first official recordings, this was an album taped on Sunday 8 December 1963 at the Richmond 'Crawdaddy Club' with The Yardbirds playing the role of backing musicians. It was not officially released until after the hits had begun.

Due to financial restrictions, many visiting American artists did not bring their regular backing musicians with them when they played British dates, but instead relied on a pick-up local band. Although this provided the opportunity for blues fans to play on stage with their idols, things were not always straightforward.

Sonny Boy – 'the wizard of the harp' – could be a difficult person to work with. He arrived to play what was then termed the 'American Negro Blues Festival' (subsequently the 'American Folk Blues Festival') at the Fairfield Hall, Croydon, on 18 October. Going on tour, he travelled with an imitation crocodile briefcase containing only his harmonica and a bottle of Johnnie Walker Scotch whisky. Rehearsal time was minimal, and when they got to the venue, Sonny Boy would often play different songs, in a different sequence, or with improvised arrangements.

Much of the biographical details about Sonny Boy Williamson II are dubious or disputed. Even his birth date is open to a number of theories – although there's a consensus that it was probably 11 March 1908 in Mississippi – yet the date of his death is clearly 24 May 1965.

In an interview from *Tapeop.com*, Giorgio Gomelsky talks about The Rolling Stones and The Yardbirds:

There were a couple of blues bands outside of London. This wasn't rock 'n' roll – this was the blues. The rock 'n' roll thing came in afterwards. It's very interesting how the possibility of recording happened. The first time that Sonny Boy Williamson came to England, he stayed with me. I took him in my car, and we went to all these places where there were blues bands. In the South End, there were The Paramounts that (later) became known as Procol Harum. In Birmingham, there was The Spencer Davis (Group), where Steve (Winwood) was like 14 and playing the organ. In Newcastle, there was a band called The Alan Price Kansas Blues Quintet, later known as The Animals. I ended up there and found a guy, Phillip Wood, who had a portable Ampex machine – mono. He had done demos for The Animals – a kind of straight, innocent character, but he had this equipment. I think it must have been the only Ampex one-inch (whatever it was at the time) portable recording device. When I saw this, I went, 'Wow! Let's drag this into the club.' And we recorded Sonny Boy with The Animals the first time that Sonny Boy went up there. I convinced Phillip to come to the next venue. I did a big thing on 28 February (which was my birthday) in 1964, in Birmingham. It was my first edition of a British Blues Festival – Sonny Boy, Rod Stewart and Long John Baldry – anybody that could play a couple of blues numbers would be on this, and that's how we convinced the Marquee to let us have a go at recording the live stuff.

There is a different track sequencing on the two editions. The UK edition is as follows, with the US edition in parentheses.

Side One
'Bye Bye Bird' (Willie Dixon, Williamson) 2:23 (1-1)
The harmonica blasts at shriek volume as the announcer makes his introduction, and The Yardbirds play basic blues progressions. 'Bye Bye Bird' had been the B-side of Sonny Boy's 1963 single 'Help Me', and was covered by the Moody Blues on their 1965 debut album *The Magnificent Moodies* with Denny Laine singing, which came after this Yardbirds version was recorded, but prior to its release!

'Mister Downchild' 3:56 (2-1)
This song was written and first recorded by 'Sonny Boy Williamson, His Harmonica & House Rockers' as early as August 1952 on the minor Trumpet Records label in Jackson, Mississippi. Eric Clapton later said that he'd repeatedly listened to Robert Lockwood's guitar playing on Sonny Boy's original Chicago records so that he could convincingly master the solo, and he vindicates himself with some style.

'Twenty-Three Hours Too Long' 5:04 (2-2)
The harmonica cuts like a flick-knife blade, leading into a slow-burning atmospheric Delta blues. His woman's been gone so long that at breakfast-time, 'th' blues start tuh walkin' all over ma bread'. Written by Bluesman Eddie Boyd, the track closes with a tasteful guitar solo from Eric, no flash or bombast, just dripping with heartfelt melancholy.

'Out On The Water Coast' 3:00 (2-3)

This is a jumpy blues taken at a lively pace, fronted by Sonny Boy's gravelly voice and raspy harmonica. He wants her to meet him down at the water coast so he can find out which one she loves the most, but where the water coast is located must remain an enigma. The tight Yardbirds backing proves more than competent at following his lead, with Eric contributing some stinging guitar picking.

'Baby Don't Worry' 4:23 (2-4)

Blasts of harmonica form solid, raw punctuation between Sonny Boy's groaned, lascivious, howled and grunted vocal lines, broken by scattered audience cheers. The range of sounds he coaxes from the mouth-iron is nothing short of awesome. The Yardbirds are largely absent. The version of the same song that Sonny Boy did live with The Animals opens with a salacious laugh.

Side Two
'Pontiac Blues' 3:45 (1-2)

This classic blues song was originally issued as a 10" 78rpm shellac, with Elmore James on session guitar, as long ago as November 1951 on Trumpet Records 145 – although Sonny Boy deliberately and wrongly announces it as 1938!

In the song, he brags that he's found out just what his Baby likes as they're motorvating down Highway 49 in the sleekly styled auto manufactured by General Motors in Detroit, which boasts hydramatic, automatic transmission. As a staple part of his set, Sonny Boy also performed the song when the blues came to town and he played the 'Club A Go-Go' with The Animals around the same time, with Hilton Valentine's guitar and Alan Price playing organ; it's preserved on the LP *Newcastle-On-Tyne, December 1963*, issued in 1976 by Charly Records (CR30013), with Sonny Boy counting the group in with '1-2-1-C'. It's informative to compare The Animals' version with The Yardbirds backing the same Chicago blues maestro on the same song. With Sonny Boy's chugging harmonica, The Yardbirds' playing is more restrained and subtle. Clapton says that Sonny Boy joked that 'these white boys wanted to play the blues so bad. And they did play them so bad.'

Astutely, Gomelsky taped live feeds from what was billed as *The First British R&B Festival: 28 February 1964* at Birmingham Town Hall, which was issued in 1989 under that name as 'An Historical Artefact' (Decal LIK54). The album includes four tracks by Sonny Boy Williamson with The Yardbirds – 'Slow Walk', 'Lonesome Cabin', 'Bye Bye Bird' and 'Pontiac Blues' – as well as an All Star Jam of 'Got My Mojo Working', plus tracks by The Road Runners, The Spencer Davis R&B Quartet, Rod Stewart and Long John Baldry. Bob Wooler handled the stage announcements.

'Take It Easy Baby' 4:18 (1-3)

Sonny Boy murmurs and moans as Clapton plays solid, sympathetic guitar figures. The vocals are rough-shouted but pleading, with breathy harmonica interjections, tipping the lyrics about her living her life too fast into the vague veiled threat that 'something bad might happen to you'. McCarty sets ticking and throbbing percussion as Clapton drips in notes around the anguished voice. The closing roar of audience applause is well-deserved.

'I Don't Care No More' 3:18 (1-4)

'A lot of you people don't understand what's happening about the blues,' Sonny Boy lectures by way of introduction, 'the blues is something that you went through with, or come in contact with – you understand? So, at this particular time, this was my trouble' – then a blast of mouth-harp leads into a near-talking blues about when Sonny Boy first met his woman. This track is virtually a solo outing for Sonny Boy, as The Yardbirds simply look on in awe and wonder, witnessing authentic street-corner wailing, and – at one point – he even hisses through his teeth for emphasis. A startling track.

'Do The Weston' 4:00 (1-5)

There were bonus tracks from the same tape included on the 2007 4CD box set *The Yardbirds Story By Giorgio Gomelsky* (Charly Records SNAJ 736CD), including 'Western Arizona', which is an alternate title for this track. The Yardbirds establish an easy jogging rhythm as Sonny Boy adds harmonica across the top. Although this appears to be a largely improvised instrumental, it does demonstrate, despite the well-documented problems, the ease with which the group and the blues veteran work together. Soon after the mid-point, Sonny Boy exclaims, 'What a closer ... well!' And he's not wrong.

The Yardbirds: In Italian!

'Paff... Bum' (Sergio Bardotti, Gian Franco Reverberi, Paul Samwell-Smith) 2:27 b/w 'Questa Volta' (Bobby Solo, Gianni Marchetti, Mogol) 2:33
Production credited to Giorgio Gomelsky, recorded in Columbia Studios, New York, on 17 January 1966
Released: 4 February 1966 (Italy). No UK or US release
Ricordi International SIR 20-010
Highest chart position: Italy: 5
This was an Italian-language song recorded specifically for the 1966 San Remo Music Festival, which was a prestigious event, launched in 1951, and which continues today. Being invited to participate was considered a good career move, in showbiz terms. Considering his dubious self-mythologised personal history, Gomelsky was, as ever, an internationalist, and he considered that doing the Festival was a vital step into the legit music business. But maybe not for a group like The Yardbirds! Gene Pitney, in his

smooth tuxedo, was better suited as the event's star. The Yardbirds played the song live on 27 January and issued it as an Italian single shortly afterwards. The track was also featured, with other songs from the Festival, on the album *Sanremo '66* (Ricordi MRL 6050).

Originally performed by Italian star Lucio Dalla, 'Paff… Bum' was adapted and given English lyrics by Paul, with a long, tinny piano introduction, and Keith singing unconvincingly about 'Paff Bum' being the 'sounds of love'. It's such light, fly-away pop that Jeff Beck refused to play on the record, so it's saved by a stinging solo from Chris. With 'the bearded one' Gomelsky credited as producer and Gianni Marchetti as arranger, there were various editions of the song, including as the German B-side of 'Shapes Of Things' (Epic 5-9910).

To hear Keith singing in Italian, flip the single over. 'Questa Volta' – which translates as 'This Time' – bears some melodic similarity to the Elvis Presley hit 'That's When Your Heartaches Begin'. But again, the guitar solo is probably the only reason you'd really want to buy this record.

The UK Release – 'Shapes Of Things'
'Shapes Of Things' (Samwell-Smith, Relf, McCarty) 2:24 b/w **'You're A Better Man I'** (Mike & Brian Hugg) 3:15
Personnel:
Keith Relf: lead vocals
Jeff Beck: lead guitar
Chris Dreja: rhythm guitar
Jim McCarty: drums
Paul Samwell-Smith: bass guitar
Production credited to Giorgio Gomelsky at Chess Studio on 21 and 22 December 1965, and Columbia Studio, Los Angeles, on 7 January 1966, and the RCA Hollywood Studio on 10 January and the B-side at Sun Studio, Memphis, on 12 September 1965 and Columbia Studios, New York, on 21 September 1965
Released: 25 February 1966
Columbia DB 7848. Not issued in the US in this form
Highest chart position: UK: 3
One of the first singles written by the band, 'Shapes Of Things' also includes one of the first-ever psychedelic guitar solos, a piercing blast of feedback-soaked noise by Beck that ranks as one of his all-time most innovative. 'We started off this Indian thing with 'Shapes Of Things' and all the other groups have hyped it off us', protested Jeff Beck to Richard Green in *Record Mirror* on 11 June 1966. 'They reckon it's the big thing to use a sitar on their records, but we don't. We've been using the sound for about two years now. I didn't listen to Indian music or anything to get the idea. I got it when I was out of my head with the music in Chicago.' The American edition of the song just missed becoming The Yardbirds' third top-ten hit in the US, stopping at number 11.

In an April coup coordinated by Samwell-Smith, The Yardbirds switched management from the inspired hands-on amateurism of Giorgio Gomelsky – who went on to manage Blossom Toes – to the more commercially streamlined and professional Simon Napier-Bell, recommended to the group by Vicki Wickham from *Ready Steady Go!* But if he found The Yardbirds as 'a reflection of Giorgio Gomelsky's neurotic mixed-up mind' (*NME*, 29 October 1983), Napier-Bell was to leave the group in a far worse state! Napier-Bell had made his major breakthrough into pop by writing the lyrics for Dusty Springfield's signature hit, hence his scurrilous and frequently amusing memoir was titled *You Don't Have To Say You Love Me* (Ebury Press, 2005), in which he tells how he co-produced The Yardbirds' *Roger The Engineer* album with Paul Samwell-Smith, through to producing the avant garde 'Happenings Ten Years Time Ago' single. He went on to contrive the confrontational career arc of John's Children – including a young Marc Bolan – before launching Wham! onto the world!

This sixth UK Yardbirds single was made a top 50 tip by the lukewarm *Record Mirror* review, which said 'chugging sort of opening beat from The Yardbirds, with a heavy, stomping beat and group vocal. It has a commercial sound but isn't the best yet from this chart-busting group. Curious guitar figures later on, and a determined sort of effort to get the excitement going. But a hit. Semi-Indian sort of attitude towards the end.'

What that review fails to mention is that the song almost takes its name from HG Wells' 1933 future-history *The Shape Of Things To Come* and that it's an anti-war protest song that both looks forward racially – 'please don't destroy these lands, don't make them desert sands' – and is self-questioningly personal: 'will I be older, come tomorrow, maybe a soldier, come tomorrow, may I be bolder than today?' All wrapped into a concise, structured detonation of full-on energies. Beck's solo grows organically and logically from the song's melodic structure, in ways that Clapton's frequently didn't (Eric's solo on 'A Certain Girl' sounds grafted in from elsewhere). While the song achieves the correct degree of suggested profundity, it falls on the correct side of being pretentious. A balance that many prog rock bands would fail to accomplish across entire albums.

'We did that in Chicago at Chess, and in those days, they got a much better sound in the American studios. Probably still do, actually', recalled McCarty. 'They've got a much better drum sound. It came off quite easily, really. We'd rehearsed it a lot already, the basic bones of the song, and we were all excited being there recording at Chess.'

Even the B-side formed its own challenging message. Dismissed by the *Record Mirror* reviewer as 'slower and effective', it confronts prejudice in a way that renewed its relevance when it was revived as a single by rabble-rousing punk band Sham 69.

The Yardbirds' single entered the charts at number 28 on 3 March 1966, rose through number 17 and number six to peak at number three on 24

March beneath The Walker Brothers ('The Sun Ain't Gonna Shine Anymore') and The Hollies ('I Can't Let Go').

The US Release – 'Shapes Of Things'
'Shapes Of Things' (Samwell-Smith, Relf, McCarty) 2:24 b/w **'New York City Blues'** (Relf, Dreja) 4:17
Production of B-side credited to Giorgio Gomelsky at the New York Columbia studio, recorded on 21 September 1965
Released: 28 February 1966 (US). Not issued in the UK in this form
Epic 5-10006
Highest chart position: US: 11
The first pressing of this American single has 'I'm Not Talkin' as the B-side, which was switched on 28 March to the newly recorded 'New York City Blues', a track that did not appear on an album until 1967 when it was included on The Yardbirds' first *Greatest Hits* collection (Epic LN24246). Critic Beverly Paterson praised its 'brutal burst of electric guitar, coaxed from the supernatural fingers of Jeff Beck', which then 'slinks and slouches into a burning blues statement.' It's been pointed out how Jimmy Page replicates the opening guitar figures on 'Since I've Been Loving You' on *Led Zeppelin III* (October 1970). And yes, this is an altogether tighter, more intense performance, a studied blues structure laced with stinging riffs that moan and groan with power, while the vocals – dropping into talking blues at one point – are convincingly pained over crisp and cohesive drumming, capturing the Yardbirds at the peak of their game. The song recounts the story of meeting a girl and bringing her home, only to be greeted by her Dad brandishing a 'big black shiny shotgun'. This is the kind of thing that might even have tempted Eric Clapton to stay with The Yardbirds!

The Yardbirds' German Single – 'Boom Boom'
'Boom Boom' (John Lee Hooker) 2:25 b/w **'Honey In Your Hips'** (The Yardbirds) 2:18
Personnel:
Keith Relf: lead vocals
Eric Clapton: lead guitar
Chris Dreja: rhythm guitar
Jim McCarty: drums
Paul Samwell-Smith: bass guitar
Produced by Giorgio Gomelsky
Released: 11 March 1966 (Germany)
CBS 1433
No chart placing
The 1988 Eric Clapton 4CD boxset *Crossroads* (Polydor 835-261-2) kicked off with three Yardbirds songs on which he'd participated, namely 'Boom Boom', 'Honey In Your Hips' and 'Baby What's Wrong', all recorded prior to the

release of the group's first single. The three tracks derive from a session recorded on 10 December 1963 at RG Jones Studio in Morden, which formed a demo that helped the group obtain their record contract. How those demos came to be a German single is a mystery, although, theoretically, Gomelsky was fired as The Yardbirds' manager in April 1966 – he was an enthusiastic gig-fixer and efficient promoter, but he was out of his depths when caught up in the devious machinations of the music industry. So, he could have pocketed the demos and offered them to record companies in Germany and Holland as a kind of damage-limitation exercise. A Dutch single was subsequently withdrawn.

By the time of the German single's eventual release, The Animals had recorded their own strident version of this primal John Lee Hooker song for their debut LP *The Animals* (October 1964), and – spun off as an American single – their 'Boom Boom' had become a minor number-43 hit on the *Billboard* chart. The Newcastle quintet largely follow Hooker's template, where, predictably, The Yardbirds' interpretation of the song is a smoother, more collective effort defined by Keith's high-profile harmonica. One of the earliest group originals, 'Honey In Your Hips' is a handclap-driven rewrite of the Johnny Otis 1958 rock standard 'Willie And The Hand Jive' (which Eric Clapton recorded for his 1974 *461 Ocean Boulevard* album), with impressive bass guitar from Samwell-Smith driving a mild Bo Diddley beat. 'When I hear the sound of a rock 'n' roll band', Keith sings, he's 'rocking up and down and around-around … to the beat of that crazy sound'. A toe-tapper.

Clapton's guitar is strongly featured on The Yardbirds' fast-shuffling 'Baby What's Wrong' (2:40) with Keith at his most blues-wailing, and as a device intended to attract major-label A&R attention, this might just have tipped the balance in the band's favour. Their take on this Jimmy Reed song eventually appeared on a 1973 double album, *History Of British Blues Volume One* (Sire SAS 3701), while a YouTube search will access a Rolling Stones demo of 'Baby What's Wrong', as well as a version by The Animals issued in 1990 as part of their *The Complete Animals* anthology (EMI 1367).

Meanwhile, Jeff Beck collapsed on stage during a French gig in Marseille.

The Single – 'Over Under Sideways Down'
'Over Under Sideways Down' (Dreja, McCarty, Beck, Relf, Samwell-Smith) 2:37 b/w **'Jeff's Boogie'** (Dreja, McCarty, Beck, Relf, Samwell-Smith) 2:25

Personnel:
Keith Relf: lead vocals
Jeff Beck: lead guitar
Chris Dreja: rhythm guitar
Jim McCarty: drums
Paul Samwell-Smith: bass guitar
Produced by Simon Napier-Bell with Paul Samwell-Smith at Advision Studios

between 19 and 20 April 1966
Released: 27 May 1966 (UK), 13 June 1966 (US)
Columbia DB 7928 (UK), Epic 5-10035 (US)
Highest chart position: UK: 10, US Billboard: 13

While Keith guested on the panel of BBC's *Juke Box Jury* on 21 May reviewing other people's new pop singles, the *Record Mirror* reviewer – either Norman Jopling or Peter Jones – awarded this new Yardbirds single 'Top Fifty Tip' status on 28 May 1966, but drew attention to 'those odd guitar-simulated sitar sounds again and a lively, almost beat-singalong treatment from the boys. Immediately catchy and not too ambitious. A very big hit even without the strength of their name. Excellently recorded. And odd lyrics. Flip is a great guitar showcase.'

This became the group's fastest-climbing hit to date; it entered the chart at number 21 on 2 June 1966, climbed to number 15, then lodged at number ten for two consecutive weeks. The Beatles' 'Paperback Writer' replaced Frank Sinatra's 'Strangers In The Night' at number one, The Rolling Stones' 'Paint It Black' was descending from number two to number six after its own spell at the top slot, The Animals ('Don't Bring Me Down'), The Mamas & The Papas ('Monday Monday') and The Merseys ('Sorrow') were all in that same very happening top ten.

With Samwell-Smith and Simon Napier-Bell credited as producers, 'Jeff's Boogie' is an instrumental credited to the five group members, although it sounds remarkably similar to Chuck Berry's 1957 'Guitar Boogie', indeed, litigiously close. But everyone from The Beatles down had borrowed from Chuck. The Yardbirds' single, naturally at the time, was released in mono. The stereo version was only issued when the track was added to the *Roger The Engineer* album.

Both 'Over Under Sideways Down' and 'Shapes Of Things' were included on a 16-track *Now That's What I Call Music*-style anthology issued in 1966 as *Go... With An All-Star LP Volume 1* (Columbia SX6062), which also gathered Wayne Gibson ('Under My Thumb'), The Attraction ('Stupid Girl'), Downliners Sect ('Glendora') and two from Herman's Hermits.

In the group's next major shake-up, Paul Samwell-Smith quit the band. Always reserved and formal by nature, he'd never felt completely comfortable on stage. He'd endured an antagonistic relationship with Eric Clapton, and after arranging 'For Your Love', he'd discovered an increasing preference for a backroom role in production. In this capacity, he formed a vital conduit between musicians and the production desk, between ideas and their consummation. Although bracketed in with Gomelsky and credited on the label as 'directed by', it was Paul who oversaw the 1965 recording of The Mockingbirds' single 'You Stole My Love' b/w 'Skit Skat' (Immediate IM015), the return favour being a 'thank you' nod to Graham Gouldman, who wrote both sides. The Yardbirds would later try – and abandon – their own version of 'You Stole My Love'. Paul was replaced in The Yardbirds lineup by Jimmy

Page. Soon, Chris Dreja moved from rhythm guitar to bass, while Page shared lead duties with Beck.

Some time earlier, on 20 February 1965, *Record Mirror* featured an advert for a single by Jimmy Page ('She Just Satisfies' b/w 'Keep Moving', Fontana TF533). With both sides co-written by Jimmy with Barry Mason, the single had a raw Kinks-style riff driving the 2:01 A-side, flipped with a 3:28 instrumental rave-up on which Jimmy played harmonica and bass, as well as guitar. Now rare and collectable, it passed by unnoticed at the time. Jimmy was a session guitarist. That same *Record Mirror* issue featured a mini artist profile of 'Jimmy Page: An Ace Guitarist'. He was credited as playing the guitar-bending sounds that elevated Dave Berry's 'The Crying Game' into the charts (although Jimmy later suggested that Big Jim Sullivan was responsible).

Subsequent researchers and archivists delving into the minutiae of 1960s discographies have attributed Jimmy's session contribution to just about every hit and cult obscurity of the period, including sessions by The Who and The Kinks. Playing three sessions a day, 15 sessions a week, Jimmy himself has lost track of what he played on, although two albums issued in 1989 and 1990, *Jimmy Page: Session Man* (US AIP Records AIP 10041, UK AIP AIPCD 1041 and US AIPCD 1053), compiled a series of battered, old, neglected sides, the first gathering both sides of 'She Just Satisfies' alongside The Zephyrs ('Sweet Little Baby' from August 1963) and Lulu & The Luvvers ('Surprise, Surprise', April 1965). The second volume has Neil Christian & The Crusaders ('Honey Hush', May 1964 and 'I Like You', April 1966) and Brenda Lee ('Is It True', October 1964). The album is more fully detailed later in this book.

Jimmy was born on 9 January 1944 in the West London suburb of Heston, although the family later moved to Feltham. Already under the spell of Scotty Moore and James Burton – respectively Elvis Presley and Ricky Nelson's guitarists – he claimed to have discovered a Spanish guitar left by the previous residents of the house when the family moved on to Miles Road, Epsom. He took a few lessons, but largely taught himself guitar by playing along to records. There's a famous clip of him as a precocious 13-year-old skiffle player on Huw Wheldon's 1957 *All Your Own* BBC show. Various short-lived groups followed, including The Paramounts (not the group that evolved into Procol Harum) and The Redcaps. He moved from backing poet Royston Ellis to playing with Neil Christian's Crusaders. A popular 1960s also-ran, Pirate Radio high-rotation plays later put Neil's 'That's Nice' up to number 14 on 12 May 1966, but at that point, a bad dose of glandular fever derailed Jimmy's career trajectory.

Building a reputation by jamming at the Marquee, he was offered session work, starting out by playing on former-Shadows Jet Harris & Tony Meehan's huge instrumental hit 'Diamonds' (which reached number one on 31 January 1963). Being spotted by producer Shel Talmy led to further studio work, which rapidly went into overdrive with The Nashville Teens ('Tobacco Road'), Van Morrison's group Them ('Baby, Please Don't Go'), Marianne Faithfull ('As

Tears Go By') and then in-house session-work for Andrew Loog Oldham's Immediate label. But, although lucrative, the anonymity of studio musicianship still left an itch for greater creative visibility. And The Yardbirds lineup shuffle offered the opportunity of stepping out of the shadows into the instant celebrity of a band with an established run of hits…

Keith Relf's Solo Single – 'Mr Zero'
'Mr Zero' (Bob Lind) 2:46 b/w **'Knowing'** (Keith Relf) 1:53
Produced by Simon Napier-Bell at De Lane Lea studio, London
Released: 13 May 1966
Columbia DB7920 (UK), Epic 10044 (US)
Highest chart position: UK: 50
Following the transatlantic success of his evocative 'Elusive Butterfly', Bob Lind suddenly found himself the go-to songwriter of choice. Former teen heartthrob Adam Faith got in first with a cover of Lind's 'Cheryl's Goin' Home', then – to issue as his own first solo single – Keith chose 'Mister Zero' from the same 1966 *Do Not Be Concerned* album (World Pacific Records WP-1841). Paul Samwell-Smith shares producer credit with Simon Napier-Bell.

Record Mirror's Richard Green reveals a story of complex rivalry in the issue dated 28 May 1966. Georgio Gomelsky had planned to record the Bob Lind song with Keith, but The Yardbirds slipped from his managerial grasp at the last moment. Undaunted, he went ahead and produced 'Mr Zero' with Susi Klee, a Zurich-born singer who was in London to improve her English. Her single was issued as Polydor BM56082 in direct competition with Keith's.

Not that Keith was necessarily planning a separate career away from The Yardbirds, it was seen as more of a side project. In the same issue of *Record Mirror*, David Griffiths interviews Keith, with a smartly cynical photo-credit comment that 'although he's recorded a solo disc, he won't be breaking away from The Yardbirds (seems we've heard that before somewhere)!' Yet, Keith is quoted as saying, 'I don't want people to think that I would ever leave the group. I'll never think in terms of leaving The Yardbirds, never think in terms of recording without them.' It's just that the song did not lend itself to a group arrangement.

Bob Lind's version had a pleasant soft-folkie charm, occasionally reminiscent of 'Norwegian Wood' with the then-fashionable surreal touches of 'tapestry kittens that hung on the wall'. Keith largely retains that simplicity of spirit, although it's embellished with the subtle production depth of bass and bell chimes, with his voice providing a rising strength of emphasis The Mr Zero of the title is a variant of Paul Simon's 'Most Peculiar Man', or maybe Dylan's 'Ballad Of A Thin Man', in that 'Little Miss Someone has packed and gone' while 'the charades are all done' and 'Mr Zero has lost.'

Issued just two weeks before The Yardbirds' 'Over Under Sideways Down' single, Keith performed 'Mr Zero' on *Ready Steady Go!* On 29 April 1966, and four weeks later, the single made its solitary appearance at number 50 on the

Record Retailer/ Record Mirror chart. Keith's own song on the B-side retains the folkie simplicity, with dancing harpsichord, as he serenades the wife he's missing while they're apart.

There are stories that Keith was not always in a good place. He'd always suffered from asthmatic health issues, which had become complicated by seeking solace through an over-fondness for booze. His out-of-control performance at Oxford's Queen's College May Ball on 18 May 1966 – with The Yardbirds sharing the bill with The Hollies – was embarrassingly shambolic, and a trigger in Paul's decision to quit. But if Keith always gave the impression of being too fragile for the world, this track provides a tantalising glimpse into his inner sensitivity.

Yardbirds aka Roger The Engineer

Personnel:
Keith Relf: vocals (except 'The Nazz Are Blue'), harmonica
Jeff Beck: lead guitar, lead vocals on 'The Nazz Are Blue', bass guitar on 'Over Under Sideways Down'
Chris Dreja: rhythm guitar, backing vocals, piano
Jim McCarty: drums, percussion, backing vocals
Paul Samwell-Smith: bass guitar (except on 'Over Under Sideways Down'), backing vocals
Production: Simon Napier-Bell and Paul Samwell-Smith at Advision Studio in London between 19 and 20 April, 31 May and 4 June and mid-June 1966
Released: 15 July 1966. Not issued in the US in this form
Columbia SX/SCX 6063
Reissued with bonus tracks as Repertoire REP 4681-WY
Highest chart position: UK: 20

Lillian Roxon called The Yardbirds 'one of the best groups to come out of England. One of the most concerned with music, they influenced the development of every group that came out of the English scene from The Beatles to The Who.' Proof of her assertion is to be found here, in what can be considered their only complete studio album. Originally eponymously titled simply *The Yardbirds*, it has subsequently become known as 'Roger The Engineer' due to the distinctive cover-art sketch of engineer Roger Cameron drawn artfully by Chris Dreja – despite the disclaimer 'all drawings are fictitious and not meant to represent in shape or form.' It was very much an in-house album, completed on four-track in just a week. There are other sketches on the reverse, framing Jim McCarty's humorously wacky sleeve-notes – 'the Chicago Blues style, Lordy-Lord, has been the influence on several of the tracks, the rest having been influenced by everything from Dylan Thomas to Watney's special.' It's the recognisable art-school whimsy inherited from Spike Milligan or John Lennon's 1965 book *A Spaniard In The Works* (Jonathan Cape).

McCarty goes on to draw pen-portrait caricatures of the group members. Paul Samwell-Smith, 'who is generally considered to have all the qualities of Burt Bacharach, Phil Spector and (comic actor) Richard Wattis all rolled into one – I wonder about the ratios!' 'Howling' Relf – as in Howlin' Wolf – who 'scores with some fine examples of lyric writing.' For Dreja, 'for the benefit of jazz fans, that's Chris, not (Erroll) Garner, on piano when used.' And himself, 'the percussion work is of a very high standard (Ego2) and I would vote Jim McCarty one of the best drummers ever allowed out.'

At one point, Paul Samwell-Smith claimed that 'our mate' Mick from a band called The Triangle played bass on half the tracks, while Paul himself and manager Simon Napier-Bell were occupied with production chores in 'the soundproof booth.'

The release of this album preceded The Beatles' *Revolver* by a few months, but it is carried by the same spirit of adventure and innovation.

Side One
'Lost Woman' (Dreja, McCarty, Beck, Relf, Samwell-Smith) 3:16
Paul Samwell-Smith had pointed out the group's intention to concentrate on songwriting, and that all future Yardbirds releases were to be their own compositions, while, with the confidence of their new management support, Keith declared to *Record Mirror* on 28 May 1966, 'We hope to make this year our year, and our ambition is to become the most popular group, second to The Beatles.' The album opens promisingly with this unusually structured track that starts with drum cymbal-shots, then a dancing bassline before Keith sings the first verses ... until it slows into an extended harmonica-driven instrumental passage that builds in intensity, with a solid guitar wall and tom-tom drums. Then, it abruptly switches back to the bass solo, and Keith drops in the closing verse, almost as a close-parenthesis to the song's wordless core. As the lyric says, within this track, it's possible to see the 'future coming, like the rising of the tide'. A spiteful Eric Clapton pointed out that it was he who had introduced his then-bandmates to a Snooky Pryor track from which the 'Lost Women' riff had been lifted.

The album review published in *Record Mirror* was simply headed 'Columbia 33SX 6063' and featured a black-and-white photo of the group to the right, with the text alongside. 'Lost Women', it says, is 'very fast, almost bordering on British rock 'n' roll. Occasional bursts of raving and a peculiar-sounding instrumental break with what sounds like the BBC Radiophonic Workshop included.' The rival *New Musical Express* headlined 'Yardbirds Produce Oriental Sound On New LP', with Allen Evans writing that 'Lost Women' has 'a short vocal by Keith Relf, then he produces a weird wail on his harmonica through a fuzz box, giving the track a real 'breath of the Orient'. It builds to an exciting end.' It's fair to suggest that music journalism was still in its infancy!

'Over Under Sideways Down' re-channelled (Dreja, McCarty, Beck, Relf, Samwell-Smith) 2:24
Behind the learned baffle of expert witnesses pontificating on literary merit, both defending and prosecuting sides in 1960's *Lady Chatterley's Lover* trial knew exactly what was at stake. And both, from their opposing side, were absolutely right – with their opinions clearly vindicated by what followed. What was at stake – let's get this straight – was not only the right to read dirty books. After this, there was a deluge, for better or worse. And the Yardbirds lyrics here form a concise manifesto for what outraged newspaper editorials were calling the 'permissive society'. Young rakehell Keith sings 'when I was young, people spoke of immorality, all the things they said were wrong are what I wanna be'. This is a proclamation of hedonism, promiscuity and

liberation: 'Cars and girls are easy come by in this day and age, laughing, joking, drinking, smoking 'til I've spent my wage'. And it was a perfect expression of the time.

'The Nazz Are Blue' (Dreja, McCarty, Beck, Relf, Samwell-Smith) 3:04
This is the song from which Todd Rundgren took the name of his first band, The Nazz. The opening 12-bar riff is iconic Elmore James, and Jeff plays what Captain Beefheart might call a long, sustained lunar note, as well as taking a rare lead vocal. The *NME* said that the track 'has a jazzy blues sound with Jeff Beck doing a good vocal. Rock-steady backing with interesting guitar sounds.' According to the vocal, he's got 150 possessions, but he can't find his woman. The lyric 'the Nazz don't help me' implies that maybe they're looking back to 'his Royal Hipness' Lord Buckley's Beat-comic routine 'The Nazz', which sends up the Biblical Carpenter-kitty messiah story. The Small Faces also took Buckley's 'Here Come The Nazz' quote and reshaped it into their hit single 'Here Come The Nice'.

At the time of the album's release, DJ John Peel was broadcasting a morning-show for KMEN in San Bernadino, where he traded on his Englishness by persuading the programmers to allow him to play a British top 20, for which he would simply choose whatever record caught his fancy that week and award it his own random placing in the rundown. 'The Nazz Are Blue' lingered in his top five 'for an unfeasibly long time, despite never having been released as a single anywhere on Earth' (as related in Peel's *Margrave Of The Marshes*, 2005, Bantam Books).

In 1977, a band called Lavender Hill Mob issued their own very respectable cover of 'Nazz Are Blue' as a single on United Artists (UAXW925Y).

'I Can't Make Your Way' (Dreja, McCarty, Beck, Relf, Samwell-Smith) 2:26
Keith bashes out time with a tambourine. Jeff's guitar winds its way behind the vocals, set to its slight oriental tuning, then he breaks out into tight, restrained solo bursts. The harmonies may just echo back to the drones of 'Still I'm Sad', but in total, it's a kind of right turn into strangeness. The lyric playfully rejects the 'straight' conventional life of people who live their lives so worthlessly, those troubled, bothered, flustered and hurried people who are chased by the taxman and the rentman. Keith claims to prefer living his life free and having no money … and in ten years' time, he'll still feel the same! To Allen Evans, writing in the *NME*, this track 'is folksy. Combined harmony vocal, sung straight, with Eastern sounds behind. Should be a popular number to cover.' While a later retrospective over-the-shoulder glance from Charles Shaar Murray for *NME* on 25 December 1976 claimed that Jeff 'transforms every song he works on: the country singalong bathos of 'I Can't Make Your Way' achieves almost epic stature because of the marvellous fiddle evocation that Beck plays beneath the vocal and the aching purity of the

deceptively simple solo. His buzzing, screeching, whining guitar is everywhere on the album, texturing when not soloing.'

The photogenic duo of Paul & Barry Ryan covered this song on their 1967 LP *Two Of A Kind* (Decca LK4878) as a shot for credibility, complete with an approximation of Beck's guitar solo.

'Rack My Mind' (Dreja, McCarty, Beck, Relf, Samwell-Smith) 3:15
From 5-9 January 1966, The Yardbirds played dates at 'The Hullabaloo Club' on LA's Sunset Boulevard. As part of their set, they played 'Over Under Sideways Down' and 'Rack My Mind'. The track starts off with an easy ticking blues structure, with Keith singing in an insinuating nasal slur. It builds to explode into a raging guitar and harmonica mid-section, locked into a groove with every element in perfect balance. The lyric starts with Keith searching his dictionary for words to describe his woman, then rackin' his mind before he decides on accusing her of being 'the world's worst woman, the devil ever made'.

Richard Green in the *Record Mirror* wrote that a 'fairly lengthy instrumental intro leads into Jeff on a fastish number. Harmonica plays its part, then the guitar takes command of the situation.' He commended the 'clean, unconfused backing.' At the same time, *NME* described it as 'Chicago-styled r&b, with harmonica and guitars' and a 'raving vocal by Keith. Good track.'

'Farewell' (Dreja, McCarty, Beck, Relf, Samwell-Smith) 1:29
'Listen closely to the words of 'Farewell'' advises Jim McCarty's sleeve notes, as an example of Keith Relf's facility at lyric writing. The track begins with simple piano phrases that the *Record Mirror* disparagingly compared to a TV glove-puppet: 'Thought this was going to be Larry the Lamb when it started with Chris on piano.' Then, the reviewer suggested that 'Bob Lind's influence seems to have crept in on a folksy number treated differently from usual for The Yardbirds.' He adds that the track is 'short'. By contrast, *NME* found it 'Dylan-influenced, with Keith singing his own lyric about a mixed-up chap who shuts himself in.' Then, they called it 'a short, sick nursery rhyme.'

'I ventured forth unto the day' has Keith adopting a self-consciously poetic style to work his way through the days of the week, although omitting Wednesday and Thursday along the way. It has an unusual construction: on the stereo edition, Keith recites quasi-significant verse in the right-hand channel, while in the left, the group add harmony sounds in the same 'Still I'm Sad' mode. Obviously, the mono mix simply has Keith's voice placed more to the fore. It closes with 'farewell to future days'. In total, it is a strange, yet oddly hypnotic track.

Side Two
'Hot House Of Omagarashid' (Dreja, McCarty, Beck, Relf, Samwell-Smith) 2:39
The wobble-board is a makeshift DIY instrument that consists simply of a thin sheet of wood, such as plywood, held between both hands and

'wobbled' to produce an oscillating, rhythmic whoop-whoop sound. It is, unfortunately, best known due to its use by its alleged inventor, Rolf Harris, on his first hit single 'Tie Me Kangaroo Down, Sport'. This Yardbirds track is another oddity, with non-verbal 'ya-ya-ya' chants played over tribal whoops and percussion against the rhythmic insistence of the wobbleboard. According to the sleeve notes, 'Chris Dreja's subtle vocal talents can be heard at the beginning of 'Hot House'', and there is a Jeff Beck solo to enliven the track's second half.

Reviewer Richard Green in *Record Mirror* seemed baffled when he wrote, 'All sorts of wild yells, screams and odd noises here. A wobble board competes with vocal ya-ya-yas throughout on an otherwise strictly instrumental track.' Allen Evans at the *NME* took a more informed stance, finding a 'bit of exotic jungle percussion (including Jeff with drum sticks on empty beer bottle on double track), then into Chris Dreja's wobble board (a piece of hardboard found in the studio) and chanting of repetitive lyrics, plus more wailing snake-charmer music by Jeff behind.'

Where did the 'Omagarashid' name come from? I'd at first suspected a literary or fantasy-fiction source. Not so, Jim tells me: 'It was invented by Chris or Paul. Probably terribly politically incorrect!'

'Jeff's Boogie' (Dreja, McCarty, Beck, Relf, Samwell-Smith) 2:25
'It has often been said that Jeff Beck is one of the leading guitarists in the country, and I'm inclined to agree with him', gags Jim McCarty on the sleeve notes. This is the mono single B-side of 'Over Under Sideways Down', made available in re-channelled stereo for the first time. *NME* described it as 'a guitar-swinging instrumental featuring lead guitar, Beck double-tracking some gay stuff, with snippets of other tunes like 'Alfie' [he uses the word 'gay' in its original definition, meaning 'happy']. Drumming by Jim McCarty is good, too.'

When he left The Yardbirds, Jeff took this nimble and inventive arrangement with him and played it as part of his Jeff Beck Group set, most notably live at the Fillmore West on 24 July 1968.

'He's Always There' (Dreja, McCarty, Beck, Relf, Samwell-Smith) 2:15
Jim McCarty poses me a question, 'Do you know which is the most successful Yardbirds song (financially)? – No? – by a mile it's 'He's Always There', sampled by the Pussycat Dolls.' For The Yardbirds, Keith's voice is echoed in a jumpy song structure that *NME* called 'insistent r&b. He fancies her. He suspects she fancies him, too. He'd like to take it one step further ... but her boyfriend is always in the way. There's a brief snatched guitar solo into the fade, extended to 2:31 in an alternate take collected on the 2021 Demon Super Deluxe edition. The winding, rasping, cricket-like earworm rhythm is propelled by the Latin American güiro instrument, which forms the motif running through the background of the Pussycat Dolls song 'When I Grow Up', which appears on their album *Doll Domination* (2008).

'Turn Into Earth' (Dreja, McCarty, Beck, Relf, Samwell-Smith) 3:06
Again, the stereo separation is eerily startling, with Keith's yearning voice in the left channel and otherworldly background voice-drones to the right. There's a stripped accompaniment, with tambourine jingle-jangling out the beat over a drumkit foot-pedal thump. Yet bizarrely, it sways to waltz-time. The poetic cosmic lyric signifies profundity by reflecting on transience in rural images of dying leaves, 'distant dreams of things to be, wandering thoughts that can't be free, I feel my mind turning away, to the darkness of my day', shifting down into a disconsolate murmur. This is what *Record Mirror* called 'slow and mournful with weirdo effects' and *NME* described as a 'slow, low key blues with a most effective echo solo vocal by Keith, backed by a choir effect (three voices double-tracked).' He also revealed the song is 'written by bassist Paul Samwell-Smith and his girlfriend Rosemary Simon.' Another strong track.

That bedsitter folkie Al Stewart released his own version of 'Turn Into Earth' – with an uncredited Jimmy Page session guitar – as the B-side of his debut single 'The Elf' (Decca F12467), which vindicated The Yardbirds' growing respect as tunesmiths in their own right. The Al Stewart track was later included on *The Psychedelic Scene* compilation album (1998, Deram 844-797-2).

'What Do You Want' (Dreja, McCarty, Beck, Relf, Samwell-Smith) 3:22
McCarty's high-hat and Samwell-Smith's bass form a solid bed for a return to the more raw, upbeat Yardbirds to add balance to an already diverse album. The stereo mix reveals a far more textured backing, with the brief bursts of Beck's distorted guitar to provide fittingly psychedelic anticipations, as Relf chants the title phrase over and over. The lyrics reflect paranoid Cold War fears of 'smoke up in the sky' and 'sounds which soar above my ears', while we 'sit spellbound by a flickering screen, watch the ever-changing scenes, listen to the rising screams, of children of today'. For *NME*, however, it was just 'a fast raver, with a shout vocal by Keith, with a chorus behind repeating the title. Jangle guitar.' An instrumental version of the song, titled 'Take 4: Instrumental Master' on *Yardbirds: The Jeff Beck Years* (2002, Fuel 2000, 02-061-196-2) allows the listener to isolate Jeff's contribution to greater advantage.

'Ever Since The World Began' (Dreja, McCarty, Beck, Relf, Samwell-Smith) 2:09
Record Mirror called this track 'another slowie with resounding doomful instrumental work.' It has distorted accusatory vocals that admonish the listener like a fundamentalist pulpit preacher delivering an anti-materialist message as the band add a supportive 'money' background chant. The *NME* review ascribed its 'gospel tinge' to how it was 'written during the session (as were some other tunes): it starts off as a dirge about the evils of money and then snaps out of it to a swinging pace.'

For Julian Cope's *Head Heritage* website, Brandon Tenold points out that 'although it is primarily The Yardbirds' guitar players who get all the credit for laying the foundation for heavy metal, one should not overlook the influence of the mope-rock vocal stylings occasionally employed by Keith Relf. Don't believe me? Then take a listen to the song that originally ended the album, 'Ever Since The World Began'. Over top of a Gregorian-inspired dirge, Relf sings the following doomy, gothic-tinged lyrics: 'Throughout the years there have been wars, power and richness (sic) have been the cause, trapped in money's evil net'. The cool medieval cloisters of a Gregorian monastery were a mighty long way from antebellum Delta blues! Then, around the 1:10 point, it switches into a dancey, swaying repetition of 'you don't need money' until its abrupt stop. A strange closer to an astonishing album.

Singles, EPs & Albums 1966-1967
The American Version – Over Under Sideways Down

Personnel:
Keith Relf: lead vocals
Jeff Beck: lead guitar
Chris Dreja: rhythm guitar
Jim McCarty: drums
Paul Samwell-Smith: bass guitar
Released: 8 August 1966 (US). Not issued in the UK in this form
Epic LN 24210/ BN26210
Highest chart position: US: 52

Released for the American market, this is the same as *Yardbirds* but with two missing tracks, slightly different mixes and different cover art. There are sufficient slight differences to the mono and stereo mixes to make both collectible to obsessives; the mono version has a searing Beck solo on 'Hot House Of Omagarashid' and better-clarity guitarwork on 'Lost Woman' and 'He's Always There' – which also has a longer fade and extended end-vocals – absent from their stereo counterparts. There are also missing opening beats from the stereo mix of 'I Can't Make Your Way' and 'Turn Into Earth'.

Soon after Jimmy Page joined the shuffled lineup, The Yardbirds commenced an American tour, arriving for three days of promo-work in New York on Tuesday 2 August, before commencing a schedule taking in Minneapolis, Chicago, Denver, Tulsa, Lubbock, San Francisco, San Jose and elsewhere. This tour was significant in that they were flying to dates on DC3s arranged thanks to Napier-Bell. Although rock touring was still in its infancy, this was still far from the large-scale, high-profile stadium tours that were to become the norm in subsequent years, and which were to elevate Led Zeppelin's rise to prominence.

In September, the Beck-Page lineup of The Yardbirds commenced a 12-date UK tour headlined by The Rolling Stones and Ike & Tina Turner, with Long John Baldry, Jimmy Thomas and Peter Jay & The New Jay Walkers also on the bill.

On 19 October, they arrived in the US for a further tour, this time as part of The Dick Clark Caravan Of Stars. This was the last of a series of prestigious 'package' tours organised by the host of the *American Bandstand* TV show. Begun in 1959, the Caravan had headlined Frankie Avalon, Lloyd Price, The Ronettes, The Shangri-Las, Paul Revere & The Raiders, The Byrds, Bo Diddley and many others. As such, it was a major showcase. But this gruelling 33-date tour, covering 16 American states in a tour bus, boasted a bill that also included Gary Lewis & The Playboys, Sam The Sham & The Pharaohs, Bobby Hebb and Brian Hyland. To Jimmy Page, 'it was the worst tour I've ever had to do. We were living on a bus, doing double gigs every day for four weeks. We didn't know where we were or what we were doing', until, after just two dates, Beck pulled out. He fled to LA to see girlfriend Mary Hughes while The

Yardbirds struggled to complete the tour as a quartet. 'I was tired of touring and on my last legs, really', Beck recalled about his decision. 'My logic was simple. Why go through shit when I could have a wonderful time with her?'

At a post-tour post-mortem, Jeff was fired for being unpunctual. Or was he? Accounts of the incident vary. While the Yardbirds continued on after this trip, the writing was on the wall soon after Beck had met Mary, and the band struggled with a relentless touring schedule and internal conflict. Beck had always been a mercurial character; he was not a team player by any stretch. In some ways, it's surprising he remained with the group as long as he did. There was a confusion of reports in the press. First, that he was hospitalised with tonsil problems, then that he was 'mentally exhausted by the changes in temperature and long hours of travelling.' Finally, *Disc* reported that 'Jeff Beck arrived back in London last Thursday after playing only the first few dates of The Yardbirds tour.' They suggest that Jimmy Page is also likely to quit, as 'their manager, Simon Napier-Bell, flew to America on Monday to discuss the group's future.' The details remained unclear.

Beck appeared with the other surviving Yardbirds when they gathered onstage for the band's 1992 induction into the Rock And Roll Hall Of Fame, relating with a tongue-in-cheek grudge how 'Somebody told me I should be proud tonight. But I'm not, 'cos they kicked me out. They did! Fuck them!'

Meanwhile, according to the official history, Jeff quit in order to form his own unit with Ronnie Wood and Rod Stewart, and they were immediately rewarded with a hit single in the form of enduring party-anthem 'Hi-Ho Silver Lining' (which reached number 14 in the UK in March 1967, Columbia DB 8151). The song's popularity would subsequently prove to be both a millstone and an embarrassment to Jeff's serious musical ambitions. The B-side – 'Beck's Bolero' – had been recorded between 16 and 17 May as a side project while he was still part of The Yardbirds, using Jimmy Page on uncredited 12-string guitar, John Paul Jones (bass), Keith Moon (drums) and Nicky Hopkins (piano). The composition was to receive further exposure when Jeff included it on his July 1968 debut solo album, *Truth* (November 1968, Columbia SX6293). Also, as a parting tip of the hat to The Yardbirds, Jeff opened the album with his own version of 'Shapes Of Things'. 'No-one ever beat The Yardbirds at their own game, except for the bands formed by their three ex-lead guitarists', observed *NME* on 7 April 1973.

The Jeff Beck Group followed the hit single with another Graham Gouldman song, 'Tallyman' (which reached number 30 in the UK in August 1967, Columbia DB 8227). Although Rod Stewart was technically the group's vocalist, producer Mickie Most had Jeff himself sing lead on both, much to Rod's chagrin. The group's third single was an instrumental cover of the lush French theme 'Love Is Blue' ('L'Amour Est Blue') – a number-23 hit in February 1968 (Columbia DB 8359), which was also an American orchestral number-one for Paul Mauriat. In a *Record Mirror* interview, Beck protested that he hadn't even wanted to record the song in the first place, and what did fans want of him anyway? Well, what his hard-core followers wanted was for him to follow his own muse. When Mickie Most teamed the Beck group with Donovan, another of the acts he produced for, it did result in a big transatlantic hit with 'Goo Goo Barabajagal (Love Is Hot)' (which reached number 12 in the UK in July 1969, Pye 7N 17778). In the States, it reached a *Billboard* number 36 on Epic 10510. After which, Jeff did follow his own eccentric muse with esoteric forays into jazz-rock fusions.

Side One
'Lost Woman'
'Over Under Sideways Down'
'I Can't Make Your Way'
'Farewell'
'Hot House Of Omagarashid'

Side Two
'Jeff's Boogie'
'He's Always There'
'Turn Into Earth'
'What Do You Want'
'Ever Since The World Began'

The Classic Single That Failed – 'Happenings Ten Years Time Ago'
'Happenings Ten Years Time Ago' (Yardbirds) 2:53 b/w **'Psycho Daisies'** (Yardbirds) 1:45
Personnel:
Keith Relf: lead vocals
Jeff Beck: lead guitar
Jimmy Page: electric guitar
John Paul Jones: bass guitar
Jim McCarty: drums
(B-side Jeff Beck, Jimmy Page and Jim McCarty only)
Producer: Simon Napier Bell at IBC and De Lane Lea Studio between 20 September and October 1966
Released: 7 October 1966. Not issued in the US in this form
Columbia DB 8024. Not issued in the US in this form
Highest chart position: UK: 43
The colour cover photo on the front of *Record Mirror* dated 2 July 1966 (number 277) shows the full five-piece Yardbirds, with Beck standing to the left – wearing an Iron Cross medal! – with Jimmy Page to the right, behind a crouching Relf, with McCarty and Dreja to the left. Jimmy Page's first single with The Yardbirds also featured one of the few band recordings on which both he and Beck appear. 'Happenings Ten Years Time Ago' also features a rare vocal outing from Beck, who supplies the spoken interlude in the middle

of the song, with additional bonus points awarded because it's John Paul Jones on bass! To David Wells, writing in *Record Collector: 100 Greatest Psychedelic Records* (2005 Diamond Publishing), 'the first truly great A-side that presented British psychedelia in all its fully-formed, mind-melting glory was almost inevitably issued by those serial pioneers, The Yardbirds.'

It opens with a crash, leading into guitar figures of vaguely oriental tuning, into a sharply precise rhythm section driving Keith's earnest vocal 'sinking deep into the world of time' with Jim providing vocal harmony. This then moves into a beautifully structured, futuristic dual guitar solo, rumbling into violin-bowed sounds, constantly switching, never pausing, as submerged dialogue flows beneath the surface (Jimmy Page had supposedly borrowed his technique of playing his telecaster with a violin bow from Eddie Phillips, of pioneering group Creation). In total, this single is as stunning a record and as ahead of the game as The Byrds' 'Eight Miles High' or Love's 'Seven And Seven Is'. At its best, Brit-psych can still be awesome; at the time, this was head-ripping.

To Wells, this was 'the first and, as it turned out, pretty much the only fruits of a short-lived lineup that featured Beck and former session hotshot Jimmy Page on twin lead guitars ... primarily an astonishing sonic duel between the two men. A thrilling manic sound collage, the song featured a barrage of relentlessly spaced-out lyrics ('is it real or in my mind? I've got to know what it all means') over a fractured, dissonant structure, wailing feedback imitating a police siren and, underneath those ego-overload duelling guitars a hilarious Beck monologue.' What the submerged dialogue represents is open to conjecture. Wells states that it is Jeff recreating comments made by a harassed doctor at a Hammersmith VD clinic. To me, I've always envisioned it as casual banter with local youths as The Yardbirds load amps into the tour van after a gig. 'A pop group, are you? Why you all gotta wear long hair?' 'Bet you're pulling the crumpet, aren't ya?' The manic laughter conjures that image in my mind.

It was 'an almost perversely non-commercial offering ... far too extreme for mass consumption', yet, as Wells accurately points out, rather than a springboard to greater things, it 'was closer to a full stop than a semi-colon.' All that pent-up potential was to be placed on 'pause'. Most of the big 1960s names had experience with failed singles. The Who had issued 'Dogs' in June 1968, which stalled at a paltry number 25. The Small Faces' second single, 'I've Got Mine' – their follow-up to 'Watcha Gonna Do About It' – had failed to chart at all. Manfred Mann's movie-theme composition for 'Up The Junction' failed to chart. The Hollies' cover of George Harrison's 'If I Needed Someone' rose no higher than number 20. They all bounced back with bigger hits. But not The Yardbirds.

One of the stranger aspects of the single's promotion was a full-page advertising tie-in in *Rave* (December 1966) for a 'Miss Disc' range of perfumes, headed by a full Beck-and-Page band photo: 'She's the chick among The

Yardbirds. She goes for groups. They go for her. She has her very own group, too. Named after her. Miss Disc.' Not quite the sweet smell of success!

One of the final tracks recorded with Jeff Beck, leaving a looming power-solo, the B-side is carried on a dense, nagging, heavy-rock riff not a million miles from that driving 'Communication Breakdown' on the first Led Zeppelin album. Yet, the lyric is a travelogue of American locations – 'New Orleans is the home of the blues, down in Mississippi I'm told it's nice, and all the meals there, they come with rice' – but in a trendy reference to the 'happening' West Coast scene, 'California's my home' and 'back in California there's nothing to lose, 'cause everything's swinging there with Mary Hughes'. Despite rumours to the contrary, 'Mary Hughes' was not street slang for marijuana, enhanced by implications of the 'Psycho Daisies' title. In fact, Mary was the TV and B-movie actress with whom Jeff was emotionally entangled, although she must have been 46 years old at the time!

There was also a degree of disenchantment setting in. As Richard Green went on to point out, The Yardbirds' live sets were increasingly becoming a 'big guitar thing, what with Jimmy Page and Jeff Beck standing on either side of the stage playing as fast and loudly as possible. 'I was more interested in the music, but the fans stared at Jimmy and Jeff', complained Keith.

The American Single – 'Happenings Ten Years Time Ago'
'Happenings Ten Years Time Ago' b/w **'The Nazz Are Blue'**
Released: 7 November 1966 (US). Not issued in the UK in this form
Epic 5-10094
Highest chart position: US Billboard: 30
The Yardbirds' discography was further complicated as American releases continued to offer different combinations of tracks. *Record Mirror* reviewer Richard Green pointed out that 'The Nazz Are Blue' 'starts like an Elmore James thing – any of his records. This track marks the singing debut of Jeff Back and he sounds like Steve Winwood. He also plays guitar.'

The Second Solo Keith Relf Single – 'Shapes In My Mind'
'Shapes In My Mind' (Simon Napier-Bell) 2:20 b/w **'Blue Sands'** ('F Groin') 2:15
Produced by Simon Napier-Bell at Sunset Sound, Los Angeles, in late August, and New York's Columbia Studio on 8 September 1966
Released: November 1966
Columbia DB8084 (UK), Epic 10110 (US)
No chart position
The second solo single from Keith, with Simon Napier-Bell producing. There is a churchy organ and disruptive effect sequences mixed in with lyrics that inevitably suggest an LSD trip: 'My eyes are closed, the colours cry, my brain explodes, my body shrinks into my head, I must have help or I'll be dead'. The Yardbirds were supposedly first given lysergic acid by Michael Hollingshead,

the Timothy Leary disciple and self-proclaimed 'Man Who Turned On The World'. Both Keith and Jim were known to be involved in 'substances'. Whatever, that content guaranteed that radio programmers steered well clear of this record!

The *NME* gave the single a favourable review: 'Sung on deep echo, with an enveloping organ sound and plucking bass well to the fore, plus a pounding beat, it has a nagging insidious effect in keeping with the bemused lyric'. The harmonica-led instrumental B-side is credited to Keith, but is actually played by a UK group called The Outsiders. A rare American red vinyl promo single version featured a different edit, where it was credited to 'Keith Relf of The Yardbirds'.

A 2020 compilation titled *All The Falling Angels* (Repertoire Records Repuk1385) gathers both sides of the 'Mr Zero' single with the UK edit of 'Shapes In My Mind', plus demos of other songs – 'All The Pretty Little Horses' (1:57), 'Only The Black Rose' (0:47), 'Glimpses' (1:23) and 'Echoes I May Find' (0:28) – plus outtakes from future projects, Together, Renaissance and collaborations with Jim McCarty.

Over Under Sideways Down (EP)

Personnel:
Keith Relf: lead vocals
Jeff Beck: lead guitar
Chris Dreja: rhythm guitar
Jim McCarty: drums
Paul Samwell-Smith: bass guitar
Released: 27 January 1967
Columbia SEG 8521. No US release
No chart position

The *Record Mirror* review of the original album observed that 'I Can't Make Your Way' is 'medium tempo with prominent tapping in the background. Vocal harmonies and a slightly Indian influence in the instrumental work.' 'He's Always There' 'features an instrument that makes a noise like a giant cricket.' While 'What Do You Want' is a 'fast rocker with plenty of raving. Jeff is joined vocally by some of the others on occasion. The kind of thing that used to get the fans going at the Crawdaddy.' While *New Musical Express* conceded only that the EP's title track has 'a swinging Arabic sound. Quite good', there's a kick in the tail that the group 'aren't doing as well as they used to' and 'they should get away from this droning sound.'

To Rod Stewart, in his 2013 autobiography, 'The Yardbirds had brought in Jimmy Page, who could play guitar a bit himself, and after the inevitable tensions between Page and Beck – two virtuosos fighting for space – and a fair bit of glaring at each other across a smouldering stage, Jeff had decided to leave.' To McCarty, 'Eric tended to be difficult. Jeff was a bit moody. Jimmy was pretty stable, actually. It was more of a business to him, really'

The New Year saw further changes. The four-piece Yardbirds spent the Christmas period in America, returning to London on 9 January as Simon Napier-Bell was ousted as manager, to be replaced by the more intimidating and confrontational former wrestler Peter Grant. The Yardbirds flew to Singapore to play the National Stadium on 17 January before embarking on one of the last of the old-style package tours of Australia, sharing a curiously mixed bill with The Walker Brothers and Roy Orbison, plus local artists The Mixtures and Thursday's Children (21 to 28 January), taking in Sydney, Melbourne, Adelaide and Brisbane. Their finale performance of 'I'm A Man' formed a direct continuity link – closing the circle through all the changes that had subsequently happened – back to the way they'd performed it on *Five Live Yardbirds*.

Tracks
'Over Under Sideways Down'
'I Can't Make Your Way'
'He's Always There'
'What Do You Want'

The Movie Soundtrack Album – Blow-Up: The Original Soundtrack Album
Personnel:
Keith Relf: lead vocals
Jeff Beck: lead guitar
Jimmy Page: electric guitar
Chris Dreja: bass guitar
Jim McCarty: drums
Yardbirds track 'Stroll On' produced by Simon Napier-Bell at Sound Techniques Studio, London, in early October 1966
Released: 10 May 1967 (UK), 20 February 1967 (US)
MGM C/CS 8039 (UK), MGM E/SE-4447ST (US)
Highest chart position: US: 92
In October 1966, through an MGM deal with producer Carlo Ponti, cult Italian movie-maker Michelangelo Antonioni came to Britain to film his first English-language project, the ultimate Swinging London movie *Blow-Up*, with David Hemmings, Vanessa Redgrave, Sarah Miles and the first onscreen glimpse of pubic hair! Although locations include Chelsea, Brixton, Belgravia, Greenwich, Peckham and, inevitably, Carnaby Street, the film's interiors were shot over a five-week period in a converted Holland Park slaughterhouse, the real-life studio of fashion photographer John Cowan.

The movie exploits often surreal twists, with Hemmings as a trendy fashion photographer who believes he's caught evidence of a murder that is only revealed when he 'blows up' photographic stills taken in the Greenwich Maryon Park. For the movie, Antonioni mocked up a replica of Windsor's mod

'Ricky Tick Club' in the Elstree studio, complete with Janet Street-Porter grooving in a silver jacket, and a guy wearing a Zoot Money T-shirt. The director initially envisaged The Who doing their autodestruct performance for the sequence, but following a little devious managerial jiggery-pokery, The Yardbirds were a last-minute substitution. 'Probably the best thing Simon Napier-Bell ever did for us', said Chris. It became one of their most iconic visual clips.

As the charismatic Hemmings approaches the club down an outside alleyway, the sound of 'Stroll On' is already audible. The audience is largely male. They watch as though mesmerised, although there are tranced-out dancers. These were not the screaming fans of *A Hard Day's Night*. Time had moved on.

Keith Relf wears a turquoise jacket and raises his arm to cue in Jeff Beck's solo. There's a crackle of distortion and Keith reaches out to assist as Jeff adjusts the Vox speaker settings. When the interference persists, Jeff bangs his guitar neck against the speakers in increasing frustration, a roadie jumps up to intervene, but he's too late, Jeff smashes his guitar down onto the stage in frustration and stamps on it and the band play on – Jimmy Page watches Jeff's antics with amusement. Jeff holds the fragments of his guitar aloft and hurls the neck into the audience. Of course, it was contrived for effect. Jeff Beck was never prone to smashing guitars; he loved and valued them way too much for that. But it looked terrific – it caught the moment. It was one of the great cinematic rock 'n' roll clips.

Caught up in the fighting melee to retrieve the guitar neck, Hemmings escapes from the club, brandishing it, walking past posters announcing John Mayall and The Yardbirds as the sound of 'Stroll On' continues. Once on Oxford Street, he simply throws the artefact away! He strove to possess it, but once he had it, it was without value to him. He dropped it casually.

The soundtrack album is essentially Herbie Hancock's movie score with 'Stroll On' as the sole Yardbirds contribution. The full movie was released as a Warner Home Video DVD in 2004.

For Jeff Beck, many years later – 10 August 2016, for his 50-year career-celebrating *Live At The Hollywood Bowl* DVD (2017, Eagle Vision EAGDV090) – he would return to 'Over Under Sideways Down' and deliver stunning re-treads of 'Train Kept A-Rollin'' (aka 'Stroll On') and 'Shapes Of Things' with Steve Tyler of Aerosmith taking vocals.

The First 'Greatest Hits' Album – The Yardbirds Greatest Hits

Released: 17 April 1967 (US). No UK release
Epic LN24246/ BN26246
Highest chart position: US: 28
The Yardbirds' first 'Greatest Hits' compilation was made up of all six American hit singles, plus three B-sides and the live 'Smokestack Lightning' from the *Having A Rave-Up* album. Hence, it is a souvenir of all three Yardbirds lead guitarists.

The Yardbirds played a live gig for the *Beat Beat Beat* TV show at the 'Stadthalle' in Offenbach, Germany, on 15 March 1967. The set was recorded and bootlegged using U-matic master tape, which has since been digitally restored, resulting in remarkable audio and visual clarity. It features two brief interviews with Keith Relf, an opening one in which he claims they're not interested in fads and fashions, only the music – 'actually, The Yardbirds tend to sort-of concentrate more on the music-making' – and one midway through the performance – translated by the show-host into German for the audience's benefit – where Keith makes management-disparaging comments. He doesn't name names, but is obviously referring to Simon Napier-Bell. To Napier-Bell, The Yardbirds were 'a miserable lot' who moaned and grumbled, got drunk and bickered endlessly with each other. He'd by then been replaced by Peter Grant, a Mickie Most associate.

This film formed a valuable souvenir of the final quartet configuration of the group, shortly after Jeff Beck had departed, featuring a 24-year-old Jimmy Page taking lead guitar. Keith Relf's reticent, self-effacing stage presentation always lacked the swagger of a Mick Jagger or the cheeky confidence of Manfred Mann's Paul Jones. He points at the audience, he shakes his tambourine, but again, there's an impression that the group perform the obligatory three hit singles – 'Shapes Of Things', 'Happening Ten Years Ago' and 'Over Under Sideways Down' – in order to get to the full extended rave-up of 'I'm A Man', where Keith is happiest just playing harmonica. But in doing so, it offers the opportunity to compare all three Yardbirds lead guitarist's interpretation of the song – first done with Eric Clapton on the *Five Live Yardbirds* album, then with Jeff Beck as the American studio single, and now with Page, where he's clearly heading in directions to be further explored in Led Zeppelin two years later.

Side One
'Shapes Of Things' (Paul Samwell-Smith, Keith Relf, Jim McCarty) 2:24
See earlier entry.

'Still I'm Sad' (Paul Samwell-Smith, McCarty) 2:59
See earlier entry. In the US, this track was relegated to the B-side of 'I'm A Man'.

'New York City Blues' (Keith Relf) 4:17
Keith Relf would never claim to be a technically proficient vocalist, but as Alan Clayson points out, his 'often torturous endowment still conveyed such exquisite brush strokes of enunciation and inflection that a fractional widening of vibrato during a sustained note could be as loaded as Joe Cocker's rawest wail', while his harmonica-playing 'slipped from suppressed lust through lazy insinuation to intimate torment' more eloquently than he could manage as a vocalist. This track, the American B-side of 'Shapes Of Things', perfectly illustrates Clayson's contention.

'For Your Love' (Graham Gouldman) 2:27
Richard Williams in *Melody Maker* described 'For Your Love' as 'their biggest
hit and, in my opinion, their best record. Its arrangement and execution
sound not in the least dated, and they've never been given credit in this
country for what they achieved.' In response to a resurgence of interest in
The Yardbirds, Charly Records issued an EP of their hit singles as *A Jukebox
Giant* in 1978 (CEP110). The four tracks were 'Still I'm Sad', 'Evil Hearted
You', 'Shapes Of Things' and 'For Your Love'.

'Over Under Sideways Down' (McCarty, Dreja, Beck, Relf, Samwell-
Smith) 2:22
The hit single was constructed in the studio. One input was hearing DJ Mike
Raven playing old rock 'n' roll records on his radio programme … and
deciding to do a 'Rock Around The Clock'-type boogie. It started with a Jeff
Beck bassline, overlaid with McCarty playing heavy off-beats coupled with
rim-tinkling à la Bill Haley. According to a Simon Napier-Bell interview, when
The Yardbirds were stuck for lyrics, they turned to him, 'I suggested they sing
a chorus of complete rubbish: 'Over Under Sideways Down, backwards,
forwards, square and round'. They thought this was a great idea: the critics
raved.' Inevitably, there are other versions of the story, including one where
Keith was obliged to bowdlerise the second line of their first draft in order to
remove the inference to various sexual positions!

Side Two
'I'm A Man' (Bo Diddley) 2:35
The American single version.

'Happenings Ten Years Time Ago' (Relf, Dreja, McCarty, Beck, Page)
2:49
The single that Tom Hibbert said was 'possibly the greatest 45 ever released'
in his *Rare Records: Wax Trash & Vinyl Treasures* (1982, Proteus Publishing).

'Heart Full Of Soul' (Graham Gouldman) 2:28
The hit single that bizarrely 'inspires a poignant and unforgettable' picture
love-story in *Valentine* (25 September 1965), in which 'Eve knew that she
could not resist the tragic, haunting call of the castle walls'. This was an
intriguing alternate take – version 3, as included on the 2019 album *Live At
The BBC Revisited* (Repertoire) – where Jeff Beck repeats his sitar-mimicking
magic on a livelier reading of the song for the June 1965 *Top Gear* radio
show.

'Smokestack Lightning' (Howlin' Wolf) 5:35
Their slow-burning take on the Wolf's signature number, lifted from the debut
Five Live Yardbirds album, features Clapton. Jeff Costello, writing in the

American *DISCoveries* magazine in November 1989, points out that The Yardbirds 'could take a song like 'Smokestack Lightning' or 'I'm A Man', whip it into a frenzy of raw energy, and at the point of apparent total chaos, stop on a dime and resolve the theme with perfect dynamics.'

'I'm Not Talking' (Mose Allison) 2:30
Where The Beatles were loveable scousers with a ready wit and a compulsive backbeat, The Rolling Stones had their insolent loutish decadence, The Kinks were wry commentators on the fads and fancies of the Swinging Sixties scene and The Who were screwed-down manic aggression. The Yardbirds always had that slight superiority suggested by the Beat Generation bebop jazz hipness of their name. For instance, there was Paul Samwell-Smith's penchant for tie-and-collar academic smartness, Jeff Beck's inspired flights of guitar experiment and Keith's detached air of far-sighted intellectual preoccupation. Powerful, but somewhat cerebral, too. This track was lifted from their American *For Your Love* album.

The Single – 'Little Games'
'Little Games' (Harold Spiro, Phil Wainman) 2:24 b/w **'Puzzles'** (Relf, Dreja, McCarty, Page) 2:02
Personnel:
Keith Relf: vocals
Jimmy Page: guitar
John Paul Jones: bass, cello arrangement
Dougie Wright: drums
Produced by Mickie Most at De Lane Lea Studios in London between February and March 1967
Released: 21 April 1967 (UK), 3 April 1967 (US)
Columbia DB 8165 (UK), Epic 5-10156 (US)
Highest American chart positions: US Billboard: 51, US Cashbox: 48, US Record World: 44
The perceived failure of 'Happenings Ten Years Time Ago' led to a major loss of self-confidence, and a resulting fall into the uncaring hands of Mickie Most, who had his own ideas about hit-making that had little to do with The Yardbirds' credibility or creativity.

It was after the Roy Orbison tour of Australasia that the label decided to pair The Yardbirds in the studio with Mickie Most at the console. Although he was born in Aldershot on 20 June 1938 and was involved in the early skiffle days at Soho's famous 'The 2i's Coffee Bar', it was during a sojourn in South Africa that Mickie had his first hits as a performer. Returning to the UK, he scored a minor hit with 'Mr Porter' (which reached number 45 in July 1963), following it with 'The Feminine Look', which happened to feature a young Jimmy Page playing session guitar. But it was as a producer that he made his real impact on 1960s pop-rock, at the mixing desk for The Animals ('House

Of The Rising Sun'), Herman's Hermits, The Nashville Teens, Donovan, Lulu and many more. For The Animals, he had steered a successful strategy with a string of powerful singles, which gave them the label leverage to follow their own r&b inclinations on albums. He was responsible for masterminding Jeff Beck into the charts with 'Hi Ho Silver Lining'. Jimmy Page was part of his regular studio crew, so it was not unnatural that Mickie Most was seen as the magic bullet required to arrest The Yardbirds' apparent chart decline.

That Keith Relf was prepared to go along with the strategy indicates that his own self-image had been shaken and impaired. Believing that if Most could contrive the group back into the top 20, it would restore their reputation and standing within the pop pantheon, and that prize was worth a little swallowing of pride. Few bands of the period (and they were 'bands' by then, not 'groups'!) could balance that trick of hit singles with respected albums … other than, maybe, The Who.

'Little Games' was a sharp, catchy, swinging London celebration about 'parties in Chelsea flats' and 'mixin' with kinky cats'. The fast-cut choppy rhythms and fine guitar solo, matched to Keith's high, detached vocals, lift its slight content. And although the song may have lacked the depth and creative innovation for which The Yardbirds had become known, it was not a record entirely without merit. It plays fast and loose with ideas of the kinky smart set, who are cool and trendily free-loving. The song boasts 'Margaret, Josephine, Susie and Catherine, they help me in my little games'. Perhaps it potentially meets the marketable American idea of what Carnaby Street cool was like, in the same way that Herman's Hermits traded on exaggerated ideas of their Englishness, or New Vaudeville Band pushed it into novelty caricature. But it did catch something of the flashy, disposable spirit of the times.

The psych-charged four-piece group-composed flip is perhaps more typical of the group vibe, from a strummed acoustic play-in, with Keith's voice sounding confident to a greater degree as he delivers quasi-profound lyrics about 'love, war, people arguing, how can they know what to hate?' He goes on to say, 'Ever since I began thinking, I wondered why things were so, but no matter how hard I contemplate, puzzles will never go' over a richly involved instrumental stew before the track closes with some killer Jimmy Page guitar flashes.

The single didn't chart, apart from on the Radio London Fab Forty, which doesn't really count, as the Pirate Radio Station's chart was not based on across-the-counter sales. There was also an attractively raw radio version of 'Little Games' – without the cello sweetening – recorded on 17 March 1967, broadcast on *Saturday Club* on 15 April (issued on *The BBC Sessions*, 1999 Repertoire REP 4777-WY). But, at best, this record must be counted as a Pyrrhic victory.

The Manfred Mann Cover – 'Ha Ha Said The Clown'
'Ha Ha Said The Clown' (Tony Hazzard) 2:19 b/w **'Tinker Tailor Soldier Sailor'** (McCarty, Page) 2:47

Personnel:
Keith Relf: vocals
Al Gorgoni: guitar
Bobby Gregg: drums
Joe Macho Jr: bass guitar
Rick Nielsen: organ
Produced by Mickie Most at the New York Columbia Studio on 13 June 1967 and EMI Abbey Road Studio on 19 June 1967. The B-side was recorded at De Lane Lea in London between March and April 1967
Released: 17 July 1967 (US)
Epic 5-10204
Highest chart position: US: 45

It almost seemed like throwing in the towel. They had given up on the UK charts to concentrate on America, where there was still interest, where the group were playing long improvisational sets – including material like 'Dazed And Confused' – at hippie venues. On Saturday 22 July 1967, The Yardbirds played in the round at the Santa Monica Civic Auditorium on a bill with The Strawberry Alarm Clock – who were shortly to score an American number-one hit with 'Incense And Peppermints' – Captain Beefheart & His Magic Band, The West Coast Pop Experimental Band and Moby Grape – who had just issued their first acclaimed album. Simone Romero recalls how 'we snuck into the Santa Monica Civic Auditorium to see The Yardbirds. It was the second show with Jimmy Page on lead guitar, who had been the bass player until Jeff Beck abruptly quit before the San Francisco concert.'

The Los Angeles Times review said, 'The Yardbirds and The Moby Grape received the most fervent applause.' 'The Yardbirds played a great show that night', recalled Moby Grape bass player Bob Mosley. Drummer Don Stevenson, to Cam Cobb in *Weighted Down: The Complicated Life Of Skip Spence* in 2024, added, 'The Yardbirds were one of those bands we went out and watched. We didn't always watch the bands we were playing with, but sometimes we made sure we did.'

Paul Jones, singer with Manfred Mann, had written a song called 'The One In The Middle' with The Yardbirds in mind. It had a teasing tongue-in-cheek lyric about the people of the town who came from miles around just to see the singer looking sweet. Keith shied away from such an embarrassing sentiment. So, Manfred Mann recorded it themselves as the title song of a chart-topping EP – Paul had no such qualms of conscience!

Meanwhile, Tony Hazzard's song 'Ha Ha Said The Clown' had been picked up by the Mike d'Abo lineup of Manfred Mann with an imaginative Shel Talmy production using Mellotron and novelty effects to striking ends. Recorded on 10 February 1967 and issued at the end of March, it rapidly climbed to a peak at number four on 26 April on the UK charts. However, because it was making little headway in America, Mickie Most suggested an opportunistic Yardbirds cover for that market. Most had faith in the short, radio-friendly singles format, which had served him so well to date. He had cut a George Harrison-penned verse from Donovan's 'Hurdy Gurdy Man' in order to make room for a Jimmy Page guitar solo (John Bonham and John Paul Jones also played on the single). Patronisingly, Most considered that 'pop fans' weren't ready for extended tracks, when all the evidence pointed to the fact that they very much were.

When the group declined to do the song, Most went ahead anyway, using American session musicians to record the backing track, then cajoled Keith Relf to dub his vocals over the top at Abbey Road. In many ways, this re-tread pales in comparison to Manfred Mann's own version; Keith's voice lacks the animated conviction that d'Abo invests in the comedy circus storyline – 'hear the jokes, have a smoke' – Keith obviously had little belief in the song and the instrumental treatment is little more than competently pedestrian. 'It was a terrible mistake', admits McCarty.

British record-buyers – myself included – were confused to see this record listed as 'Bubbling Under' the *Billboard* top 50, and how the group that had recorded 'Happenings Ten Years Time Ago' could have been reduced to this state. While even The Yardbirds themselves were more concerned with playing West Coast counter-culture venues alongside the emerging heavy underground bands, where what had once been called their 'rave-up' style was being spun out into long improvisational free jamming.

Again, the group-penned flip is maybe more convincing, shown to greater advantage on the *Little Games* album. For a long time, these two tracks were sought-after but difficult to acquire for British record-buyers, until they were added as bonus tracks to the expanded CD edition of the *Little Games* album.

Little Games

Key Personnel:
Keith Relf: vocals, harmonica, percussion
Jimmy Page: guitar
Chris Dreja: bass (with exceptions), backing vocals
Jim McCarty: drums (with exceptions), percussion, backing vocals
Produced by Mickie Most at Olympic and De Lane Lea Studios on 5 March and
between 29 April and 1 May 1967
Released: 24 July 1967 (US). No UK release
Epic LN 24313 mono, BN26313 stereo
Highest chart position: US: 80

Although the wheels had fairly obviously come off The Yardbirds project,
they still had time for one more album, which points out new possibilities
that were never to be realised. Bizarrely, this was only their third official
album, excluding fix-ups and compilations. If *Five Live Yardbirds* had been
Eric Clapton's album, and *Roger The Engineer* was Jeff Beck's, *Little Games*
should have been the album that showcased Jimmy Page. And, in many ways,
that is exactly what it is.

Although the group successfully blocked the release of this album in the
UK, its release went ahead in the States despite their opposition. In the
greater world outside, things were changing in seismic ways. The Beatles' *Sgt
Pepper's Lonely Hearts Club Band* and The Jimi Hendrix Experience's *Are You
Experienced* were soon followed by Pink Floyd's *The Piper At The Gates Of
Dawn*, while in America, Jefferson Airplane's *Surrealistic Pillow* and The
Doors' debut album were both in the *Billboard* top ten. All of them were
changing the very nature of what a rock album could aspire to be. However,
Little Games was essentially a patchwork of ideas, some of them very good,
but blended with Mickie Most's failed ambition to get a hit single at all costs.
Left to their own devices, things might have been different.

Largely absent and out-of-touch with what was happening on the UK scene at
the time, The Yardbirds' American live sets were standing favourable
comparison with the best of the West Coast counter-culture bands, particularly
the brief dual-lead guitar period with Page bouncing off Beck, and within just
over a year's time – freed from producer and record label interference – Jimmy
Page would begin studio sessions that would become the first Led Zeppelin
album. In the meantime, he saw the *Little Games* package as something of an
embarrassment. Was this *really* the band for which he'd forsaken his lucrative
session career? No, that was the band who crafted intelligent thought-provoking
pop-rock of the calibre of 'Shapes Of Things' or 'Happenings Ten Years Time
Ago'. Sure, Graham Gouldman's songs were pop, but The Yardbirds had been
capable of turning them around into singles of startling originality.

In 1985, the Fame label – a subsidiary of Mickie Most's RAK Records –
issued a UK edition of the ten *Little Games* tracks fleshed out with related

singles and B-sides (Fame FA41-3124-1), the sleeve-notes ironically drawing attention to the 'blistering guitar work on 'Think About It' that hints at the shape of things to come with Led Zeppelin.' In 1992, EMI-America issued a 2CD edition, *Little Games Sessions & More*, expanded with the singles, plus outtakes and alternate mono/stereo mixes, including instrumental 'Never Mind' (2:46). It also contained 'I Remember The Night' (3:01, by Anthony Pirollo) – a piano-led spoof cockney-French romance with whistle and kazoo that builds into an 'all together now' pub singalong. There were instrumental demos of 'LSD' (1:00); and 'You Stole My Love' (2:55, by Graham Gouldman) – a catchy 1965 Mockingbirds song recorded for Immediate IM015 that has the swaying tempo-change quality that is the Gouldman hallmark. The single bears the credit 'Directed by G Gomelsky and Paul Samwell-Smith', while Julie Driscoll sings backing vocals. It unfortunately only exists by The Yardbirds in numerous uncompleted instrumental takes with acoustic and stinging electric guitar; as well as three tracks by Together – McCarty and Relf's duo project.

Side One
'Little Games' (Harold Spiro, Phil Wainman) 2:25
Bobby Gregg and Dougie Wright play drums on this album version of the title song, while John Paul Jones adds bass and cello arrangements. Phil Wainman would later become known for his work with Sweet. He wrote 'Little Games' with pianist Harold Jacob Spiro. The line 'my temperature's rising but that's not surprising, when you do what you do to me' seems like a deliberate tip of the hat to Irving Berlin's song 'Heat Wave' as performed by Ethel Merman in 1938 ('the temperature's rising, it isn't surprising, she certainly can can-can').

'Smile On Me' (Dreja, McCarty, Page, Relf) 3:16
Despite the songwriter credit, this track adapts 'Killing Floor' and 'Shake For Me' by Howlin' Wolf ('I got a cool-shaking baby, shake like jello on a plate'), the energies that Jimmy Page would take forward into Led Zeppelin under the guise of 'The Lemon Song'. The original blues artists themselves continually plundered, refashioned and adapted songs from each other and from their tradition, so the fact that their white blues-boy copyists took similar liberties with the songs is hardly a revelation. And this track does present The Yardbirds at their most rocking, with pounding McCarty drums and a ferocious Page guitar solo, which indicates one of the directions The Yardbirds could have taken, if fates had been kinder.

'White Summer' (Page) 3:56
Chris Karan contributes pattering tabla to Jimmy Page's reworking of the haunting traditional Irish folk lament 'She Moved Through The Fair', which he'd learned from hearing Davey Graham sing it live at the famous 'Troubadour' Club in Earl's Court ... or maybe from the EP *From A London Hootenanny* (1963, Decca DFE8538), where it was listed as 'Round 861;

Henry H141'. He'd also studied the fretboard technique on the Bert Jansch version.

Jimmy was the only group member present in the De Lane Lea Studio (28-29 April 1967) when it was recorded, using a modal tuning to achieve a sensitive sitar sound. And it's a rich, unaccompanied track of some acoustic nimble dexterity and clever fingering flourishes. With an uncredited oboe player echoing the melody line, it succeeds in being both beguiling and pensive. A raw take of the track was later included on *Cumular Limit* (August 2000, Burning Airlines Pilot 24), a 2CD anthology of demos and live TV feeds. The Yardbirds played 'White Summer' live as part of a BBC radio *Saturday Club* show dated 5-6 March 1968, which was later included on the *Yardbirds: Live And Rare* album (March 2019, Repertoire Records REPUK1364). An in-concert version was recorded at the New York 'Anderson Theatre' on 30 March 1968, which was controversially included on *Live Yardbirds: Featuring Jimmy Page* (1971, US Epic E30615) – an album that Jimmy took out an injunction against the label to stop, although editions have subsequently emerged. When he played this instrumental as part of The Yardbirds' set, Jimmy used a 1961 Danelectro 3021 guitar, and he seamlessly took 'White Summer' over into the transitional Led Zeppelin dates, where it became part of a mash-up medley with 'Black Mountain Side'.

Among many other interpretations, 'She Moved Through The Fair' was recorded by Fairport Convention (on *What We Did On Our Holidays*, 1969), by Sandy Denny in a solo acoustic take and by Pentangle (on *In The Round*, 1986), until it formed the basis of 'Belfast Child', a number-one hit single for Simple Minds in 1989.

'Tinker, Tailor, Soldier, Sailor' (Page, McCarty) 2:49
Lyrically spun out around the nursery rhyme that predicts the child's future career, this former B-side of the 'Ha Ha Said The Clown' single decides 'I don't want a trade at all' in preference to 'living off the road' – 'perhaps I'll come to a great success, or possibly a dreadful mess', with crashing guitars over galloping drum patterns, all enhanced by a resonating Jimmy Page bowed guitar solo to give it depth.

'Glimpses' (Dreja, McCarty, Page, Relf) 4:24
The recited lyrics have that pastoral, cosmic mystification that Keith would take further into Renaissance, consisting of two brief four-line verses, with a long, repetitive coda. The curious line 'time is just a cumulus limit, which with one glimpse can overcome' will give its name to a Yardbirds rarities album (detailed later in this book). The track opens with bass figures, sharp drumming, drone voices, sheets of Jimmy's hallmark 'bent' guitar distortions and a treated voice reciting the poem, with disconcerting rumbles and a burst of submerged dialogue that in later years would be termed a 'sample'. The tempo accelerates towards the explosive close. A powerfully inventive track.

Side Two
'Drinking Muddy Water' (Dreja, McCarty, Page, Relf) 2:53
Although credited to all four Yardbirds, this is a tribute reimagining of Muddy
Waters' 'Rollin' And Tumblin'', as if there's a need to be reminded that this
band had started out most blueswailing. And yes, it retains all the dirty
harmonica-driven r&b energies they'd started out with as Keith sings 'I been
drinking muddy water, I don't know how long for, since I been running,
Babe, I been treating you like a dog'. Ian Stewart adds piano. To Jimmy Page,
this was a 'little pocket of resistance' to Most's 'run them off quickly and make
money' strategy.

There's a version recorded live at the New York Anderson Theatre, plus a
Studio Sketches 'version two' included on the *Yardbirds '68* double-CD issued
in 2017 through Jimmy Page's own label as JPRLPCD3. Significantly, the
album – which cannibalises rare tracks from the hastily withdrawn *Live
Yardbirds: Featuring Jimmy Page* and *Cumular Limit* – includes three Led
Zeppelin in-waiting songs: 'Dazed And Confused', 'White Summer' and the
acoustic Jimmy Page instrumental 'Knowing That I'm Losing You' –
supposedly based around his break-up with Jackie DeShannon, which would
become 'Tangerine'.

'No Excess Baggage' (Roger Atkins, Carl D'Errico) 2:32
John Paul Jones plays bass for a song by the Brill Building songwriter duo
responsible for The Animals' hit single 'It's My Life' in October 1965. It has a
naggingly simple riff with a catchy pop song construction about moving,
seeing the world while he can and tasting the fruits of life, while the band
provide answering vocal backing to Keith's high, clear assertions. It provides
a simple, uncluttered moment in the midst of deeper, more complex material.
Even the Jimmy Page guitar solo is concise and efficient rather than
outstanding.

'Stealing Stealing' (Dreja, McCarty, Page, Relf) 2:42
Ragtime boogie-woogie piano and kazoo provide a novelty, sing-along, skiffle,
good-time feel to this fun throwaway track. The writer credits don't mention
Gus Cannon, yet the song is clearly stolen from a track recorded in
September 1928 by the Memphis Jug Band, which had already been adopted
by Bob Dylan as early as 1962 (and included on his *Great White Wonder II*
bootleg), possibly via Dave Van Ronk's version, and later performed by The
Grateful Dead in 1966. Stealing indeed! It could be generously argued that its
inclusion here blends a previously unsuspected humour into The Yardbirds'
catalogue.

'Only The Black Rose' (Relf) 2:52
There's a strained 47-second unplugged demo of this song on Keith's solo *All
The Falling Angels* album, showing his voice at its most vulnerably frail. Yet,

this is the song, above all, that provides the direct link that takes him from The Yardbirds into Renaissance. The richness of folk-psych acoustic guitar provides depth as he metaphorically strips himself naked: 'When I am blind, soothe my brow, when thoughts hurt my brain'. There's the sickly romance of the doomed poet – 'stillness everywhere now… as flowers bloom and die' – conjuring images of the famous Henry Wallis painting *Death Of Chatterton*. It's a song made more affecting by its flaws.

'Little Soldier Boy' (McCarty, Page, Relf) 2:39
Appropriately, martial drumming introduces a kind of anti-war fairy-tale about teddy bears, wind-up toys and a wooden soldier who organises a war across the nursery floor that destroys them all, until – as 'smoke clouds rolled across the sky' – he also falls into the fire. With mouth-trumpet noises to add to the game, this simplified metaphor is probably more well-intentioned than it is successful.

Above: Jimmy Page joins the lineup in time to fly out to Canada on the first leg of a 1966 American tour. (*Getty*)

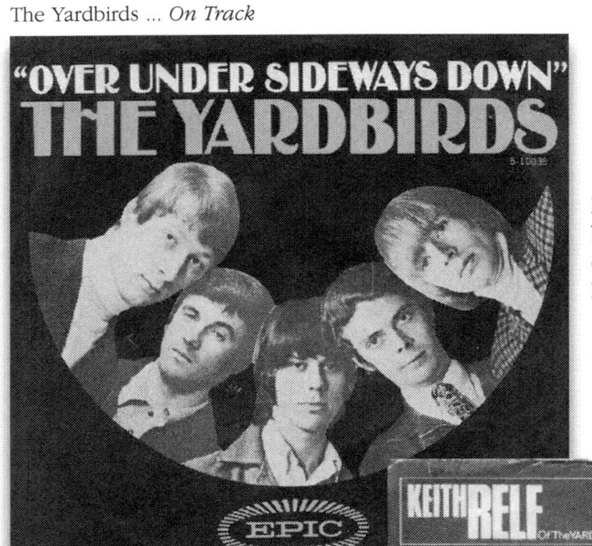

Left: The last of The Yardbirds' big hit singles: the American edition of 'Over Under Sideways Down'. (*Columbia/Epic*)

Right: Keith Relf's debut solo venture with a song written by American folkie Bob Lind. (*Columbia/Epic*)

Left: Chris Dreja's cartoon artwork of studio engineer Roger Cameron has led to the album initially titled *Yardbirds* becoming known as *Roger The Engineer*. (*Columbia*)

Right: Repackaged for American release, the *Roger The Engineer* album became *Over Under Sideways Down*. (*Epic*)

Left: The Yardbirds' finest single – 'Happenings Ten Years Time Ago' – which inexplicably failed to become a major hit. (*Columbia*)

Right: A *Greatest Hits* compilation, as seen from an American perspective. (*Epic*)

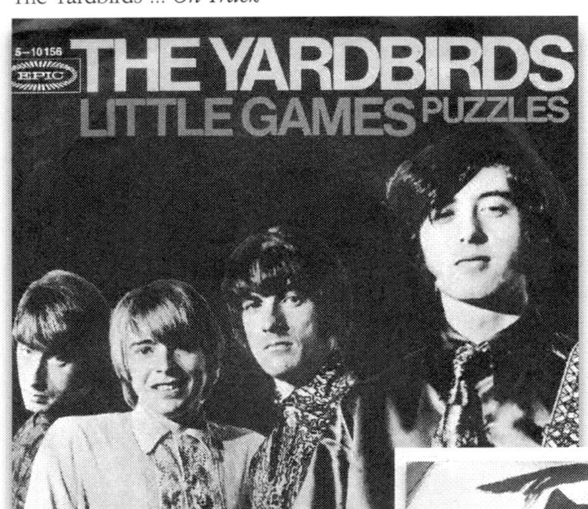

Left: The four-piece Yardbirds, with Jimmy Page and with a Mickie Most production, on the 'Little Games' single. (*Columbia/Epic*)

Right: The Italian sleeve for The Yardbirds' ill-advised cover of a Manfred Mann hit. (*Epic/Ricordi*)

Left: The final studio album, *Little Games*, wasn't even initially issued in the UK. (*Epic*)

Singles, EPs & Albums 1967-1968

The Yardbirds Sing Nilsson – 'Ten Little Indians'

'Ten Little Indians' (Harry Nilsson) 2:14 b/w **'Drinking Muddy Water'** (Relf, Page, McCarty, Dreja) 2:56

Personnel:

Keith Relf: vocals

Jimmy Page: guitar, reverse echo guitar

John Paul Jones: bass, orchestral arrangement

Clem Cattini: drums

Produced by Mickie Most at the London Olympic Studio on 25 September, the B-side produced at the De Lane Lea Studio between March and April 1967

Released: 16 October 1967 (US). No UK release

Epic 5-10248

Highest chart position: US: 96

Harry Nilsson was enjoying a gratifying ripple of celebrity status, with Beatles patronage in response to his inventive mash-up of 'You Can't Do That', and a song conspicuously covered by The Monkees ('Cuddy Toy'). 'Ten Little Indians' is the opening track on his *Pandemonium Shadow Show* album (December 1967, RCA Victor LPM-3874). With a ten-nine-eight countdown glance at Agatha Christie – her 1939 novel *And Then There Were None* had provided the narrative strand for the 1965 movie *Ten Little Indians* (with pop star Fabian). And by way of the biblical Ten Commandments, as Nilsson has the Indians 'lookin' at another man's wife', taking another's life and then taking 'the name of god in vain'. Over martial drumming, The Yardbirds replicate Nilsson's arrangement to an extent, until the bizarre oscillating Jimmy Page guitar solo that takes the track into the fade. There's an implied narcotic reference in the 'seven little Indians all trying to get their kicks, one thought he'd found another way to get to heaven, then there were six'.

Only two Yardbirds are actually present on the record. Dreja and McCarty would tell how they'd turn up for a recording date, only to discover that Mickie Most had already cut the track using session musicians. In a later Renaissance interview with *ZigZag* magazine, Keith bewailed how 'we were just a group being sent out to promote Mickie Most's records. He was involved in our management, and was our producer, and on two or three 'Yardbirds' records, he used session men to do the backings, while we were touring, and then just got me to overdub my voice. Incredible, isn't it?'

Drummer Clem Cattini goes back as far as playing on Johnny Kidd & The Pirates' 'Shakin' All Over', one of Britain's first convincing rock 'n' roll singles. Then – as part of Joe Meek's house band – he played on The Tornados' transatlantic number one, 'Telstar'. As a session drummer, it's claimed he's featured on some 42 UK number-one hits, and on records by everyone from PJ Proby and Dusty Springfield to The Ivy League and Tom Jones. Yet, 'Ten Little Indians' does constitute a more assured step than the single it follows.

Despite the group flying into New York for a single Madison Square Gardens gig, chart rewards proved hard to come by.

The flip side is simply lifted from the *Little Games* album.

The Final Yardbirds Single – 'Goodnight Sweet Josephine'
'Goodnight Sweet Josephine' (Tony Hazzard) 2:40 b/w **'Think About It'** (Jimmy Page) 3:45
Personnel:
Keith Relf: vocals
Jimmy Page: guitar
Chris Dreja: bass
Jim McCarty: drums
Produced by Mickie Most at London's Pye studio in mid-March, while the B-side was recorded at De Lane Lea in late January 1968
Released: 1 April 1968 (US)
US Epic 5-10303, UK Columbia DB 8368
Highest chart position: US: 127

The valedictory Yardbirds single is another disappointing product of Mickie Most's pop vision. Like 'Ha Ha Said The Clown', it's slick and radio-light, with just a slight flirty hint of swinging London promiscuity. An ideal hit for someone, but nowhere near right for the group who had once recorded 'Shapes Of Things'. Cobbled together in the studio, with Clem Cattini playing drums, John Paul Jones on bass and Nicky Hopkins on keyboard on early takes, the full four-piece lineup were nevertheless there in TV promotional clips, with Keith sporting a moustache and a flamboyant Jimmy Page in lace ruffles making the most of his solo.

As a bonus, on the American mix, Jimmy's guitar is heavily phased. There's also a live *Saturday Club* version on the 2CD *Live At The BBC And Beyond* album (2016, Repertoire REPUK 1309), recorded on 15 March and broadcast on 16 March 1968, introduced by veteran radio presenter Brian Matthew. I remember hearing the *Saturday Club* broadcast – it was a regular fixture on my listening agenda. I liked the song, and I liked the performance, but not in the way that I'd loved 'Shapes Of Things' or 'Happenings Ten Years Time Ago'.

This isn't to discredit the track. There's a catchy little guitar figure leading into 'Goodnight sweet Josephine, she's the queen of Clapham, every night she goes out with men to trap 'em in her net of ecstasy ... If Josephine could, she'd give you her blood, I know that she would'. Some critics have read that to mean she's a prostitute, or maybe one of those good-time girls who just wants to have fun. Tony Hazzard offers his own explanation as to how the song came about: 'I used to drink in a little pub called The Rose And Crown in Clapham Old Town, South London. It tended to be frequented by the CID (police). I think I got the idea from spending time there.' He later recorded his own versions of 'Ha Ha Said The Clown' and 'Goodnight Sweet Josephine' on his album *Tony Hazzard Sings Tony Hazzard* (CBS 63608).

The Julian Cope *Head Heritage* website calls the song a 'a music hall booze-up/sing-along about some heart o' gold, brazen barroom round-heels arranged with ale-soaked tack piano, although it's hilarious for Pagey's supersonically-phased guitar that dwarves even The Small Faces' 'Itchycoo Park'.' The track closes with 'Goodnight sweet Josephine, we love you to distraction, whatever she does, the police will take no action, they're all in love, with Josephine'.

About the Page-composed B-side, Cope's *Head Heritage* continues that it's …

… an entirely different matter altogether, for here there are three multi-tracked guitars and it's the razor-sharp, rave-up to end all rave-ups. 'Think About It' is crazy and has a radioactive guitar half-life of millennia. It's a searching, prototypical proto-metal and proto-everything else that blitzes like psychedelia and/or punk, depending on your mood.' Cope advocates the way the compassionate and searching lyrics, similar in approach to 'Mister, You're A Better Man Than I' and 'Shapes Of Things' break down into a wordless vocal bridge referencing The Yardbirds' earlier ventures into Gregorian chant, before building up to a solo that denies nothing and unleashes carnage in its wake … leaving the three remaining founding members in the dust (or two, as I believe it was John Paul Jones and not Dreja on bass). The track ends 'on a typical '67 backwards rhythm track, a slight harmonica blows in the fade's background as though bidding a sweet farewell to a chequered career that at least ended on an exquisitely demented note. It's The Yardbirds at their most insane. Ever.

Again, there's a *Live At The BBC* radio edit, introduced by Brian Matthew, where the nagging blues riff structure is clearer and more prominent, while the lyrics pose pseudo-profound questions about 'when will the clouds all roll away? When will the good people have their say? I hope you're still around to see the day'. But The Yardbirds would not be around much longer.

During their final American tour, during the spring of 1968, The Yardbirds performed Jake Holmes' 'I'm Confused' (later adapted into 'Dazed And Confused') and 'White Summer', which were both repertory blueprints for Page's New Yardbirds. A 30 March concert at the New York Anderson Theater (later CBGB's Second Avenue Theater) was taped for possible release as a live album by Epic, but when the band listened to the playback, they vetoed the project. Epic did attempt to issue the album in 1971, by which time Led Zeppelin had taken the US by force. The label dusted off the tapes, slapped Jimmy Page's name on the cover and sat back to wait for the profits to roll in. But the first thing to arrive was a court order from Zeppelin restraining the issue of the album. Epic withdrew it at the last moment in response to Jimmy Page's injunction.

With both Jeff Beck and Paul Samwell-Smith gone, it was as though a third element was missing, too, as though the group had lost its grounding, its lodestone, which had always been for the blues. However imperfectly replicated, it had been their core ingredient, their roots. By now, they were introducing new covers into their sets, but there was little to unify their choices or give them consistency, although the blues was still a powerful motivator within rock, with Peter Green's Fleetwood Mac evolving it with new innovations – 'Oh Well', 'Man Of The World' and the *Then Play On* (1969) album, as well as the enduring 'Albatross'. Jethro Tull began from the same blues origins, although they very quickly adapted into newer forms under Ian Anderson's fertile imagination. Jimmy Page ensured that the blues was an essential part of the Led Zeppelin mix.

The Yardbirds had hung out with the avant-garde Andy Warhol art Factory scene, and a 4:11 recording survives of The Yardbirds playing the as-yet unknown Velvet Underground junkie-anthem 'I'm Waiting For The Man', with Jim's relentless Mo Tucker drumming heavily laced with Keith's harmonica, as part of their 31 May 1968 set at the Los Angeles Shrine Exposition Hall. John Cale had brought an acoustic demo of the song to London during the summer of 1965, hoping to score a record company deal, and although there was no contract forthcoming, the demo was circulated through the rock community, where it may well have come to The Yardbirds' attention. It proves that the Yardbirds' flame of innovation still burned.

The sunshine face of hippie drug culture, seen through the kaleidoscopic lens of The Grateful Dead, Jefferson Airplane, Love and Big Brother & The Holding Company, had commercial traction, but The Velvet Underground's wasted New York art-chic would have to wait for David Bowie's patronage to give them legitimacy. Unless The Yardbirds could have got in first? Would an opportunistic cover of 'I'm Waiting For The Man' have returned them to the top ten? Who Knows? The question must remain open to conjecture.

Perhaps Keith felt restricted by the group's limitations and was feeling the need to stretch further. He'd done the gentle folk lullaby 'Hush-A-Bye (All The Pretty Little Horses)' for a BBC radio *Saturday Swings* broadcast on 17 April 1965. Now, they were covering Bob Dylan's 'Most Likely You'll Go Your Way (And I'll Go Mine)' on a 1967 edition of *Saturday Club*. Dylan had been known to filch from Robert Johnson songs, but for The Yardbirds, it seemed an uncertain fit. Manfred Mann had used Dylan songs most effectively – 'If You Gotta Go, Go Now', 'Just Like A Woman' and even an EP cover of 'With God On Our Side' (on *The One In The Middle* EP, June 1965, HMV 7EG890). Would 'Most Likely You'll Go Your Way (And I'll Go Mine)' have been a candidate to reverse The Yardbirds' chart fortunes? Again, that must remain open to conjecture.

Their first three hits had been with Graham Gouldman songs. Now, they worked on studio demos of another – 'You Stole My Love' – which Graham had already recorded with his Mockingbirds group. There is a surviving complete backing track. But either The Yardbirds lost interest, couldn't find a satisfyingly novel arrangement, or they simply put it on one side and never got around to completing it.

There's a rare track recorded on 5 April 1968 in New York during The Yardbirds' final studio session called 'Avron Knows' (3:49). It takes its name from a hippie who 'thinks he's trippy', a character the band met while touring in Florida. Avron provided inspiration for this tongue-in-cheek sniping at the insincerity of certain factions of the emerging counter-culture, of 'stupid flower-power'. 'He thinks he's free', sings Keith, 'well so do we', chant the others. 'He's where it's at', sings Keith, 'stupid pratt', chant the others. It features both Keith and Jim on vocals, with snarling guitar. Of the new material they were playing, this track provides further conclusive evidence of unflagging creativity (it was eventually issued on *Yardbirds '68* in 2017). There is also an instrumental version, 'Avron's Eyes'.

However, disheartened, The Yardbirds split on Sunday 7 July after a gig in Luton at the College of Technology. To Lester Bangs, writing in *Rolling Stone* magazine on 9 July 1970, The Yardbirds 'came up with a strange, compelling melange of British beat vitality, hard Chicago blues and electronic apocalypse; and thus, with a minimum of hoopla, The Yardbirds turned a corner in the history of rock 'n' roll.' Now that history was over.

Initially, Page and Dreja retained the group name and planned to play a ten-day Scandinavian tour as The New Yardbirds. But Dreja dropped out to become a photographer. Page recruited fellow session musician and arranger John Paul Jones as bassist (born on 3 June 1946 in Sidcup). Page asked Terry Reid to be vocalist, but although he declined, Reid suggested Robert Plant (born on 20 August 1948, from West Bromwich). Page and Chris Dreja, with new manager Peter Grant (Simon Napier-Bell continued to manage Jeff Beck), saw Robert perform as part of a band called Hobbstweedle in Birmingham. As a consequence, with only his rail fare in his pocket, Plant left the Midlands for talks at Jimmy Page's Pangbourne boathouse in Berkshire. It was Plant who suggested drummer John Bonham (born on 31 May 1948 in Eromwich, Staffs), who had been playing in back-up bands for Joe Cocker, Chris Farlowe and Tim Rose.

This was The New Yardbirds lineup that first rehearsed together on 19 August 1968 – the day prior to Plant's 20th – and this was the lineup that fulfilled the Scandinavian contractual obligation dates. When they played the Gladsaxe Teen Club in Denmark (on 7 September 1968), the set was a curious mix of The Yardbirds' 'Train Kept A-Rollin'', 'For Your Love' and 'White Summer/ Black Mountain Side' with the transitional 'Dazed And Confused', plus future Zeppelin material – 'Communication Breakdown', 'I Can't Quit You Babe', 'You Shook Me' and 'Babe I'm Gonna Leave You'. There was also the strange inclusion of 'Flames', a song originally recorded by Elmer Gantry's Velvet Opera in November 1967 (Direction 58-3083). By then, it seemed that Jimmy considered the 'Yardbirds' name more of a millstone than an advantage...

Yet, Jimmy Page still found time to fill his session quota. He was part of a stellar lineup featured on *No Introduction* (1968, Spark SRLM 107) by Leeds-born former Joe Meek protégé Keith David DeGroot. It was an album largely made up of vintage rock 'n' roll and rockabilly numbers, on which Jimmy was playing alongside Nicky Hopkins, John Paul Jones, Albert Lee, 'Big' Jim Sullivan, Chris Hughes and Clem Cattini (the drummer from 'Ten Little Indians'). He drew a session fee with a similar sideman crew (Cattini, Lee, Stevie Winwood, Matthew Fisher, etc.) for Joe Cocker's debut 12" *With A Little Help From My Friends* (Regal Zonophone SLRZ1006). Furthermore, although recording began in May 1969, when Jimmy hooked up with Jeff Beck, as well as John Bonham, Nicky Hopkins and Noel Redding for *Lord Sutch & Heavy Friends* (May 1970, Atlantic 2400-008), the issue date for the re-launch of the veteran shock-rocker's career lapped over the decade's end. Jimmy Page co-wrote a number of the tracks with the 'Screaming' Lord, who was pictured on the album sleeve leaning up against his Union Jack-customised Rolls-Royce. The album's failure led to Sutch redirecting his energies to his Monster Raving Loony Party.

At the dawn of the 1970s, Mickie Most's pop vision was to be vindicated elsewhere, with new names Hot Chocolate and Most's RAK label roster: Suzi Quatro, Smokie, Mud and others, including Kim Wilde. But his association with The Yardbirds had not been productive. He imposed his own idea of what he thought the group should be, in direct conflict with the group's own image of itself.

'If, in the final analysis, The Yardbirds were too flawed a band to qualify as truly great, then at least let them be remembered as a band in which great things happened', wrote Charles Shaar Murray by way of an epitaph in *NME* on 25 December 1976.

Meanwhile, Relf and McCarty planned their own band…

Keith Relf And Jim McCarty's Single As Together – 'Henry's Coming Home'

'Henry's Coming Home' (Relf, McCarty) 2:54 b/w **'Love Mum And Dad'** (Relf, McCarty) 0:47
Released: November 1968
Columbia DB 8491
No chart position.

A short-lived duo experiment for Keith and Jim during the indecisive transitional period following the collapse of The Yardbirds. Former Shadows drummer Tony Meehan was credited as arranger and conductor, while Paul Samwell-Smith was on hand as producer. In fact, Paul had been doing very well for himself. He got co-writer as well as producer credit on songwriter Barry Mason's psych-whimsy single 'Over The Hills And Far Away' b/w 'Collection Of Recollections' (October 1966, Deram DM104), which delves back into the doomy Gregorian chant feel. Paul was also listed as one of the superstar guests playing on the *McGough & McGear* album (March 1968, Parlophone PMC7047) by the former Scaffold duo. Moreover, a unique B-side by former Manfred Mann singer Paul Jones, 'The Dog Presides' (b/w the Gibb brothers' 'And The Sun Will Shine', 1968, Columbia DB8379), not only features Samwell-Smith's bass, but Jeff Beck's guitar, Paul McCartney's drums and a Peter Asher production. But, while his production work was taking off, Paul was still close enough to The Yardbirds family to be a part of this project, which reunites three members of the original lineup.

There's an anecdote that during The Yardbirds' final days, Keith had told Jimmy Page that he enjoyed The Turtles' hit song 'Happy Together', and that he wanted to record something in a similar vein. Much to Jimmy's horror! This single – as Together – could be seen as evidence of that ambition. Jim sings on the easy-jogging fly-away A-side, with a West Coast ba-ba-ba chorus. 'Love Mum And Dad' has a slower, dreamy, folksy feel, with John Mark's acoustic guitar and rattling drums. It's a song written in the epistolary form of a letter, into which Jim interjects a semi-spoken 'they never understand a single word we say'. To Yardbirds biographer Alan Clayson, the track forms 'quite an articulate speech of the heart – about inner-city isolation being preferable to an adolescence of small-town dreariness and perpetual domestic 'atmosphere'.'

A couple of further tracks by the duo survived as bonus tracks on albums by their next joint project, Renaissance. Keith's *All The Falling Angels* LP gathers both sides of the 'Together' single alongside 'Shining Where The Sun Has Been' (2:47), a lively acoustic strum despite its rough, unpolished demo qualify, plus 'Together Now' (3:01) – a hippie-dippy confection that marks the first appearance of Jane Relf, who provides pastoral high-flying backing vocals with lyrics 'tell me the time, dandelion clocks say it's quarter to nine'. There is a 'symphonic version' of the song issued as by Renaissance on their 2022 *Live At Fillmore West & Other Adventures* 4CD set, Repertoire Records (REPUK1419). A further track – 'Line Of Least Resistance' (2:12) – is the demo of a Relf-McCarty composition with Jane's voice and tambourine that was subsequently recorded as the only single (October 1970, Regal Zonophone RZ3028) by a band called Reign that included vocalist Andy Banks, bassist Tim Renton, drummer Andy Renton of Hapshash & The Coloured Coat, and guitarist Robin Le Mesurier – son of Hattie Jacques with John Le Mesurier. It's a pleasant folk-rock track, very much in the Together 'la-la-la-la' vein.

It does seem that, once freed of Mickie Most's coercive influence, the duo's individual confidence had returned.

Aftermath & Renaissance

Jimmy Page After The Yardbirds – Led Zeppelin
Led Zeppelin

Personnel:
Robert Plant: vocals, harmonica
Jimmy Page: Fender Telecaster electric, Gibson J-200 acoustic and Fender
ten-string pedal steel guitars, backing vocals and production
John Paul Jones (John Baldwin): bass, organ and backing vocals
John Bonham: drums, timpani and backing vocals
Plus:
Viram Jasani: tabla (on 'Black Mountain Side')
Chris Dreja: back cover photo
Peter Grant: executive producer at Olympic Studios
Glyn Johns: engineering and mixing
Released: 12 January 1969 (US), 31 March 1969 (UK)
Atlantic 588171 (UK), Atlantic SD-8216 (US)
Highest chart position: UK: 6, US: 10

Could this have been the next Yardbirds album? Page was there. John Paul
Jones had various in-and-out connections with the group, usually in a session
or arranger capacity. Certainly, Robert Plant was a powerfully bombastic voice
compared to Keith Relf's more subtly restrained style. 'Dazed And Confused'
had been a stand-out of the final Yardbirds live dates, extended with
improvisations in what could be seen as a direct link to their early rave-up
innovations, a process documented on the *Yardbirds In '68: Live At The BBC
And Beyond* (Repertoire Records REP 2366, 2018), with Page's guitar battling
Relf's harmonica onstage at the French TV sessions at Bouton Rouge on 9
March 1968.

But, freed of the pressures and expectations of management, record label
and hit-seeking bought-in producers, the musicians were able to follow their
own muse for the first time. And their aim was true.

The album was begun at 11 pm on 25 September, and recording lasted for
36 hours of Olympic studio time through to October. Liberated from Mickie
Most's controlling hand, with Jimmy Page credited as producer – with Glyn
Johns as engineer – the results were epic. During recording sessions for the
as-yet unsigned band, Jimmy Page heard Who drummer Keith Moon using the
term 'going down like a lead Zeppelin' to describe a disastrous gig. He liked
the term and adapted it to rename The New Yardbirds. The final 'New
Yardbirds featuring Jimmy Page' gig was a Surrey University Great Hall 'First
Big Dance Of Term' (Friday 25 October), although the newly titled and
equally new lineup had already played their first gig at The Marquee on 18
October, and were then immediately acclaimed during their opening
American tour from 26 December in Boston, Mass, with Vanilla Fudge and
MC5.

The rest is rock 'n' roll legend ...

Side One
'Good Times Bad Times' (Jimmy Page, John Paul Jones, John Bonham, Robert Plant) 2:43
'Babe, I'm Gonna Leave You' (Ann Bredon, Page, Plant) 6:40
'You Shook Me' (Willie Dixon, JB Lenoir) 6:30
'Dazed And Confused' (Page, inspired by Jake Holmes) 6:27

Side Two
'Your Time Is Gonna Come' (Page, Jones, Plant) 4:41
'Black Mountain Side' (Page) 2:06
'Communication Breakdown' (Page, Jones, Bonham, Plant) 2:26
'I Can't Quit You Baby' (Willie Dixon) 4:42
'How Many More Times' (Page, Jones, Bonham, Plant) 8:28

The Continuing Adventures Of Keith Relf And Jim McCarty – Renaissance

Renaissance – Renaissance

Personnel:
Keith Relf: lead vocals, guitar, harmonica, backing vocals
Jane Relf: lead and backing vocals, percussion
Jim McCarty: drums, percussion, backing vocals, brief second lead vocals on 'Innocence'
John Hawken: piano, harpsichord
Louis Cennamo: bass
Paul Samwell-Smith & Andy Johns: producers at Olympic Sound Studios in London
Released: November 1969
Island ILPS-9114 (UK), Elektra EKS-74068 (US), Island 87-609ET (Germany)
Highest chart position: UK: 60

Is this a natural evolution from The Yardbirds' quieter, more pastoral moments, a complexification of their relentless quest for innovation and experimentation? Or a new beginning? The choice of the name – Renaissance, both a revival and a renewal – hints at something of both. Keith plays lead guitar, as though he's grown tired of truculent and moody guitarists who quit to hunt their own place in the superstar constellation. And he seems more content to be integrated into the band, as a musician rather than being out front as the focal point. As in the song the revived Yardbirds later recorded as a tribute to him, Keith had 'a sadness hidden behind his gaze' ('An Original Man' on the *Birdland* album).

It was the final months of the 1960s, caught on the cusp of the new decade, an unprecedented moment in the evolution of the music that had started out as teen-beat rock 'n' roll, the brakes were off as never before. The musicians were young, talented and ambitious, eager to make their mark within the new possibilities. Prog was not yet seen as pompous or overblown. If they were musically good, they were keen to push those abilities to the max, and audiences were largely carried along by their forays into neo-classical symphonic twiddly bits or jazz-improvisational exploits. For now, at least, the sky was no limit at all. It was not until the advent of punk hit the reset button in late 1976 that it said so far, and no further.

Born on 7 March 1947, Jane Relf was Keith's younger sister, who had operated as part of The Yardbirds Fanclub set-up. John Christopher Hawken (born in Bournemouth on 9 May 1940) also has an intriguing history. His earliest semi-pro group – The Cruisers, which also featured future-Renaissance member Michael Dunford – evolved into The Nashville Teens, who played the Hamburg 'Star Club'. Joined by Barry Jenkins, who later replaced John Steel in The Animals, the Nashville Teens toured with Chuck Berry and Carl Perkins and scored major chart hits with John D Loudermilk songs 'Tobacco Road' (which reached number five on the *NME* chart on 22 August 1964) and 'Google Eye' (which reached number 13 on 14 November 1964), both comfortably before The Yardbirds had enjoyed anything like a chart presence. The group created confusion while touring America simply by being an English beat-group from the south coast with nothing whatsoever to do with the Tennessee Country music city!

There was a point in 1968 when Chris Dreja – in league with pedal steel player BJ Cole – considered Hawken for a country-rock side-project they were planning. It came to nothing, but it did serve as an introduction into The Yardbirds circle, and it was soon after that he was invited to McCarty's Thames Ditton home for a sounding-out meeting, which evolved into Renaissance.

Side One
'Kings And Queens' (10:55) McCarty, Relf

We're greeted by cascades of neo-classical piano, interspersed with what Alan Clayson called 'cunning dynamic shifts and couplets with obscurely supernatural overtones.' This is fantasy turned into vinyl. There's a sequence of 'movements' that link and interact – prog rock when it was still at its most progressive. Portentous as hell. For the listener, the Pre-Raphaelite posey lyrics conjure up mental images of knights in chromium-plated armour, maidens locked in some far tower and minstrels who rhyme songs of reason that change with the weather. Keith, seen as the troubadour, plays a Gibson ES-335 guitar. He has long, blonde hair and a ragged beard. Jane beats a tambourine and is serenely beautiful. The bassline chases the piano phrases. They share tight vocal harmonies in which the voices become indistinguishable. To the *NME* reviewer, the track 'begins in a baroque style, progressing to heavy semi-classical pieces, jazz-influenced phrases and some vocals.' This is musicianship from a planet distant in time and space that – at close to 11 minutes – never overstays its welcome.

'Innocence' (7:05)

With clicking McCarty drums and a depth of sound that intensifies, this is a song of considerable delicate complexity with bass and tempo-change keyboard interactions. It slows almost to a halt, develops into a quiet sequence, then picks up momentum and dances around the poetic lyric passages extolling childlike perception with subtle nuances. It's a track that proves rock music can also be prettily decorous. The *NME* reviewer called it 'a lot softer and slower, simpler, but as interwoven as a web – a really nice number.'

Side Two
'Island' (5:57)

Jane sings incredibly high and pure, with Keith adding emphasis as required. There's a spinet-like piano solo, ghosted by bass in complex interplay. Jane drops into scat-phrasing with the warm sounds of windsong, where tears are borne on the breeze. With access to the kind of cutting-edge technology and lavish studio time not available to The Yardbirds, Paul's 16-track production nevertheless stays crisp with excess kept to the minimum, allowing the band's basic personnel to shine. The piano's tonal range was split onto three separate tracks. 'We divided the drums onto three tracks, too – it was a fairly new experiment', Keith explained to *ZigZag*. 'The Beatles did it on *Abbey Road* ... by separating the bass, middle and treble of the piano; it can be mixed so that it pans across between the speakers or the 'phones, and each track can be moved around and so on. It produces a really big sound.'

When the track was issued as a single, the *Melody Maker* review said: 'A beautiful piano introduction by John Hawken, once of the Nashville Teens, helps send off the twin talents of Jane and Keith Relf on one of the most distinctive tracks from their recent well-received album. A hit? Who knows in these troubled times?' To the *NME,* it was 'a sort of heavy folk number that reminds me of a thing Joan Baez once did.'

'Wanderer' (4:00) John Hawken, McCarty
With its baroque keyboard elaborations, this is what *Melody Maker's* Karl Dallas dismissed as 'a wonderful piece of keyboard-dominated kitsch', with an occasional medieval flavour. Jane's vocals are as high and pure as morning dew on the leaves of an enchanted forest. The American label, Elektra, invested in a full-page advert in *Rolling Stone* magazine announcing the band as 'risen from the ashes of The Yardbirds'. Their review was less enthusiastic, while conceding 'the basic compositions have a tantalising tinge of that old Yardbirds quality.'

'Bullet' (11:24)
NME called this 'a goodly album and a praiseworthy debut from the young group', while pointing out that 'Bullet' 'shows the group in many different lights, each member having the chance to express himself – an opportunity which is used to effect.'

Louis Cennamo (born on 5 March 1946) was already a veteran of Jimmy Powell & The Five Dimensions, whose blues-rock shows, with vocalist Rod Stewart, were a highly-rated mod attraction. He joined Renaissance after a long spell doing session work for the likes of James Taylor, Al Stewart and Chuck Berry, plus Mike Patto (of Spooky Tooth) and Viv Prince (of The Pretty Things) in a short-lived Chicago Line Blues Band, whose sole single for the Philips label covered Little Anthony & The Imperials' 'Shimmy Shimmy Ko Ko Bop' in 1966. It was bass player Louis who played a significant part in shaping the classically influenced Renaissance song arrangements. In the coda to 'Bullet', Alan Clayson finds 'the post-serialist tonalities of such as Penderecki and Ligeti.' As one of the band's live performance highlights, 'Bullet' was often visually and sonically the set closer, showcasing Keith's harmonica, Jim's drum solo, and Louis' technique of using a violin bow on his bass. Louis would continue to use the violin bow on his bass with later bands.

Bonus Tracks On The CD Reissue
'The Sea' (3:00)
Piano-led, both ponderous and a country-lilt, with supernaturally high Jane Relf vocals.

'Island' (3:37)
The single's edit.

Innocence Bonus Tracks
'Shining Where The Sun Has Been'
A pre-Renaissance demo by Keith Relf & Jim McCarty recorded as Together.

'Prayer For Light'
'Walking Away'
Two post-Renaissance tracks by Relf and McCarty – written and sung by Jim – intended for the unreleased 1971 movie *Schizom*.

'All The Fallen Angels'
Keith's 1976 demo, also featured on the 1979 album *Enchanted Caress* as by Illusion.

The Second Renaissance Album – Illusion
Illusion
Personnel:
Keith Relf: lead vocals, guitar, backing vocals (not present on track 4)
Jane Relf: lead vocals (on tracks 1, 5 and 6), backing vocals, percussion
Jim McCarty: drums, percussion, lead vocals (on track 2), backing vocals (not present on track 4)
John Hawken: keyboards (not present on track 6)
Louis Cennamo: bass (not present on track 4)
Personnel on 'Mr Pine': Terry Crowe (vocals), Michael Dunford (guitar), Neil Korner (bass), Terry Slade (drums, percussion)
Recorded at Olympic Studios during Spring and Summer 1970
Producers: Keith Relf & Andy Johns
Released: 1971
Island Records 6339-017, Island Records (UK 1977, HELP 27) gatefold sleeve, Renaissance Records (US 1997, RMED00168)
No chart position.
1970 opened positively with a well-received American tour. Renaissance was clearly a commercially viable proposition, yet as sessions began for album two, there were unresolved problems and tour fatigue. Paul Samwell-Smith,

who had done much to negotiate the Elektra deal, felt himself slighted when Keith and Jim decided to self-produce the sequel. Then, Keith, McCarty and Cennamo left the band to seek pastures new. Hawken called up his former Nashville Teens bandmates in to help out, with Terry Crowe (vocals), Michael Dunford (lead guitar) and Neil Korner (bass) supported by session drummer Terry Slade (drums). After fulfilling contractual obligations to tour Europe in support of the album, Jane Relf quit, too, replaced for five months by American singer Marie-Louise 'Binky' Cullum, as Renaissance II, before former cabaret singer Annie Haslam assumed the vocal role.

With McCarty helping out, Jane Relf issued a one-shot September 1971 solo single, 'Without A Song From You' b/w 'Make My Time Pass By' (Decca F13231). Charmingly decorous, both sides were gathered onto her compilation *The Jane Relf Collection 1969-1995* (US 200, Bell & Whistle Records JRJRC 196995).

Jim McCarty wrote 'If You've Got A Little Love To Give', which appeared on the September 1972 album *Dave Clark & Friends* (Columbia SCX6494), a last gasp project that included the Dave Clark Five's October 1969 hit 'Put A Little Love In Your Heart'.

Finally, in October 1970, Hawken himself took up an invitation to join Spooky Tooth, severing the band's final original connection.

Side One
'Love Goes On' (Keith Relf) 2:51
It opens with a light strum and moves into a repeated 'ba-ba-ba' good-time west-coast summer chorus until Jane's strong voice takes the verse. It might seem instantly forgettable, but once it gets into your head, it stays there.

'Golden Thread' (Keith Relf, Jim McCarty) 8:15
This features stately, quasi-classical piano and Jane's ethereal, wordless voice, with McCarty taking on the vocals as the instrumentation rises to peaks of intensity before falling away to quietude. The golden thread is what connects us: 'We walk the golden thread, and keep our footing firm and away, if you trip, I'll fall, you'll do the same for me one day'.

'Love Is All' (McCarty, Betty Thatcher) 3:40
It starts with a trickling piano, then the solo voice breaks into an inspirational ensemble chorus to extol the virtues of a love, which is 'the sky and the air'. Then – in a further metaphor – it becomes 'the way and the song'. Outlined by vaguely fuzzed guitar, it all builds into a big fade-out repetition. All you need is love.

'Mr Pine' (Michael Dunford) 7:00
It comes in sequences: a medieval harpsichord with pattering hand drums, folksy harmony vocals with spoken inserts, then an organ passage spaced by

strummed acoustic guitar, bookended by the third movement's return to harpsichord. Who is the elemental Mr Pine? He spends his summers drinking wine and he has a friend called Gypsy Joe who wears an earring through his nose. And together, they make for a genuinely enchanting journey.

Side Two
'Face Of Yesterday' (McCarty) 6:06
With descending twiddly piano bits, Jane's voice ascends into stratospheric highs in order to paint vivid word-pictures of a sculptor moulding a dream, a builder shaping a life and a man of music 'who wrote a score for several instruments or more' but found only disharmony, in a charming overabundance of prettification. Coming increasingly to the fore as a songwriter, Jim would later write songs intended for Dorris Henderson, formerly of Eclection, a folk-rock band that split in 1969.

'Past Orbits Of Dust' (McCarty, Keith Relf, Thatcher) 14:39
We are greeted by stinging, dancing keyboards from Don Shinn (standing in for John Hawken) over a solid drum pulse, with harmony vocals regaling cosmic visions of wonder, leading into a spirited jazzy swing as Jane sings solo verses about 'chasing seas of joy, ghosting through the void' and 'under glowing moons, solar afternoons, fate and love go by, shooting stars of time'. Pattering drums interact with the buoyant bassline through an intermission, which strengthens into the next vocal sequence. With scintillating soft-loud instrumental interactions of startling ingenuity, this track is truly impressive. In an interview with journalist Nick Watts of *Melody Maker*, Keith explained that 'a lot of people thought the music was very pretentious and contrived, but I think that was because they wanted us to blow more. Our thing, however – Jim and I – is arranging. We did all our blowing with The Yardbirds.'

This curiously fragmented second album was originally issued in Germany in 1971. It received wider release in 1973 but was not issued in the UK until 1977. The third album issued by Renaissance – *Prologue*, in October 1972 (Sovereign SVNA 7253) – featured none of the original personnel, with Francis Monkman (formerly of Curved Air), John Tout and Annie Haslam taking lead vocals. The only remaining connection was that Jim McCarty co-wrote two tracks – 'Kiev' and 'Bound For Infinity' – with Cornwall-based poet Betty Thatcher. The duo also wrote 'On The Frontier' for the next album, *Ashes Are Burning* (October 1973, Sovereign SVNA 7261). Jim co-wrote 'Things I Don't Understand' with Michael Dunford for the fifth Renaissance album, *Turn Of The Cards* (July 1974, BTM Records RCA 1000).

Renaissance actually achieved a number-ten hit on the UK charts with 'Northern Lights' (Warner Bros K17177) on 19 August 1978, taken from their *A Song For All Seasons* LP (Warner Bros K56460), which also logged their highest album chart position, at number 35, during that same month. Renaissance continued to record and tour until they disbanded in 1987. *Time-Line* (April 1983, IRS Records SP70033) was their 11th and final studio album.

Other Yardbirds Offshoots
The Return Of 'Top' Topham – Ascension Heights
Ascension Heights
Released: 1970
Blue Horizon S 7-63857
No chart position.

As The Yardbirds' legend evolved to ever greater proportions, the group's original guitarist – mentioned in interviews and features – assumed an almost mythic reputation enhanced by his total invisibility. In fact, he was doing very nicely indeed. Torn between art and music, after graduating from Guildford and Epsom Art Schools, he became an interior designer and painter. He painted murals, one for an Epsom church, another for a Piccadilly Circus Greek restaurant. Later, he accepted a commission from a Saudi businessman for an 'erotic bathroom mural' in a Knightsbridge mansion. He used models from the Royal Ballet School and adopted a pre-Raphaelite style to decorate the onyx alcoves with Greek nymphs.

But blues was a hard habit to kick. He toured Germany as part of The Winston G band, then played with The John Dummer Band, and became a session player with Mike Vernon's Blue Horizon label. His name appears on the credits of *Christine Perfect* (Blue Horizon S 7-63860), her 1970 solo album recorded after leaving Chicken Shack, but before joining Fleetwood Mac. Top also played and recorded with sometime one-man-band Duster Bennett. He's there on the live album *Bright Lights* (1969, Blue Horizon 7-63221), recorded at the Angel Hotel in Godalming, and he appeared on Duster's 1970 *12 DBs* album (Blue Horizon 7-63868), which includes Duster's take on Ray Charles' 'I Chose To Sing The Blues' and Ray Davies' 'Act Nice And Gentle'.

Then, this one-off solo album became something of an all-star project, with Duster Bennett (harmonica), both Colin Allen and John Marshall (drums), Terry Noonan, Butch Hudson, Greg Bowen and Nigel Carter (trumpets), Mike Vernon (percussion), Alan Skidmore, Tony Coe, Danny Moss and Steve Gregory (tenor saxes), Chris Pyne, Danny Elwood and Jack Thirlwell (trombones), Pete Wingfield (piano) and Herbie Flowers (bass), plus Annette Peacock, Leslie Duncan and Sunny Leslie on backing vocals. It's an easy, low-ambition album, more studio after-session wind-downs with a group of friends tossing ideas around rather than following them to see where they might lead.

From a rasping 'Roadrunner' ascending fret play-in that leads to a pleasant bluesy instrumental with an earworm hook, the album moves through chiming guitars in free spacey jams with no particular place to go, but enjoying the trip. There's an incursion into clean-picking Shadows territory with a jog-along Western movie feel ('Hop House'). Duster Bennett adds tasteful harmonica, while the title track itself is a big, wide-screen, string-laden production job, with horns, background voices and stinging guitar. 'Tuxedo Junction' is not quite the 1940 hit as The Glenn Miller Band might recognise it, until the album winds down with a cover of Marvin Gaye's Motown hit.

Topham's return was then interrupted by serious illness. But he was destined to re-enter the story later:

Side One
'Sawbuck' (2:17)
'Mini-Minor-Mo' (2:10)
'Hop House' (3:35)
'Ridin' The Blinds' (2:30)
'Hot Ginger' (4:05)
'Funks Elegy' (3:06)

Side Two
'Ascension Heights' (3:36)
'Tuxedo Junction' (3:15)
'Globetrottin'' (3:47)
'Mean Old Pullman' (2:13)
'How Sweet It Is (To Be Loved By You)' (2:48)

The expanded edition of *Ascension Heights* (Blue Horizon 88697359082, 2008) also included a strange 'Christmas Cracker' (3:08), which works funk improvisations around 'Rudolph The Red-Nosed Reindeer' and the slow, bluesy vocal 'Cracking Up Over Christmas' (2:40, written by Mike Vernon). There were also four tracks that Top had recorded simply as a session player for the Peterborough-Bluesman Lloyd Watson: demos of 'Heart Of Stone' (2:54), 'You Gonna Ruin Me Baby' (2:43), the aching 'Long And Lonely Year' (4:38) and 'Anything For You' (2:27). It seems that these 'bonus tracks' are the only form in which these songs were ever issued.

Keith And Jim Continued...
Meanwhile, Keith and Jim completed the score for a skiing movie called *Schizom*, telling of two young men who get lost on a mountain. The film was never actually commercially released, but the soundtrack, recorded at London's Advision Studios, was completed on 30 September 1970, with Brian Hodgson (bass), Terry Cox (drums), John Mark (guitar) and Ann Odell (piano), with the voices of both Keith and Jim as well as Jane Relf and Kay Garner. The tapes remained in limbo for decades until they were eventually released on CD in 2012 as Easy Action Ears 038.

The album *Schizom* as by Keith Relf & Jim McCarty (all tracks written by Relf & McCarty):

1. 'Opening Sequence (Prayer For The Light)'
2. 'Voice Links'

3. 'Ski Sequence'
4. 'High Mountain Sequence'
5. 'Disco Sequence'
6. 'Guitar Links'
7. 'Classical Sequence'
8. 'Cymbal Effects'
9. 'Carnival Sequence'
10. 'Cymbal Effects 2'
11. 'Dream Sequence (Walk Away)'
12. 'Lower Village'
13. 'Carnival Sequence 2'
14. 'Cymbal Effects 3'
15. 'Upper Village'
16. 'High Mountain Theme'
17. 'End And Out Sequence'
18. 'The High Mountain Theme (Demo)'
19. 'Walking Away (Demo)'
20. 'Try Believing (Demo)'

Keith also worked with VCS3 and Moogs on an electronic soundtrack for an animated cartoon – 'a fantasy about a little girl being spirited away to the moon' – although there's no evidence of that ever emerging.

Later, a *Melody Maker* news paragraph from September 1972 noted that Jim McCarty had not only formed a new group called Shoot, but that he'd switched to playing keyboards, the better to present his own material. The group consisted of bassist Bill Russell (ex-Savoy Brown), drummer Don Burrell (replaced by Craig Collinge) and guitarist Dave Greene. Chris Dreja would be manager and producer. An album, *On The Frontier* (1973, EMI EMA753), was made up of nine songs written or co-written by Jim, plus one by Dave Greene.

The album *On The Frontier* by Shoot:

Side One
1. 'The Neon Life' (Jim McCarty) 3:52
2. 'Ships And Sails' (Jim McCarty) 3:39
3. 'Living Blind' (Jim McCarty) 4:39
4. 'On The Frontier' (Jim McCarty, Betty Thatcher) 4:20
5. 'The Boogie' (Jim McCarty) 4:10

Side Two
1. 'Midnight Train' (Jim McCarty, Greene) 3:37
2. 'Head Under Water' (Greene) 1:06
3. 'Sepia Sister' (Jim McCarty) 5:21
4. 'Old Time Religion' (Jim McCarty) 3:45
5. 'Mean Customer' (Jim McCarty, Greene) 7:26

A May 1973 Shoot single took Jim's co-composition 'On The Frontier' (b/w 'Ships And Sails' (EMI 2026)), which was a song that had been done on the Annie Haslam Renaissance album *Ashes Are Burning*.

Although the punk storm had yet to break, Shoot found themselves victims of a music industry bias. Jim McCarty of Clinton Ave, East Molesey, Surrey wrote an angry letter to *Melody Maker* about their music being 'denied the right of BBC radio exposure by a panel of experts who are evidently turning down two-thirds of all singles released on the grounds that they are 'not what the public wants to hear", which means that musicians are 'concentrating on the US for radio promotion of their work.'

The Album That Keith Relf Did Next – Armageddon

Armageddon

Personnel:
Keith Relf: lead vocals, harmonica
Martin Pugh: electric and acoustic guitars
Louis Cennamo: bass, electric bowed bass
Bobby Caldwell: drums, percussion, piano, backing vocals
Released: 1975
A&M Records AMLH 64513 (UK), A&M Records SP-4513 (US)
No chart position

On 26 March 1973, one-time Yardbird Jeff Beck teamed up with bass player Tim Bogert and drummer Carmine Appice – both former members of Vanilla Fudge and Cactus – to issue the only studio album by the power-trio, *Beck, Bogert & Appice* (Epic EPC 65455). Abandoning the restraint he'd shown on his earlier Jeff Beck Group albums, this short-lived supergroup went directly for the heavy rock jugular. If it seemed almost like Beck was cashing in on the immense commercial potential of his reputation, it worked because the album hit number 12 on the US chart and was certified gold. Predictably, once the exercise had run its course, Jeff quit and returned to the more jazz-rock fusion world where his real muse lay, leaving the label with only a *Live In Japan* double-set and a few tracks collected onto Jeff's 1991 *Beckology* compilation. But if Jeff Beck could monetise his legend, why couldn't other ex-Yardbirds?

Keith Relf produced a July 1971 single by five-piece Smoke Stack Crumble, 'Got A Bad Leg' b/w 'Whisky Macaroni' (Dawn DNS 1013), with hard riffing guitars and hoarse vocals. He also gets producer credits for *Magical Love* (1973, Matrix Records TRIX1SP) from heavy-rock band Saturnalia, with former members of Horse, plus singer Aletta Lohmeyer, on what was claimed to be the first 3D picture-disc. Then, Jim McCarty was on hand for percussion on slow-paced track 'Rosie' when Keith produced the very pleasant eponymous album for folk-rockers *Hunter Muskett* (1973, Bradley's Records BRADL1003).

Since his work with Renaissance, Louis Cennamo had performed and recorded with Colosseum on the jazz-rock fusion band's epic *Daughter Of Time* album (November 1970, Vertigo 6360-017). From there, he joined Martin Pugh in heavy rock band Steamhammer, with whom he recorded the largely instrumental album *Speech*, which consisted of just three long tracks, including 'Penumbra', which takes up the whole of the first side, runs to 22:42 and consists of five 'movements'. Keith Relf was credited as production assistant, as well as adding backing vocals. Less blues and more freaky psychedelic – featuring Louis' bowed bass – it found a home on the German Brain label (1972, Brain 1009).

It was through that connection with Keith that Louis convened Armageddon. Keith was by then based in Los Angeles, from where he phoned Martin Pugh and Cennamo, who were sharing a London flat. They recruited American drummer Bobby Caldwell from Captain Beyond, while Louis's earlier role as a member of The Herd proved useful when Peter Frampton helped them make management and record label introductions. Although based in California, the album was recorded at London's Olympic Studios.

Louis recalled how the brief band link-up was troubled by Caldwell and Pugh's drug habits, and how Keith's enduring asthma problems were worsening into emphysema, making it difficult for him to draw breaths sufficient to sing.

The album sleeve shows the four band members sitting or sprawling in the foreground, while behind them there is the shattered desolation of smouldering post-apocalypse ruins, recalling The Yardbirds' 'Shapes Of Things' lyrics – 'please don't destroy these lands, don't make them desert sands' – while the very concept and band name feeds on that same all-pervasive Cold War fear of nuclear conflict.

Side One
'Buzzard' (Caldwell, Pugh, Relf) 8:16
A manic guitar figure, slightly phased, leads into galloping instrumental interplay, and a lyric about a lurking menace poised to strike. This makes for a satisfyingly enticing promise of things to come, as Keith's harmonica simplifies and takes it down to close with an unexpectedly sharp reiteration of the opening riff.

'Silver Tightrope' (Caldwell, Pugh, Relf) 8:23
This is a slow-paced ballad with supernaturally high-pitched vocals delivering sci-fi lyrics, accompanied by shimmering guitar. 'I thought I heard them softly calling, the voices of the spheres, as light years flash forever falling, away from waking fears', as it builds into a heavier climax. To Alan Clayson, this track 'was worth the whole price of the album – a reconciliation between thunderclap aggression and sedate pulse, in which Keith swerved adeptly from murmured trepidation to strident intensity.'

'Paths And Planes And Future Gains' (Caldwell, Pugh, Relf) 4:30
Where Renaissance took and evolved from The Yardbirds' more pastoral moments, Armageddon extended out from the core band's advanced proto-tremors of heavy metal, with relentlessly solid electric riffing used to describe some kind of supernatural clash, where 'silver trumpets call, herald shining bright' to face the 'awesome foe'. Less adventurous than The Yardbirds and certainly a step down from the virtuoso intricacies of Renaissance, this musical genre was nevertheless filling stadia, and carried promise that – in Armageddon's case – was not to be realised.

Side Two
'Last Stand Before' (Caldwell, Cennamo, Pugh, Relf) 8:23
Again, the basis of the track is a naggingly repetitive riff, with its hard edges softened by harmony vocals and by Keith's strategic harmonica soloing. The

lyrics – about 'rock 'n' roll, moving your soul' – are personalised through four-line verses about low-life characters named Henry, Lucy and Jumping Jack Flash.

'Basking In The White Of The Midnight Sun' (Caldwell, Pugh, Relf) 11:30
a) 'Warning Coming On' (1:00)
b) 'Basking In The White Of The Midnight Sun' (3:03)
c) 'Brother Ego' (5:10)
d) 'Basking In The White Of The Midnight Sun (Reprise)' (2:18)
If the vocals are sometimes less than audible across this epic, segmented prog-metal opus, the inner sleeve fortunately included the full lyric sheet. There are full-on riffing guitars spinning off into snarling twiddly solos that make full dexterous use of effects pedals, around forceful drums and throbbing bass patterns.

With better management support and strategic tie-in live date promotion, the story could have been different – this is a band that promised more than it achieved.

Not Quite Renaissance – Illusion
Out Of The Mist and Illusion

Personnel:
Jane Relf: vocals
Jim McCarty: vocals, acoustic guitar, percussion
John Knightsbridge: acoustic and electric guitars
John Hawken: keyboards, piano, synthesiser, Mellotron
Louis Cennamo: bass
Eddie McNeill: drums
Out Of The Mist release date: 1977, Island
Illusion Release date: 1978, Island
No chart positions.

By a curious process, as the evolved lineup of Renaissance drifted apart, the original core members found themselves drawn back together again, with Keith and Jane Relf, Jim McCarty, John Hawken and Louis Cennamo. They recruited guitarist John Knightsbridge (later of McCarty's pick-up band Ruthless Blues), with Eddie McNeil freeing McCarty from the drum stool in order to concentrate on guitar. This renaissance of Renaissance took the name of the prog band's second album in order to establish continuity and firmly imprint legitimacy, not to mention that the other Renaissance still continued. Angus MacKinnon's 26 March 1977 *NME* review of the album drew the appropriate comparisons: 'Illusion's failure is puzzling ... they still outclass the current Renaissance. Jane Relf's a considerably more soulful singer than Annie Haslam, whilst both pianist Hawken and bassist Cennamo could play their opposite numbers out of court.' Illusion played The Marquee on 17 March and toured supporting Bryan Ferry. Available on vinyl and cassette, the album was advertised as 'a rare combination of haunting melody, almost classical piano and spiralling guitar work. Take the time to listen and you'll become addicted.'

Unfortunately, the full project was to remain unrealised, as by this time, Keith Relf – who had joined fresh from his stint with Armageddon – died on 14 May 1976, aged just 33, electrocuted while playing his guitar through an improperly-earthed amp in his basement rehearsal space at the West London home he shared with wife, April (Mannino). He was found alongside his guitar by Jason, his eight-year-old son.

Maybe the music world had become immune to tragedy after the deaths of Otis Redding (10 December 1967), Brian Jones (3 July 1969), Jimi Hendrix (18 September 1970), Janis Joplin (4 October 1970), Jim Morrison (3 July 1971) and 'Mama' Cass Elliot (29 July 1974). The *NME* headlined 'Tragedy Of Yardbirds Star: Keith Relf Dies At 33', with a photo of a bearded Keith crouching with one hand clutching the mic-stand and the other hand lifting a bottle to his lips. Maybe too many tears had already been shed. A new lineup of The Yardbirds would tribute Keith as 'An Original Man' on their 2003 *Birdland* album.

Meanwhile, the album opens with the trickling piano of 'Isadora'. It's a track with the gift of simplicity, and all the better because of it. Some listeners may guess at Isadora Duncan … or a lost lover, or just a romantic fantasy. Only Jim knows for sure. 'Twas a lost lover!' he confides to me when I enquire. For 'Roads To Freedom', the lyric 'running away from what we've been, every day we live again, we're free' seems autobiographical in that – with the band released from the need to be epic or to deliver virtuoso musicianship – these tracks are more effortlessly pleasing. 'Face Of Yesterday' is a direct return to the song from the Renaissance album from which Illusion had taken its name, with the addition of subtle strings. Synths drone and circle, with ripples of piano and the remnant of prog complexity in the tight tempo-change arrangements, but Jim's songs work best on this more human scale.

Side One
'Isadora' (Jim McCarty) 6:56
'Roads To Freedom' (McCarty, John Hawken) 3:53
'Beautiful Country' (McCarty, Hawken) 4:21
'Solo Flight' (McCarty, Hawken) 4:23

Side Two
'Everywhere You Go' (McCarty) 3:18
'Face Of Yesterday' (McCarty) 5:45
'Candles Are Burning' (McCarty) 7:10

There was a second album, simply titled *Illusion* (1978, Island Records ILPS9519), with the same personnel, and produced by Paul Samwell-Smith:

Side One
'Madonna Blue' (McCarty) 6:46
'Never Be The Same' (McCarty) 3:18
'Louis' Theme' (Louis Cennamo, Jane Relf) 7:41

Side Two
'Wings Across The Sea' (McCarty) 4:49
'Cruising Nowhere' (McCarty) 5:01
'Man Of Miracles' (Keith Relf, McCarty, Hawken) 3:27
'The Revolutionary' (McCarty, Hawken) 6:15

Then the band fragmented and went their separate ways. A further collection of previously unissued 1979 demo material – *Enchanted Caress* (Brisk Productions SRT9CD2174) – surfaced and was remastered in 1989. It featured a unique instrumental take on 'Slaughter On Tenth Avenue' (3:34), the 1957 noir movie theme, also done by Mick Ronson, but with added sax and machine-gun street sounds. The album credits Keith Relf as producer and included his last recorded track, 'All The Falling Angels' (5:26).

There were two cassette collections compiled by Richard Mackay of *Yardbirds World* fanzine taken from Keith's 7" reel-to-reel home-recordings, issued as *Keith Relf Musical Spectrum*, with 'Renaissance Rehearsal', a blurred 'Collector Of The Light' (2:37), co-written with Cennamo, an eerie acid-folk guitar instrumental, 'Night Journey' (2:24), and a nakedly personal 'Think What You're Achieving' (2:34), plus fragments such as the improvised 'Electric Guitar' (3:02), 'Guitar Workout', 'Cherokee' and 'Electronic From'. *Musical Spectrum Vol.II* was subtitled '1965-1976'. Variant editions have been subsequently copied and circulated in different forms.

Both Illusion albums were reissued as a single CD in 1994 as Demon EDCD369. There was to be one final flourish in 2001 when Jim McCarty, Jane Relf, Louis Cennamo and John Hawken reunited as Renaissance Illusion for the album *Through The Fire* (Spiral SCD923), made up of ten McCarty compositions recorded variously at RMS Studio, Chiswick Reach and Rooster Studios.

John Hawken, who had enjoyed success as keyboard player with The Strawbs for their *Hero And Heroine* (1974) and *Ghosts* (1975) albums, died on 15 May 2024. David Cousins tributed Hawken 'not only for your playing, but also for your sense of humour, which brought tears to my eyes every time we met up.'

Not Quite The Yardbirds Album – Box Of Frogs

Box Of Frogs

Personnel:
Paul Samwell-Smith: bass guitar, backing vocals, percussion, synthesiser,
producer
Jim McCarty: drums, percussion, backing vocals
Chris Dreja: rhythm guitar, percussion, backing vocals, photography
John Fiddler: lead & backing vocals, acoustic & electric rhythm guitar,
percussion, synthesiser, assistant producer
Additional musicians:
Jeff Beck (lead guitar on 1, 3, 6 and 9), Rory Gallagher (slide guitar on 5 and 7),
electric sitar (on track 7), Max Middleton (keyboards on 2, 4, 5, 7) and others
Released: June 1984
Epic EPC 25996 (UK), Epic BFE 39327 (US)
Highest chart position: US: 45

Like a 'barrel of monkeys', a box of frogs means unpredictable fun. Yet, in some
ways, this album seems a calculated step towards generic stadium rock. 'It
didn't have the edge', Samwell-Smith admitted to *Mojo* magazine in June 2024.

During the summer of 1983, Dreja, McCarty and Samwell-Smith reunited
as The Yardbirds for two sold-out gigs (Wednesday 22 and Thursday 23
June) as part of the Marquee 1958-1983 Anniversary celebrations Among
the songs they performed were Chuck Berry's 'Back In The USA', Taj Mahals'
'Statesboro' Blues' and a new song, 'Back Where I Started', before closing
with a rousing 'Heart Full Of Soul'. Then, encouraged by the response, and
enjoying playing live together again, augmented by John Fiddler (vocals)
and Mark Feltham from Nine Below Zero (harmonica), they formed a new
band – Box of Frogs – and signed to Epic, or, as *Melody Maker* helpfully
explained, 'some ole Yardbirds and their guests comprise this casual
receptacle of tailless amphibians.'

Samwell-Smith had other calls on his time. Utilising the production skills
he'd acquired working on Yardbirds studio sessions, he'd gone on to
produce the debut album – *Evensong* (Island ILPS9136) – by psychedelic-
folk outfit The Amazing Blondel, as well as their *Fantasia Lindum* album
(1971, Island ILPS9156). 'Amazing Blondel play real Elizabethan music. In
order to do this, they've made an exhaustive study of the music itself
They've also gone to amazing lengths to get the right instruments. On their
latest album, they've composed a series of beautiful Elizabethan songs',
announced the press advert.

Paul was involved with Ian Matthews during the recording of his 1971
album *If You Saw Thro' My Eyes* (Vertigo 6360-034), although Ian himself
takes producer credit. Paul produced Cat Stevens' major comeback album
Mona Bone Jakon (April 1970, Island), following it by producing *Tea for the
Tillerman* (November 1970), *Teaser And The Firecat* (October 1971) and
Catch Bull At Four (September 1972), which helped steer the former teen

prodigy into the more mature singer-songwriter arena. Jethro Tull broke their rule of self-producing only once, when Paul was invited in to produce their *The Broadsword & The Beast* album (1982, Chrysalis). Paul co-produced and added backing vocals to Carly Simon's October 1986 hit 'Coming Around Again', written for the Jack Nicholson movie *Heartburn*. He produced most of the eponymous debut album for *All About Eve* (February 1988, Mercury-Phonogram), which spawned four top 40 singles, including 'Every Angel', which he remixed. Among other projects, he produced the 1988 album *Gladsome, Humour & Blue* (Kitchenware Records KWCD 08) for Martin Stephenson & The Daintees.

However, his loyalty to his former bandmates and to The Yardbirds' legacy continued to exert a powerful gravitational force. Reviewer Russell Rhodes said, 'Take three former Yardbirds (McCarty, Dreja, Samwell-Smith), a onetime Medicine Head and British Lioner (John Fiddler), put them together, shake them around, add some basic bluesy riffs for taste, season well with guest musicians and what have you got? You got yourself a Box Of Frogs. And a fine spawn it is, too.'

'The reason we're talking about The Yardbirds now is because we had that edge', Paul told *Mojo*.

'Back Where I Started' (Samwell-Smith, Dreja, McCarty, Fiddler) 3:54
An 'On The Road' feel to a hard-beater with mouth-harp and slithering slide guitar. John Fiddler had been a tousled raggle-taggle hippie in the eccentric Medicine Head duo, who – supported by DJ John Peel – scored a couple of odd hits with '(And The) Pictures In The Sky' and 'One And One Is One'. As a direct link, Keith Relf had not only been producer for their second album, *Heavy On The Drum* (1971, Dandelion Records DAN8005), but he occasionally played bass on their live dates. Needless to say, in the Box Of Frogs promotional video, John's hair has been shorn into an acceptably 1980s mullet.

'Harder' (Fiddler, Ray Majors) 3:44
With as hard drum-kicks and as sharp guitar riffs as a lost Rolling Stones outtake, this is a well-tooled dose of swaggering stadium Rock, strutting with punching drums and zipping slide guitar.

'Another Wasted Day' (Samwell-Smith, Dreja, McCarty, Fiddler) 4:12
A sly, insidious blues opens out into stabs of horns and flash guitar soloing from a guesting Jeff Beck, who was credited on the original release as 'J Frog'. It resembles The Yardbirds with a sharp twist of lime.

'Love Inside You' (Fiddler) 2:47
With Dzal Martin adding tasty slide guitar and Max Middleton on keyboard, this is a slickly-produced mid-paced exercise in crafted Rockism.

'The Edge' (Samwell-Smith, Dreja, McCarty, Fiddler) 4:02
Rory Gallagher plays some stinging slide guitar so close to the edge it tips over the brink, in a terrain where black cats' trails are lethally crossed. Simultaneously punch-drunk snarling and burning all over the relentless drum-pulse.

'Two Steps Ahead' (Samwell-Smith, Dreja, McCarty, Fiddler) 4:33
Jeff Beck again, and unmistakably so, making up a Yardbirds quorum, although it could be argued that this album is more preconceived and rock mainstream than The Yardbirds ever were, despite some of the 'Hey' chants that might just recall 'Over Under Sideways Down' at a stretch, and some effectively distorted strangeness during the instrumental break.

'Into The Dark' (Samwell-Smith, Dreja, McCarty, Fiddler) 4:07
There's a vague reggae influence lurking about the percussion, but with Rory Gallagher guesting with electric sitar to create a novel synthesis. 'Looking out of my window at the world outside' is sung across skanking rhythms and shimmers of sitar.

'Just A Boy Again' (Samwell-Smith, Dreja, McCarty, Fiddler) 5:38
'Everybody in the world says I'm crazy, 'cos I play the Jack of Hearts' is sung over acoustic folky-blues power-chords, darkness and light changes edged by Peter John Vettese's honky-tonk piano, but always punched out by McCarty's rock-steady drumming.

'Poor Boy' (Samwell-Smith, Dreja, McCarty, Fiddler) 4:26
Jeff Beck returns for another snarling bite of high-energy blues-rock, protesting that he's broke, the sheriff is knocking on his door – to a chorus of 'Oh, shit!'. There's then a sideways glance at The Who stutter – 'why don't he just f-fade away?' and even hints as far as Robert Johnson with 'ever the devil's took my soul.' There's a howl of anguish that dissolves into a solid guitar barrage ripped by Geraint Watkins' piano runs. A fine tongue-in-cheek closer.

The Singles – Box Of Frogs
'Back Where I Started' b/w **'Nine Lives'** & **'The Edge'**
Epic TA 4562
This single was issued in 1984 in 12" and 7" (minus 'Nine Lives') format. Paul Du Noyer wrote the 4 August 1984 *NME* review: 'What I like about Box Of Frogs, apart from the name, is the way their 'Back Where I Started' has these ex-Yardbirds simply picking up where they left off, the psychedelic end of the late 1960s blues boom, rather than making any unnecessary stabs at sounding modern.' The *Melody Maker* reviewer added: 'The crickets chirrup, the guitar weeps. Derivative in the way that only a great blues is allowed to be, lurching riff, gutsy harp and impassioned vocals.'

'Into The Dark' b/w 'X-Tracks Medley' (made up of 'Two Steps Ahead', 'Just A Boy Again', 'Harder', 'Another Wasted Day' and 'Back Where It Started')
Epic TA 4678
This single was issued in 12" and 7" formats.

The Second Box Of Frogs Album – Strange Land
Strange Land
Personnel:
Paul Samwell-Smith: bass, production, backing vocals
Jim McCarty: drums, keyboards, backing vocals, percussion
Chris Dreja: rhythm guitar, percussion
John Fiddler: vocals
Plus additional musicians:
Rory Gallagher (lead guitar on tracks 2, 4 and 6, electric sitar on 5 and 6), Steve Hackett (lead guitar on 3 and 9), Jimmy Page (lead guitar on track 7), Graham Gouldman (rhythm guitar and backing vocals on track 6), Max Middleton (synthesisers), Geraint Watkins (piano), Carroll Thompson and Julie Roberts (backing vocals on tracks 2 and 4)
Released: 1986
Epic EPC 26375 (UK), Epic BFE 39923 (US)
No chart position.
For their second and final shot as Box Of Frogs, the nucleus of the band opted for the formula as before, a step towards mainstream blues-rock, with an impressive roster of guests who are eager to write themselves into The Yardbirds' history. John Fiddler's departure during the studio sessions also opened the door for the inclusion of such diverse fill-in vocalists as Ian Dury, Roger Chapman and Graham Parker.

'Get It While You Can' (Gary O'Connor) 3:50
This is bass-heavy swaggering 1980s pomp-rock with polished harmonies, slick guitar and Graham Parker-style vocals. 'Time means nothing to the ones like me, just the will to survive, the need to be free' with hard-rock cliches about how he gets his loving on the run. The Yardbirds were never this obvious.

'You Mix Me Up' (Samwell-Smith, Dreja, McCarty) 3:22
With jumpy, jerky funk rhythms allied to radio-friendly female back-up voices, this track proves that Box Of Frogs could deliver flawlessly machine-tooled rock attuned to the zeitgeist of the time. Strongly percussive, with John Fiddler taking the vocals.

'Average' (Samwell-Smith, Dreja, McCarty, Fiddler) 4:18
Art-punk maverick Ian Dury seems an unlikely fit for the unaccustomed rock setting of this trio of former Yardbirds, yet as his assured vocals suggest, this

is 'nice, nice', and the combination results in a standout track. The mid-point guitar barrage is interrupted by a phone call suggesting that 'there has to be more to my life' than the quotidian average. There is supposedly a demo version by Chris Dreja & Jim McCarty that leans more towards a Kinks treatment of the song, but the introduction of Ian Dury's distinctive enunciation lifts it well above average.

'House On Fire' (Samwell-Smith, Dreja, McCarty, Fiddler) 4:21
The Yardbirds never survived into the era of adult-oriented stadium rock, but the stomping drums, wailing guitar interplay and down-dirty vocals here provide hints of what might have been, enforced by peerless production gloss. Dreja, McCarty and Samwell-Smith declined to tour in support of Box Of Frogs – much to Fiddler's chagrin – but the lyric 'today New York, tomorrow Hong Kong' suggests the touring lifestyle, with lurching rhythms split by a sly soul voice mid-point break, then a lengthy fade.

'Hanging From The Wreckage' (Samwell-Smith, Dreja, McCarty, Fiddler) 3:39
Sitar sounds reverberate as ensemble harmony ghost-voices chant the title, while strings pluck and surge. The lyric advocates 'looking forward not looking back … There was no turning back', making this track a beguiling excursion into futuristic sonic textures that capture something of The Yardbirds' earlier spirit of invention and innovation.

'Heart Full Of Soul' (Graham Gouldman) 3:50
The three Yardbirds acknowledge their shared history, but with a radical reworking of their classic 1965 hit. There are Peter-John Vettese's low electronic rumblings and dancing emulator synths, plus Family-man Roger Chapman's trademark bleating vocal delivery, while Rory Gallagher retains the electric sitar tuning for a new decade. Graham Gouldman himself adds rhythm guitar and backing vocals.

'Asylum' (Samwell-Smith, Dreja, McCarty, Fiddler) 4:49
There's punching percussion, while synth-sirens establish panicky atmospherics, with a lengthy distorted Jimmy Page guitar solo. This track is a strangely brewed production that manages to incorporate John Fiddler singing about 'dancing to the beat', and yes, it is danceable, until the false fade fools your feet.

'Strange Land' (Samwell-Smith, Dreja, McCarty, Fiddler) 4:51
This track takes the tempo down a peg, but it's still relentlessly forceful, with Roger Chapman's hoarsely braying vocals, infused with maybe just a lyrical touch of SF writer Robert A Heinlein's 1961 novel *Strangers In A Strange Land*. Dzal Martin's guitar is beguilingly melodic throughout.

'Trouble' (Samwell-Smith, Dreja, McCarty, Fiddler) 5:40
Steve Hackett contributes guest guitar to this snarling, hard stadium-rock album closer. Paul Samwell-Smith's production is consistently pin-sharp from first track to last, with the dive-bombing guitar runs here served up with confident attitude, overlaid with weirdly, unsettling vocal harmony effects.

Bonus Tracks On The Cassette Edition
'I Keep Calling'
'20/20 Vision'

The Box Of Frogs Single – 'Average'
'Average' (3:51) b/w **'Strange Land'** (4:44) **and 'I Keep Calling'** (3:02)
Released 1986
Twelve-inch single Epic-TA7248
No chart position.
With Ian Dury at his most lascivious on the A-side, plus braying Family vocalist Roger Chapman guesting on the flip of both 7" and 12" editions, this is something of an all-star single, with all it needed to become a sizeable hit. Yet, inexplicably, it failed to achieve its full chart potential.

Keith Relf's Final Single – 'Together Now'
'Together Now' b/w **'All The Fallen Angels'**
Released: 1989
MCCM 89-002 (USA)
No chart position.
Although issued as Keith's third solo single, the A-side was originally recorded in 1968 by Together – with Jim McCarty – while the flip was recorded on 2 May 1976, just ten days before Keith's death.

Above: The final Yardbirds lineup. Left to right: Jimmy Page, Keith Relf, Jim McCarty and Chris Dreja. (*Getty*)

Above: A value-for-money
1966 'package' tour, which opened at the Royal Albert Hall on 23 September and ran to 9 October. At the Ipswich 'Gaumont', ticket prices ranged from

Left: After The Yardbirds, a new beginning was heralded with Renaissance and their self-titled debut. (*Island/Elektra*)

Right: It was during the recording of the second album, *Illusion*, that the first Renaissance lineup began to fall apart. (*Island/Renaissance Records*)

Left: Issued in July 1975, *Armageddon* was to be the band's only album. (*A&M*)

Right: In June 1984, Chris Dreja, Jim McCarty and Paul Samwell-Smith were joined by John Fiddler to become Box Of Frogs. Patty Dryden provided the album artwork. (*Epic*)

Left: The second Box Of Frogs album – *Strange Land* (1986) – included contributions from many guest stars. (*Epic*)

Right: Recorded on 2 May 1976, just ten days before Keith Relf's death, 'All The Fallen Angels' was finally released in 1989. (*MCCM*)

Left: Recorded live in London in 1992, *Reunion Jam* was released in December 1999. (*Mooreland Street Records*)

Right: Chris Dreja and Jim McCarty were joined by guests – including Jeff Beck – for the 2003 studio album *Birdland*. (*Favoured Nations*)

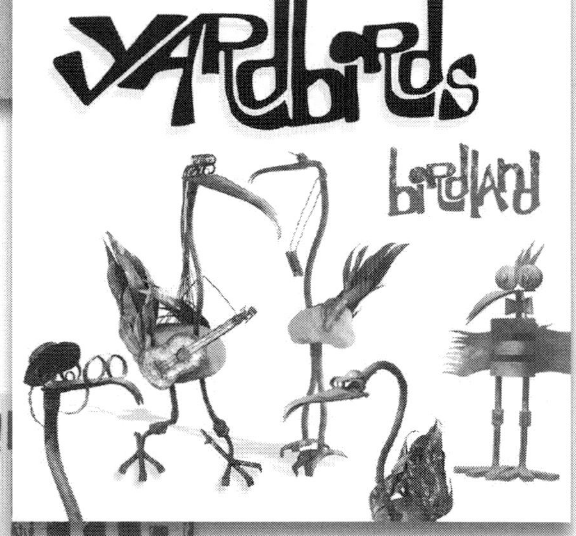

Left: Another instalment of live Yardbirds, released in 2007, which looks back to 'Shapes Of Things' and 'For Your Love'. (*Voiceprint/Mooreland Street Records*)

Yardbirds Compilations

The Yardbirds: Featuring Performances By Jeff Beck, Eric Clapton, Jimmy Page

Personnel:
Keith Relf: lead vocals
Eric Clapton: lead guitar
Jeff Beck: lead guitar
Jimmy Page: lead guitar
Chris Dreja: rhythm guitar
Jim McCarty: drums
Paul Samwell-Smith: bass guitar
Released: 31 August 1970 (US)
Epic EG-30135
Highest chart position: US: 155

This presents 20 tracks between 1964 and 1967 not already included on 1967's
The Yardbirds Greatest Hits. Later, Charly Records released two separate albums,
The Yardbirds Featuring Eric Clapton (1982, Charly LPS1053) – also issued as
Eric (Slow-Hand) Clapton (1975, Charly CR300.012) – and *The Yardbirds
Featuring Jeff Beck* (1977, CR30013). Charles Shaar Murray of the *NME* praised
'the sheer punk energy of the music and the yobbo joy that the band must have
had in playing it. By 'modern standards' – haha – both musicianship (the lead
guitars and Paul Samwell-Smith's striding, up-front bass excepted) and recording
sound primitive in the extreme, but it has a storming powerdrive and a surging,
raging ballsy power which, by its very rawness, puts to shame the manufactured,
waddling armour-plated muscle of yer modern deluxe heavy bands.'

Side One

1. 'Drinking Muddy Water' (Dreja, McCarty, Page, Relf, produced by Mickie
Most) 2:50
2. 'Hot House Of Omagarashid' (Dreja, Beck, McCarty, Relf, Samwell-Smith,
produced by Simon Napier-Bell & Paul Samwell-Smith) 2:37
3. 'I Wish You Would' (BB Arnold, produced by Giorgio Gomelsky with music
director Samwell-Smith) 2:18
4. 'The Train Kept A-Rollin' (Tiny Bradshaw, Lois Mann, Howard Kay,
produced by Giorgio Gomelsky with music director Samwell-Smith) 3:26
5. 'Smile On Me' (Dreja, McCarty, Page, Relf, produced by Mickie Most) 3:17

Side Two

1. 'Jeff's Boogie' (Beck, produced by Simon Napier-Bell & Paul Samwell-
Smith) 2:25
2. 'I Ain't Got You' (Calvin Carter, produced by Giorgio Gomelsky with music
director Samwell-Smith) 1:55
3. 'What Do You Want' (Dreja, Beck, McCarty, Relf, Samwell-Smith, produced
by Simon Napier-Bell & Paul Samwell-Smith) 3:24

4. 'White Summer' (Jimmy Page, produced by Mickie Most) 3:49
5. 'Got To Hurry' (O Rasputin, produced by Giorgio Gomelsky with music director Samwell-Smith) 2:26

Side Three
1. 'Little Games' (Spiro, Wainman, produced by Mickie Most) 2:25
2. 'Lost Woman' (Dreja, Beck, McCarty, Relf, Samwell-Smith, produced by Simon Napier-Bell & Paul Samwell-Smith) 3:13
3. 'Only The Black Rose' (Keith Relf, produced by Mickie Most) 2:48
4. 'Farewell' (Dreja, Beck, McCarty, Relf, Samwell-Smith, produced by Simon Napier-Bell & Paul Samwell-Smith) 1:29
5. 'I Ain't Done Wrong' (Relf, produced by Giorgio Gomelsky with music director Samwell-Smith) 3:39

Side Four
1. 'A Certain Girl' (N Neville, produced by Giorgio Gomelsky with music director Samwell-Smith) 2:17
2. 'Ever Since The World Began' (Dreja, Beck, McCarty, Relf, Samwell-Smith, produced by Simon Napier-Bell & Paul Samwell-Smith) 2:03
3. 'Tinker, Tailor, Soldier, Sailor' (McCarty, Page, produced by Mickie Most) 2:41
4. 'Turn Into Earth' (Dreja, Beck, McCarty, Relf, Samwell-Smith, produced by Simon Napier-Bell & Paul Samwell-Smith) 3:05
5. 'Here 'Tis' (Ellas McDaniel, produced by Giorgio Gomelsky with music director Samwell-Smith) 5:04

The Yardbirds! Featuring Jimmy Page
Personnel:
Keith Relf: lead vocals
Jimmy Page: lead guitar
Chris Dreja: rhythm guitar
Jim McCarty: drums
Released: 13 September 1971 (US)
Epic E 30615
No chart position
This was recorded in New York City in 1968, only to be withdrawn shortly after release, but was frequently bootlegged until it was superseded by *Yardbirds '68* (32017), which adds 'Heart Full Of Soul' (1:48) and a second CD, 'Studio Sketches'.

Side One
1. 'The Train Kept A-Rollin'' (Tiny Bradshaw, Lois Mann, Howard Kay) 3:10
2. 'Mr, You're A Better Man Than I' (Mike & Brian Hugg) 6:50
3. 'I'm Confused' ('Dazed And Confused' inspired by Jake Holmes) 6:47
4. 'My Baby' (Mort Shuman, Jerry Ragavoy) 5:01

Side Two

1. 'Over Under Sideways Down' (Chris Dreja, Keith Relf, Paul Samwell-Smith) 2:39
2. 'Drinking Muddy Water' (Chris Dreja, Keith Relf, Jimmy Page, Jim McCarty) 3:16
3. 'Shapes Of Things' (Paul Samwell-Smith, Keith Relf, Jim McCarty) 2:48
4. 'White Summer' (Jimmy Page) 4:19
5. 'I'm A Man' (Ellas McDaniel) 11:59, includes a sequence of 'Moanin' And Sobbin'.

CD 'Studio Sketches'

1. 'Avron Knows' (Page, Relf, McCarty) 3:49
2. 'Spanish Blood' (Page, McCarty) 3:15, instrumental with McCarty spoken verses
3. 'Knowing That I'm Losing You' (Jimmy Page) 2:54, instrumental from which Led Zeppelin's 'Tangerine' evolved
4. 'Taking A Hold On Me' (Page, McCarty) 3:02, with Jim McCarty vocals
5. 'Drinking Muddy Water: Version Two' (Page, Dreja, Relf, McCarty) 2:49
6. 'My Baby' (Ragavoy, Shuman) 2:59
7. 'Avron's Eyes' (Page) 2:56, instrumental
8. 'Spanish Blood' (Page, McCarty) 3:11, instrumental

Remember... The Yardbirds

Personnel:
Keith Relf: lead vocals
Eric Clapton: lead guitar
Jeff Beck: lead guitar
Chris Dreja: rhythm guitar
Jim McCarty: drums
Paul Samwell-Smith: bass guitar
Released: 18 June 1971
Regal Starline SRS5069
No chart position

Twelve 'electronically reprocessed' tracks that predate *Roger The Engineer*, from 'I Wish You Would' to 'Shapes Of Things'. Richard Williams in *Melody Maker* wrote, 'Many people will buy this album for Clapton and Beck, and good luck to 'em, but I prefer to think of The Yardbirds as an organic unit, always about three weeks ahead of their time.'

Side One

1. 'Heart Full Of Soul' (Gouldman) 2:27
2. 'Smokestack Lightnin'' (Chester Burnett) 5:35
3. 'I Wish You Would' (Arnold) 4:14
4. 'Good Morning Little Schoolgirl' (Love, Level) 2:44

5. 'Evil Hearted You' (Gouldman) 2:23
6. 'For Your Love' (Gouldman) 2:26

Side Two
1. 'Shapes Of Things' (McCarty, Relf, Samwell-Smith) 2:25
2. 'Still I'm Sad' (McCarty, Samwell-Smith) 3:00
3. 'My Girl Sloopy' (Russell, Farrell) 5:33
4. 'A Certain Girl' (Neville) 2:16
5. 'I Ain't Done Wrong' (Relf) 3:38
6. 'I'm A Man' (McDaniel) 4:36

Golden Eggs
Personnel:
Keith Relf: lead vocals
Jeff Beck: lead guitar
Jimmy Page: lead guitar
Eric Clapton: lead guitar
Chris Dreja: rhythm guitar
Jim McCarty: drums
Paul Samwell-Smith: bass guitar
Released: 1973
Unofficial bootleg album (US)

At a time when a lot of Yardbirds material had fallen out of print – when Roy Carr was bewailing in the *NME* that 'there is still no comprehensive reissue programme of their material', and when various illicit vinyl combinations extracted from Bob Dylan's *Basement Tapes*, as well as illegally-taped Rolling Stones concert albums were enjoying respectable under-the-counter sales – a Los Angeles-based bootleg label, Trademark Of Quality, issued this knowing compilation of tracks, made up of rescued B-sides and a solo Keith Relf single, beside 'Stroll On' from the *Blow-Up* soundtrack, plus songs from The Yardbirds' later Jimmy Page phase. The front-cover cartoon artwork, by William Stout, shows a fox licking its lips as it prepares to devour a nest of newly-hatched chicks – a visual pun on Mickie Most's attitude towards the band – while the reverse side has a unique caricatured Yardbirds Family Tree from their Eric Clapton beginnings through to Led Zeppelin. The bootleg itself was instantly bootlegged in a monochrome sleeve by the rival Phony Graf label!

This was followed two years later by *More Golden Eggs* (TMQ,1975), featuring the rare 1965 Jimmy Page solo single and The Yardbirds' Italian singles. The William Stout cover art portrays birds with The Yardbirds' heads. An interview with Keith Relf is printed on the reverse.

Side One
1. 'Steeled Blues' (Jeff Beck) 2:37
2. 'Putty (In Your Hands)' (J Patton, K Rodgers) 2:17

3. 'Mr Zero' (Bob Lind) 2:45, the Keith Relf solo single produced by Paul Samwell-Smith with Simon Napier-Bell
4. 'No Excess Baggage' (C D'Errico, R Atkins) 2:29
5. 'Think About It' (Jimmy Page) 3:47
6. 'Stroll On' (Dreja, Beck, Page, Relf) 2:43
7. 'The Nazz Are Blue' (Dreja, Beck, Mcarty, Relf, Samwell-Smith) 3:00
8. 'Knowing' (Keith Relf) 1:53, the B-side of the Keith Relf solo single
9. 'Little Soldier Boy' (McCarty, Page, Relf) 2:33

Side Two
1. 'Puzzles' (Keith Relf) 2:01
2. 'Stealing, Stealing' (Dreja, McCarty, Page, Relf) 2:21
3. 'Sweet Music' (Bowie, Cobb, Lance) 2:28
4. 'Ha Ha Said The Clown' (Tony Hazzard) 2:23
5. 'Rack My Mind' (Dreja, Beck, McCarty, Relf, Samwell-Smith) 3:10
6. 'Ten Little Indians' (Harry Nilsson) 2:13
7. 'Goodnight Sweet Josephine' (Tony Hazzard) 2:44
8. 'Glimpses' (Dreja, McCarty, Page, Relf) 4:22

Shapes Of Things

Personnel:
Keith Relf: lead vocals
Eric Clapton: lead guitar
Jeff Beck: lead guitar
Chris Dreja: rhythm guitar
Jim McCarty: drums
Paul Samwell-Smith: bass guitar
Released: 9 December 1977
Charly CDZ1 (UK), Bomb Canada 104.5 (Canada)
No chart position

The sleeve announces, 'A collection of classic Yardbirds recordings 1964-56', made up of 24 tracks predating *Roger The Engineer*, with five session outtakes not included on albums released during the band's lifetime, including 'Someone To Love' in two parts, a percussive group-composed work-out at 2:21 and a bluesy instrumental with Beck's lead guitar at 4:14. Both are rehearsal backing tracks that turned into 'Lost Women'. On 26 November 1977, *NME*'s Charles Shaar Murray pointed out that 'Part 2 features Beck getting highly engrossed in his rhythm part and grooving on that to the point where it would've thrown the song out of whack if it'd been used for the finished product.' Murray also praises Samwell-Smith, 'who can be heard here playing a lot of stuff that most people think Jack Bruce introduced to the vocabulary of the rock bass player', and that The Yardbirds' 'simple, energetic playing and superb grasp of the neglected art of dynamics stretched their gifts a lot further than might be supposed.'

In 1984, *Shapes Of Things* was expanded into a 72-track seven-LP boxset (BOX104) with *The First Recordings* (LP1); *Sonny Boy Williamson With The Yardbirds* (LP2); *Five Live Yardbirds* (LP3); *For Your Love* (LP4); *Having A Rave-Up With The Yardbirds* (LP5); *Shapes Of Things* (LP6); and *Odds And Sods* (LP7). It including three takes of 'Good Morning Little Schoolgirl' (backing track, backing plus harp, master), two takes of 'Heartful Of Soul' (sitar version, master), three takes of 'Got To Hurry' (take one backing track, take 2 backing track, master). There's also a previously unreleased 'Chris' Number', instrumental 'Pounds And Stomps' ('He's Always There' variant), plus two tracks by the Authentics featuring Jimmy Page ('Without You' and 'Climbing Through'). It provides a 'black box flight recorder of The Yardbirds ascent from struggling club days to temporary toppermost of the poppermost' – according to *NME*'s Paul Du Noyer – with a 36-page illustrated booklet.

London 1963: The First Recordings

Personnel:
Keith Relf: lead vocals
Eric Clapton: lead guitar
Chris Dreja: rhythm guitar
Jim McCarty: drums
Paul Samwell-Smith: bass guitar
Released: 17 July 1981 (Germany)
L&R 44.001
No chart position

An album taped live at the Richmond 'Crawdaddy Club' on 7 and 8 December 1963, with tracks 3 and 4 from side two being recorded at the RG Jones Studio in Morden on 10 December 1963 as demos. Despite its near-bootleg origins, the sound quality is remarkably good, and it carries the live immediacy of the performance atmosphere intact. To Lester Bangs of *Rolling Stone* on 9 July 1970, 'the early Yardbirds were loose and raw and played with a breathtaking natural energy that has never been matched by any of their progeny. Some of Clapton's very best work is here – I doubt if he has ever outdone the famous 'Smokestack Lightnin'' jam – and the whole group cook with a joyously driving conviction that propels them like a single pulsating organism out on some then-unheard-of limbs and back again with breathtaking ease.'

Side One

1. 'Smokestack Lightnin'' (Chester Burnett) 6:48

'Let's have a big hand for The Yardbirds, please', then Keith's harmonica cuts like a blade. This is a different take of the *Five Live Yardbirds* standout performance, illustrating just how flexible their live format could be.

2. 'You Can't Judge A Book By Looking At The Cover' (Willie Dixon) 2:56

The only version of this Bo Diddley classic that The Yardbirds committed to vinyl, with rattling maracas and inventive, burning, growling guitar runs from Clapton. 'I look like a farmer, but I'm a lover'.

3. 'Take It Easy Baby' (Rice Miller Williamson) 4:12
With Sonny Boy Williamson.

4. 'Talkin' About You' (Chuck Berry) 1:56
A reliable beat-group standby that The Yardbirds later did as part of their *Reunion Jam* sessions, punctuated by an animal howl.

Side Two
1. 'Let It Rock' (Chuck Berry) 2:17
Clapton accurately replicates Chuck Berry's runs and riffs with respectful fidelity.

2. 'I Wish You Would' (Billy Boy Arnold) 5:55
An extended take on their familiar track with Keith's wailing harmonica playing against Clapton's powerful guitar, it builds into powerful climaxes, aided by background audience sounds.

3. 'Boom Boom' (John Lee Hooker) 2:24
A studio demo that emphasises a more harmonic approach to the vocals than on the officially released versions.

4. 'Honey In Your Hips' (Yardbirds) 2:18
Eric Clapton plays guitar on this Keith Relf eulogy to the joys of dancing 'to the beat of that crazy sound'.

5. 'Who Do You Love' (Ellas McDaniel aka Bo Diddley) 4:13
With audience sounds, Clapton's guitar is restrained and unflamboyant while soloing, although Keith is moved to comment, 'That's very nice', to a bottleneck slide sequence.

The Yardbirds: The Single Hits
Personnel:
Keith Relf: lead vocals
Eric Clapton: lead guitar
Jeff Beck: lead guitar
Chris Dreja: rhythm guitar
Jim McCarty: drums
Paul Samwell-Smith: bass guitar
Released: 1982
Charly Records CFM102
No chart position

A unique gilt-edged 10" LP of ten tracks from 'Good Morning Little Schoolgirl' to 'You're A Better Man Than I', taking in 'I Ain't Got You', 'Got To Hurry', 'Still I'm Sad', etc., from what *NME*'s Andy Gill, on 10 April 1982, called 'one of the few original units operating in 1960s pop.' John Tobler adds liner notes.

Jimmy Page: Session Man

Released: 1989 and 1990

AIP Records AIPCD1041 and AIPCD1053

Within the tsunami of new beat-group signings as the 1960s boom picked up momentum – with session time at a premium and new groups unused to the strictures of studio discipline – it was frequently expedient to employ a hip, young guitar-slinger well-versed in the idiom who could be relied upon to supply a precise fill or neat solo as and when required. As such, Jimmy Page's session history is confusingly labyrinthine and the subject of fierce argument among devotees who claim he played on this or that record, a debate confused by the fact that a session musician very often turned up in the studio to add their contribution to a backing track without ever knowing which record it eventually ended up as part of. Compiling a collection of the singles Jimmy played on is further complicated by licensing deals and legal copyright issues. There was an earlier bootleg anthology issued in 1979 by Slipped Disc Records called *James Patrick Page: Session Man*, but this authorised version was released through a subsidiary of the specialist Bomp! Records label.

Volume 1

1. 'Don't You Dig This Kinda Beat' by Chris Ravel & The Ravers (August 1963) 1:50

This was an early incarnation for Chris Andrews, who went on to write hits for Adam Faith, Sandie Shaw and The Fortunes, as well as scoring his own number-three hit with 'Yesterday Man'. As the B-side of 'I Do', it was issued as Decca F11696.

2. 'Sweet Little Baby' by The Zephyrs (August 1963) 2:40

Jerry Donahue of this group later played with Fairport Convention, then with the reformed Yardbirds. Pete Gage, later of Vinegar Joe, was also a member. 'Do I love that girl? Yes, I love her, yes sirree' – there's even an exhortation to 'come on and do the Twist.'

3. 'Roll Over Beethoven' by Pat Wayne With The Beachcombers (December 1963) 2:57

At a time when everyone from The Beatles on down were doing this Chuck Berry song – it was track one on side two of *With The Beatles* a month earlier – this Birmingham group issued it as Columbia DB7182.

4. 'Somebody Told My Girl' by Carter-Lewis & The Southerners (October 1963) 2:39

Issued on Oriole CB1868, the prolific songwriting duo of Ken Lewis and John Carter went on to become Ivy League and The Flower Pot Men. It opens with a strong guitar hook leading into appealingly close Everly-style harmony vocals, broken by the spikey guitar solo.

5. 'My Baby Left Me' by Dave Berry & The Cruisers (January 1964) 2:03

The Sheffield-born singer was covering the Arthur 'Big Boy' Crudup song previously done for 'Sun Records' by Elvis Presley, produced by Mike Smith and issued as Decca F11803. The follow-up to his debut hit with Chuck Berry's 'Memphis Tennessee', this single peaked at number 37. The swaggering beat is propelled by the forceful, chopping guitarwork.

6. 'Once In A While' by The Brooks (March 1964) 2:39

The song was written in 1937 by Michael Edwards with Bud Green lyrics, and had been recorded by Sarah Vaughan and Nat King Cole. The Brooks had been The Brook Brothers – Geoff and Ricky – who had a number-five UK hit in March 1961 with Howard Greenfield-Barry Mann's humorous 'Warpaint', in an Everly Brothers style. Produced by Mike Smith, this was issued as Decca F11868.

7. 'Money Honey' by Mickie Most & The Gear (March 1964) 2:23

Written by Jesse Stone, this hard-hitting song was first recorded by Clyde McPhatter & The Drifters in 1953, then by Elvis Presley on his 1956 debut LP. Mickie gave it a thumping Nashville Teens sound with a sharp guitar solo.

8. 'That's Alright' by Mickie Most & The Gear (March 1964) 2:10

With 'Money Honey', this constitutes both sides of Mickie's single issued as Columbia DB7245. This B-side was written by Miki Dallon, who also played piano alongside bassist Alan Cartright as The Gear.

9. 'I Just Can't Go To Sleep' by The Sneekers (October 1964) 1:58

A Ray Davies song produced by Shel Talmy that closely follows the original Kinks arrangement. Talmy was producing The Kinks albums at the time, so he was well-positioned to requisition Ray's songs for his other clients.

10. 'A Certain Girl' by The First Gear (October 1964) 2:21

Yes, this is another smoother interpretation of The Yardbirds' first B-side, produced by Shel Talmy. The instrumental break has some novel stop-start guitar and snap drum-thump effects, but The Yardbirds – Jimmy's future colleagues – retain the edge.

11. 'Leave My Kitten Alone' by The First Gear (October 1964) 2:23
The B-side of their 'A Certain Girl'. First recorded in 1959 by Little Willie John, who co-wrote the song, 'Leave My Kitten Alone' was done by The Beatles in 1964, but was not issued by them until the 1995 *Anthology 1* package. It's a jog-along treatment with Dave Walton's lead vocals – 'I love my little kitten just like you hound-dogs love your bone' – answering harmonies and a blistering guitar solo.

12. 'How Do You Feel' by The Primitives (January 1965) 2:24
A four-piece beat-group from Oxford, with the B-side of their 'You Said' single on Pye 7N15755. It has fast-paced, high-pitched harmonies, rapid-fire drums and fluid guitar.

13. 'Zoom, Widge And Wag' by Bobby Graham (January 1965) 2:36
Written by session drummer Bobby Graham with Jimmy Page, this percussive mod instrumental with cinematic flourishes was issued as the B-side of Bobby's cover of jazz drummer Louis Bellson's 'Skin Deep' as Fontana TF521.

14. 'She Just Satisfies' by Jimmy Page (February 1965) 2:03
Both sides of Jimmy's solo single. Jimmy met Jackie DeShannon at Abbey Road Studios in 1964, where the successful American songwriter of hits such as The Searchers' 'When You Walk In The Room' was there to demo some new songs. Jimmy is credited as playing on her 'Don't Turn Your Back On Me'. They began dating through into 1965, with Jimmy travelling to Los Angeles where she introduced him into the rock music community, and they co-wrote a number of songs together, eight or nine titles including 'I've Got My Tears To Remind Me', 'Leaves Come Tumblin' Down', 'Stop That Girl' and 'In My Time of Sorrow' – later recorded by Marianne Faithful. It's widely assumed that he wrote 'She Just Satisfies' inspired by her example. Recorded at Philips Studios in Marble Arch, London, Jimmy played all the instruments, including the harmonica, apart from the drums, which were provided by another session veteran, Bobby Graham.

15. 'Keep Moving' by Jimmy Page (February 1965) 3:31
Largely a badass, bluesy, harmonica-led instrumental with occasional yells to 'keep moving', allegedly from Jackie DeShannon herself, although the songwriter credits go to Barry Mason/Jimmy Page on both sides.

16. 'Night Comes Down' by The Mickey Finn (March 1965) 2:12
Mickey Finn is Marc Bolan's future colleague in T. Rex, on a song written by producer Shel Talmy with singer-songwriter Jon Mark, but Finn turns it into a brutal slice of mod verging on freakbeat while teetering on the brink of mania. It was released as Columbia DB7510.

17. 'Little By Little' by The Pickwicks (October 1965) 2:29

A song written by Gordon Mills and produced by Larry Page for the Coventry four-piece that Page decked out in promotional Dickensian gear. The Pickwicks themselves deny that Jimmy Page was involved in their sessions, and that it was Harry Friar who played guitar, but the rumour that Jimmy was involved ensured that the single – Warner Bros WB151 – subsequently became highly collectable.

18. 'Surprise, Surprise' by Lulu & The Luvvers (April 1965) 2:20

A Rolling Stones song with a beat-group setting and a Jimmy Page guitar solo midway. After her breakthrough hit with the Isley Brothers' 'Shout', the singer, born Marie McDonald McLaughlin Lawrie, joined Sandie Shaw, Cilla Black and Dusty Springfield as the trendy queens of UK Pop.

19. 'Little Games' by The Yardbirds 2:30

A BBC recording from 18 April 1967.

20. 'Most Likely You'll Go Your Way (And I'll Go Mine)' by The Yardbirds 2:56

A BBC recording from 4 April 1967.

21. 'Dazed And Confused' by Jake Holmes (June 1967) 3:36

Although Jimmy Page did not play on this track, it was included on the compilation due to its significant role in the transition from The Yardbirds to Led Zeppelin.

Volume 2

1. 'Bald Headed Woman' by The Sneekers (October 1964) 2:31

The fuzz-tone distorted Shel Talmy-penned B-side of their only single on Columbia DB7385. The group later changed their name to The Frays.

2. 'See You Later, Alligator' by Wayne Gibson & The Dynamic Sounds (August 1964)

Jimmy Page played on Wayne's cover of Del Shannon's 'Kelly', which reached number 48 on the UK charts during March 1964. This Bill Haley cover was the B-side (Pye 7N15680). Wayne's cover of The Rolling Stones' 'Under My Thumb' also became a belated number-17 hit in 1974.

3. 'I Can Tell' by The Zephyrs (August 1963) 2:43

A beat-group single of a Bo Diddley song that opens with an anguished howl, this was issued as Columbia DB7199

4. 'Castin' My Spell' by The Talismen (April 1965) 1:55

The upbeat flip of their 'Masters Of War' single.

5. 'The Feminine Look' by Mickie Most (May 1963) 2:26
A song originally recorded in 1962 by 1950s British pop star Terry Dene, revived during Mickie Most's shot at becoming a pop star in his own right: 'She wiggles when she walks, and she flirts when she talks'. It was issued as Columbia DB7117.

6. 'I'll Go Crazy' by The Untamed (May 1964) 2:23
A group from Worthing in West Sussex, with a Shel Talmy-produced cover of a James Brown song issued as Stateside SS431. This track stands out as the hit-that-might-have-been.

7. 'Talking About You' by The Redcaps (November 1963) 2:24
Crude Birmingham beat-group r&b, the Chuck Berry song produced by Mike Smith for Decca F11789.

8. 'Honey Hush' by Neil Christian & The Crusaders (May 1964) 2:04
Jimmy Page toured as one of Neil's Crusaders for around two years while Neil – born Christopher Tidmarsh – seemed to be constantly on the verge of a breakthrough that never quite happened.

9. 'I Like It' by Neil Christian & The Crusaders (April 1966) 2:13
Written by Miki Dallon, this was the French B-side of Neil's only UK chart hit, 'That's Nice', which peaked at number 14.

10. 'This Sporting Life' by Mickey Finn (March 1963) 2:32
Pleading organ-led mod soul produced by Shel Talmy, Columbia DB7510.

11. 'Baby I Go For You' by The Blue Rondos (November 1964) 2:15
Some claim it was Blue Rondo's Roger Hall who played the midway guitar fusillade, and not Jimmy Page. Nevertheless, this Joe Meek RGM production was issued as Pye 7N15734.

12. 'I'll Come Running Over' by Lulu & The Luvvers (November 1964) 2:41
Using a stomping 'Bread And Butter' beat for a Bert & Ilene Berns song, this track was featured on Lulu's debut album, *Something To Shout About* (Decca LK4719), which was produced by Peter Sullivan with Bobby Graham drumming.

13. 'Is It True' by Brenda Lee (October 1964) 2:20
Following the British invasion of the US charts, 'Little Miss Dynamite' was one of the first American stars to visit London, hunting for the new sound. She was rewarded with a number-17 hit with this Carter-Lewis song, produced by Mickie Most, with powerful Jimmy Page wah-pedal guitar and Bobby Graham on drums.

14. 'I Took My Baby Home' by The Pickwicks (January 1965) 1:50

An early raucous Ray Davies song (B-side of The Kinks' 'Long Tall Sally') issued as the B-side of 'Little By Little' (Warner Bros WB1521).

15. 'The World Keeps Going Round' by The Lancastrians (January 1966) 2:15

Another Ray Davies song, issued as Pye 7N17043. The Lancastrians were from Altrincham in Cheshire, and the closest they came to a hit was with their cover of Gale Garnett's 'We'll Sing In The Sunshine', which peaked at number 44 in the UK during December 1964, produced by Shel Talmy with both Jimmy and Big Jim Sullivan present. Jimmy also played guitar on its B-side, 'Was She Tall' (Pye 7N15732).

16. 'Masters Of War' by The Talismen (April 1965) 2:21

The Bob Dylan song was edited to A-side radio-friendly length and issued as Stateside SS408, with a wailing harmonica solo.

17. 'You Said' by The Primitives (January 1965) 2:24

Harmonica-led r&b/garage rock that is very much in the Pretty Things style.

18. 'Train Kept A-Rollin'' by The Scotty McKay Quintet (1968) 2:28

An alias used by American rockabilly musician Max K Lipscomb, who was once a member of Gene Vincent's Blue Caps, to record this cover credited to The Yardbirds for Falcon FIC-101.

19. 'Everybody Knows' by Sean Buckley & The Breadcrumbs (May 1965) 2:09

Shel Talmy's freakbeat production graces this track along with a stinging guitar solo, issued as Stateside SS421.

20. 'Nothin' Shakin' (But The Leaves On The Trees)' by Billy Fury (April 1964) 2:41

Liverpool's first British rock star, Billy Fury, revived this 1958 Eddie Fontaine song in fine rocking style.

21. 'White Summer' by The New Yardbirds

Although credited as 'Live at the Marquee', 18 October 1968, this track was lifted from a Led Zeppelin bootleg.

Over Under Sideways Down: A Comprehensive Collection 1963-1968

Personnel:

Keith Relf: lead vocals

Eric Clapton: lead guitar

Jeff Beck: lead guitar
Jimmy Page: lead guitar
Chris Dreja: rhythm guitar
Jim McCarty: drums
Paul Samwell-Smith: bass guitar
Released: March 1991
Raven Records CDRV12

A single-CD anthology with the Beck-Page lineup cover photo in which only Jimmy is smiling! Its 75-minute playing time includes 'Baby What's Wrong', 'I Wish You Would', 'A Certain Girl', 'Good Morning Little Schoolgirl' through to 'Puzzles', 'Drinking Muddy Water', 'Train Kept A-Rollin'', 'Ten Little Indians' and 'Think About It'.

Journalist Paul Sexton, in *Select* in March 1991, pointed out that this release was 'tooting its horn as the first anthology of the complete Yardbirds story, this 28-track collection is part of the British launch of Australia's Raven reissue label, out here via Topic. Noted critic Glenn A Baker's compilation plots a clear graph of the group's history-making progression – from Jimmy Reed and Mose Allison blues covers to the eternal pop of Graham Gouldman's 'For Your Love' and 'Evil Hearted You', and out the other side into the 'hip Herman's Hermits' sound, as Baker called it, of their last releases.'

The credits are as they appear on the album:

1. 'Baby What's Wrong' (Jimmy Reed) 2:39
2. 'I Wish You Would' (Billy Boy Arnold) 2:18
3. 'A Certain Girl' (Naomi Neville) 2:18
4. 'Good Morning Little Schoolgirl' (Bob Love, Don Level) 2:46
5. 'Got Love If You Want It' (James Moore) 2:33
6. 'I Ain't Got You' (Calvin Carter) 2:00
7. 'I'm Not Talking' (Mose Allison) 2:32
8. 'Train Kept A Rollin'' (Howard Kay, Lois Mann, Tiny Bradshaw) 3:10
9. 'I Ain't Done Wrong' (Keith Relf) 3:38
10. 'For Your Love' (Graham Gouldman) 2:30
11. 'Heart Full Of Soul' (Graham Gouldman) 2:28
12. 'Evil Hearted You' (Graham Gouldman) 2:25
13. 'Still I'm Sad' (Paul Samwell-Smith) 2:59
14. 'I'm A Man' (Ellas Mcdaniel) 2:37
15. 'Shapes Of Things' (Jim McCarty, Keith Relf, Paul Samwell-Smith) 2:26
16. 'Over Under Sideways Down' (Yardbirds) 2:23
17. 'You're A Better Man Than I' (Brian & Mike Hugg) 3:18
18. 'Happenings Ten Years Time Ago' (Yardbirds) 2:56
19. 'Nazz Are Blue' (Yardbirds) 3:03
20. 'Rack My Mind' (Yardbirds) 3:14
21. 'Psycho Daisies' (Yardbirds) 1:46
22. 'Stroll On' (Chris Dreja, Jeff Beck, Jimmy Page, Keith Relf) 2:43

23. 'Little Games' (Harold Spiro, Phil Wainman) 2:25
24. 'Puzzles' (Jim McCarty, Jimmy Page, Keith Relf) 1:59
25. 'Drinking Muddy Water' (Yardbirds) 2:53
26. 'Tinker, Tailor, Soldier, Sailor' (Jim McCarty, Jimmy Page) 2:40
27. 'Ten Little Indians' (Harry Nilsson) 2:17
28. 'Think About It' (Jim McCarty, Jimmy Page, Keith Relf) 3:45

Yardbirds... On Air

Personnel:
Keith Relf: lead vocals
Eric Clapton: lead guitar
Jeff Beck: lead guitar
Jimmy Page: lead guitar
Chris Dreja: rhythm guitar
Jim McCarty: drums
Paul Samwell-Smith: bass guitar
Tracks recorded between 1965 and 1968 at the BBC Studios
Released: 7 May 1991
Band Of Joy BOJCD200
Reissued in expanded 3CD edition in 2019 as: The Yardbirds: Live At The BBC
Revisited (Repertoire Records REPUK1369)
Then in June 2024 as a 4CD box set: The Yardbirds: The Ultimate Live At The
BBC (Repertoire Records REPUK1464)
No chart position

It's strange to envisage from a 21st century point of view that for all of the
1950s and most of the 1960s, there was no commercial radio sector in Britain
at all, that the BBC had an absolute broadcasting monopoly, divided down
into The Home Service (now BBC Radio 4), which catered for news, drama
and discussion, the classical music Third Programme (now BBC Radio 3) and
The Light Programme, which alone included patronising popular music
content in amongst comedy such as *The Goon Show* and the *Mrs Dale's Diary*
radio soap opera. So, for most of The Yardbirds' active career, their only
access to airtime was through *Saturday Club*, *Easy Beat*, *Top Gear*, *Pick Of
The Pops* or *The Joe Loss Pop Show* (which featured The Rolling Stones live on
17 July 1964!). Jim McCarty recalled, 'I remember doing this ('Over Under
Sideways Down') on *The Joe Loss Pop Show*, midday on the Light Programme,
when we were the interval 'pop' band. Ross MacManus (Elvis Costello's pater)
had been singing the hits of the day, then we came on, and the Joe Loss
Orchestra joined in, with Joe conducting, which was very bizarre. The Band
Of The Coldstream Guards also did a cover version. Someone at our fan club
sent me a copy of that recently, but the *Joe Loss* episode must be a real
collector's item.'

It was possible to hear Radio Luxembourg, which broadcast pop in English
during the evenings, although the further north the listener happened to be

located, the patchier the reception. The advent – and subsequent outlawing
– of pirate radio, broadcasting from ships moored outside territorial waters,
pressured 'Auntie Beeb' to restructure and launch the more pop-friendly
Radio 1 from 30 September 1967. But to hear the first broadcast of a new
Yardbirds single, or to hear a live radio session, it was necessary to tune into
the BBC. Hence, the vast radio archive of studio-quality recordings with live
performances including rare songs never officially released.

An example of such material includes a fascinating *Saturday Club* take on
Bob Dylan's 'Most Likely You'll Go Your Way (And I'll Go Mine)' (at 2:51),
introduced by Brian Matthew. Part of their later live set, they adhere closely
to the original *Blonde On Blonde* arrangement.

CD 1

1. 'Boom Boom'* 3:28
2. 'I'm A Man' (version 1)* 3:04
3. 'Little Queenie'* 3:19
Tracks 1-3: Fourth National Jazz & Blues Festival, 9 August 1964
4. 'I'm Not Talking' (version 1)* 2:31
Track 4: *Saturday Club*, recorded on 16 March 1965, broadcast on 20 March
1965
5. 'I Ain't Got You' 1:59
6. Interview: Keith Relf talks with Brian Matthew about the band's
background, 0:58
7. 'For Your Love' 2:17
8. 'I'm Not Talking' (version 2) 1:46
Tracks 5-8: *Top Gear*, recorded on 22 March 1965, broadcast on 10 April 1965
9. 'Hush-A-Bye (All The Pretty Horses)'* charmingly attractive acoustic
12-string traditional lullaby, with pattering congas, 'birds and butterflies
fluttering round his eyes', 2:03.
10. 'I'm A Man' (version 2) 4:00
11. 'Runaround/Bottle Up And Go'* raving r&b group composition, with
standout Jeff Beck steel guitar, 2:07
12. 'Spoonful'* written by Willie Dixon and first recorded by Howlin' Wolf,
Keith acquits himself well on this song, which would later be associated with
Cream, 3:19
Tracks 9-12: *Saturday Swings*, recorded on 9 April 1965, broadcast on 17
April 1965
13. 'Steeled Blues'* 2:35
14. 'I Wish You Would' (version 1) 2:40
15. Interview: Paul Samwell-Smith talks to Brian Matthew about recording
and the US tour 0:59
16. 'Heart Full Of Soul' (version 1) 2:24
Tracks 13-16: *Saturday Club*, recorded on 1 June 1965, broadcast on 5 June 1965
17. 'I'm Not Talking' (version 3)* 2:29

18. 'Louise'* 3:01

Tracks 17-18: *Saturday Swings*, recorded on 4 June 1965, broadcast on 12 June 1965

19. 'Heart Full Of Soul' (version 2)* 2:50

Track 19: *The Ken Dodd Show*, recorded on 9 June 1965, broadcast on 20 June 1965

20. Interview: Keith Relf talks about touring and the 'Heart Full Of Soul' single*, 0:57

21. 'Heart Full Of Soul' (version 3) 2:19

22. 'I Ain't Done Wrong' 2:27

23. 'I've Been Trying'* 3:01

Tracks 20-23: Top Gear, recorded on 21 June 1965, broadcast on 26 June 1965

CD 2

1. 'Too Much Monkey Business' (with introduction) 2:28

2. 'Too Much Monkey Business'* 2:21

3. Interview: Keith Relf talks about touring and recording* 0:47

4. 'Love Me Like I Love You' (version 1), a raw, rough-edged beat-group rave-up with a drum flourish at the end. An original Dreja, Beck, McCarty, Relf, Samwell-Smith composition, 2:49

5. 'I'm A Man' (version 3, with introduction) 2:29

6. 'I'm A Man' (version 3)* 2:27

7. 'I Wish You Would' (version 2)* 2:33

Tracks 1-7: *You Really Got...*, recorded on 6 August 1965, broadcast on 30 August 1965

8. 'Love Me Like I Love You' (version 2)* 2:49

Track 8: *The Beat Show*, recorded on 9 August 1965, broadcast on 12 August 1965

9. 'Evil Hearted You' (with introduction) 2:25

10. 'Evil Hearted You'* 2:18

11. Interview: Paul Samwell-Smith talks to Brian Matthew about the 'Still I'm Sad' single 0:51

12. 'Still I'm Sad' 2:52

13. 'Hang On Sloopy' (with Brian Matthew introduction) 3:32

14. 'The Stumble'* 1:56

Tracks 9-14: *Saturday Club*, recorded on 27 September 1965, broadcast on 2 October 1965

15. 'Smokestack Lightnin'' 5:00

16. 'Smokestack Lightnin'' (edited version) 3:45

17. Interview: The Yardbirds give their New Year's resolutions, 0:47

18. 'You're A Better Man Than I' (version 1) 3:09

19. 'The Train Kept A-Rollin'' 2:39

Tracks 15-19: *The Sound Of Boxing Day*, recorded on 18 November 1965, broadcast on 27 December 1965

20. 'Dust My Blues' (edited version), although derived from Robert Johnson, the Elmore James revision became a standard part of the British blues repertoire, and was later a showcase for Jeremy Spencer's slide guitar with Fleetwood Mac. Here, Jeff Beck takes vocals with devastating guitar riffs and runs that show where they got 'The Nazz Are Blue' from: 'I get up in the morning, I believe I'll dust my blues', 3:02
21. 'Dust My Blues'* 2:43
22. 'You're A Better Man Than I' (version 2) 3:11
23. 'Shapes Of Things' (version 1) 2:23
Tracks 20-23: *Saturday Club*, recorded on 28 February 1966, broadcast on 5 March 1966

CD 3

1. Interview: Keith Relf talks about his solo single, 0:48
2. 'Over Under Sideways Down' (version 1) 2:10
3. 'Baby, Scratch My Back', 'Here's our bill-topping group', announces Brian Matthew as they lead into a 'tongue-in-cheek' harmonica-laced version of the Slim Harpo song with 'chicken scratch' guitar, 3:25
4. 'The Sun Is Shining' (edited version), 'On this all-British swinging show, we got the blues, and we're loving it' – a slow blues credited to Elmore James with stinging soloing, Jeff takes the raw vocals, 2:43
5. Interview: Keith Relf talks about their US tour, 1:20
6. 'Shapes Of Things' (version 2) 2:17
7. 'The Sun Is Shining' (Elmore James song) 2:43
8. 'Jeff's Boogie' (version 1)* 2:18
Tracks 1-8: *Saturday Swings*, recorded on 6 May 1966, broadcast on 21 May 1966
9. 'Over Under Sideways Down' (version 2) 2:09
10. Comment: Barry Fantoni talks about Jeff Beck's guitar playing, 0:14
Tracks 9-10: *A Whole Scene Going*, recorded and broadcast on 8 June 1966
11. 'Jeff's Boogie' (version 2)* 2:32
Track 11: *The Joe Loss Pop Show*, recorded on 9 June 1966, broadcast on 1 July 1966
12. 'Drinking Muddy Water' 2:39
13. Interview: Keith Relf talks about touring, their flop single and their 'Little Games' single*, 0:59
14. 'Little Games' 2:25
15. 'Most Likely You Go Your Way (And I'll Go Mine)' (with introduction 'we're delighted to welcome back to the show that great group The Yardbirds') 2:55
16. 'Most Likely You Go Your Way (And I'll Go Mine)'* 2:48
Tracks 12-16: *Saturday Club*, recorded on 4 April 1967, broadcast on 15 April 1967
17. 'Think About It' (version 1) 3:08

18. Interview: Jimmy Page talks about touring America: 'Perhaps they've adopted us', 1:47
19. 'Goodnight Sweet Josephine' 2:31
20. 'My Baby' 2:58
21. 'Think About It' (version 2) 3:23
22. 'White Summer' (with John Peel intro and outro, 'for children of all ages who are playing in parks anywhere', says Peel)* 4:31
23. 'Dazed And Confused' (with John Peel outro, 'that's an amazing performance')* 5:58
Tracks 17-23: *Top Gear/Saturday Club*, recorded on 5 and 6 March 1968, broadcast on 10 March 1968.
*Tracks not previously included on REP1309 or remastered from newly discovered archival source.

Little Games Sessions And More

Personnel:
Keith Relf: lead vocals
Jimmy Page: lead guitar
Chris Dreja: rhythm guitar
Jim McCarty: drums
Released: 8 April 1991 (US)
EMI USA 0777-7-98213-27
No chart position
'*Little Games* is the wreckage of what was supposed to have been The Yardbirds' third album', say Charles Shaar Murray & Roy Carr in *NME*'s 'Yardbirds Consumers Guide' (7 April 1973). This package salvages both mono and stereo mixes of the original album, plus non-album singles and alternate takes.

Yardbirds: Where The Guitar Gods Played

Personnel:
Keith Relf: lead vocals
Eric Clapton: lead guitar
Jeff Beck: lead guitar
Jimmy Page: lead guitar
Chris Dreja: rhythm guitar
Jim McCarty: drums
Paul Samwell-Smith: bass guitar
Released: 26 November 1991
A*Vision
A documentary film made up of performances and interviews, TV appearances and archive footage, issued as a Rhino DVD in 2003, and re-released in 2008 as an unauthorised *The Story Of The Yardbirds*.

1. 'Louise' (1964)
2. 'I Wish You Would' (1964)

3. 'I'm A Man' (1964)
4. 'Heart Full Of Soul' (1965)
5. 'Still I'm Sad' (1965)
6. 'For Your Love' (1965)
7. 'My Girl Sloopy' (1965)
8. 'Train Kept A-Rollin'' (1966)
9. 'Shapes Of Things' (1966)
10. 'Happenings Ten Years Time Ago' (1966)
11. 'Stroll On' (1966)
12. 'Happenings Ten Years Time Ago' (1967)
13. 'I'm Confused (Dazed And Confused)' (1967)
14. 'I'm A Man' (1967)
15. 'For Your Love' (1965)

Train Kept A-Rollin': The Complete Giorgio Gomelsky Productions

Personnel:
Keith Relf: lead vocals
Eric Clapton: lead guitar
Jeff Beck: lead guitar
Chris Dreja: rhythm guitar
Jim McCarty: drums
Paul Samwell-Smith: bass guitar
Released: 11 May 1993
Charly CD LIK BOX3
No chart position
'Clocking in at nearly five hours,' writes *Q* magazine's Mat Snow in October 1993, 'this box charts the band's progress from ramshackle Home Counties Blueswailers backing a drunken Sonny Boy Williamson in Richmond in 1963 to the early psychedelia of 'Shapes Of Things' two years later, with numerous rarities and unheard bits and bobs on the way.' With 90 tracks sequenced in chronological order, the box set includes most of the available pre-*Roger The Engineer* tracks, including the US hit single 'I'm A Man', plus 'Sweet Music' and the ludicrous Euro-fodder of 'Questa Volta' and 'Paff… Bum', alongside previously unreleased 1963-1964 demos, live recordings and alternate takes. Digitally remastered from the original tapes, the box also housed an exclusive Yardbirds T-shirt, a metal badge and a 64-page booklet filled with detailed track annotations! Compiled with expert care by Phil Cohen with commentary by Gomelsky himself, it was later reissued as *The Yardbirds Story* (2002).

Cumular Limit

Personnel:
Keith Relf: lead vocals
Jimmy Page: lead guitar
Chris Dreja: bass guitar

Jim McCarty: drums
Released: 25 August 2000
Burning Airlines Pilot 24
A compilation made up of New York Columbia Studio demos from April 1968, with an enhanced CD of four live songs from a 1967 German TV show, plus informed Gregg Russo sleeve notes. The album offers an opportunity to contrast Keith Relf with Robert Plant's interpretation of 'Dazed And Confused' over serious Jimmy Page guitar distortion; Jimmy had obviously already worked out the song's Led Zeppelin arrangement! 'Spanish Blood' (3:12) resembles a western movie theme with Jim reciting his own words: 'my horse stood motionless as I watched her through the olive branches'. It ends in an exasperated 'that was the wrong fucking verse!' to which bandleader/ producer Manny Kellem responds, 'Ah, I'm gonna leave that.'

CD 1
1. 'Tinker, Tailor, Soldier, Sailor' (alternate version) 2:48
2. 'Shapes Of Things' 2:24
3. 'Happenings Ten Years Time Ago' 3:19
4. 'Over Under Sideways Down' 2:16
5. 'I'm A Man' 6:09
Tracks 2-5 Live in Offenbach, Germany, 16 March 1967
6. 'White Summer' (alternate version) 3:55
7. 'Ten Little Indians' 2:16
8. 'Glimpses' (alternate version) 5:16
9. 'You Stole My Love' (full instrumental version of Graham Gouldman's Mockingbirds song) 2:31
10. 'Avron Knows' 3:46
11. 'Spanish Blood' (Jim McCarty composition) 3:16
12. 'My Baby' (impassioned Keith vocal on a Mort Shuman & Jerry Ragovoy song, first recorded by Garnet Mimms in 1966) 2:57
13. 'Taking A Hold On Me' (Jim McCarty vocal on a Yardbirds composition) 3:06
Tracks 10-13 are previously unissued 1968 New York studio recordings
14. 'Dazed And Confused' (live in France, 9 March 1968) 5:50

CD 2
1. 'Shapes Of Things'
2. 'Happenings Ten Years Time Ago'
3. 'Over Under Sideways Down'
4. 'I'm A Man'
Video footage shot live in Offenbach, Germany, 16 March 1967

Ultimate!
Personnel:
Keith Relf: lead vocals

Eric Clapton: lead guitar
Jeff Beck: lead guitar
Jimmy Page: lead guitar
Chris Dreja: rhythm guitar
Jim McCarty: drums
Paul Samwell-Smith: bass guitar
Released: 31 July 2001
Rhino R2 79825
Fifty-two tracks from 1963 demos through to the last 1968 single.

Live! Blueswailing July '64

Personnel:
Keith Relf: lead vocals
Eric 'Slowhand' Clapton: lead guitar
Chris Dreja: rhythm guitar
Jim McCarty: drums
Paul Samwell-Smith: bass guitar
Released: 23 September 2003
Castle Music CMQCD 793 (UK) and Castle Music 06076-81331-2 (US)
Previously undiscovered recordings that have tentatively been identified as from a Marquee performance on 7 August 1964 with the Clapton lineup. Again, the sound quality is authentically raw, with humorous between-numbers banter. In a 'brief period' after 'Got Love If You Want It', Keith says that Eric's guitar needs to be retuned; it's a black Fender Jazzmaster, a 'brand new guitar – you may have noticed – cost him about £300, 'cos that's a lot of money, y'know.' By contrast, Keith's harmonica cost him just 10s 9d (53p)! Then, to fill the pause, Keith recounts an anecdote from an earlier Kenton gig where Chris Dreja's Gibson guitar, lying on the stage floor during a maracas number, was wrecked by a falling red speaker cabinet plunging off Sam's bass amplifier. They had to complete the set with Chris just playing a tambourine.

Neil Slaven contributes liner notes.

1. 'Someone To Love Me' (Snooky Pryor) 1:22
2. 'Too Much Monkey Business' (Chuck Berry) 3:01
3. 'Got Love If You Want It' (James Moore aka Slim Harpo) 2:31
4. 'Smokestack Lightnin'' (Chester Burnett) 5:24
5. 'Good Morning Little Schoolgirl' (Sonny Boy Williamson) 2:35
6. 'She's So Respectable/Humpty Dumpty' (O'Kelly, Ronald and Rudolph Isley) 5:18
7. 'The Sky Is Crying' (Elmore James) 6:41

Live At B.B. King Blues Club

Personnel:
Chris Dreja: rhythm guitar

Jim McCarty: drums
Billy Boy Miskimmin: harmonica
Ben King: lead guitar
John Idan: bass and vocals
Released: 30 March 2007
Favoured Nations FN2580-2
Tracks recorded live in an XM digital broadcast from New York City on 19
July 2006, mixed by Joel Singer and mastered by Jason Relf with Sophie
Marchant.

1. 'Train Kept A-Rollin" (Kay, Mann, Bradshaw) 3:40
2. 'Please Don't Tell Me 'Bout The News' (Jim McCarty) 4:34
3. 'Drinking Muddy Water' (Dreja, McCarty, Relf, Page) 3:55
4. 'Crying Out For Love' (McCarty) 4:23
5. 'Heart Full Of Soul' (Gouldman) 2:39
6. 'My Blind Life' (Chris Dreja) 3:58
7. 'The Nazz Are Blue' (Dreja, Beck, McCarty, Relf, Samwell-Smith) 4:12
8. 'Mr, You're A Better Man Than I' (Brian and Michael Hugg) 3:12
9. 'Mr Saboteur' (McCarty) 5:14
10. 'Shapes Of Things' (McCarty, Relf, Samwell-Smith) 2:43
11. 'Mystery Of Being' (McCarty) 4:08
12. 'Rack My Mind' (Dreja, Beck, McCarty, Relf, Samwell-Smith) 5:51
13. 'Over Under Sideways Down' (Dreja, Beck, McCarty, Relf, Samwell-Smith) 3:09
14. 'Back Where I Started' (Dreja, McCarty, John Fidder, Samwell-Smith) 8:30
15. 'For Your Love' (Gouldman) 3:27
16. 'Still I'm Sad' (McCarty, Samwell-Smith) 1:43
17. 'Dazed And Confused' (Jimmy Page) 4:44
18. 'I'm A Man' (Ellas McDaniel) 5:10
19. 'Happenings Ten Years Time Ago' (Beck, McCarty, Page, Relf) 3:39

Glimpses 1963-1968

Personnel:
Keith Relf: lead vocals
Eric Clapton: lead guitar
Jeff Beck: lead guitar
Jimmy Page: lead guitar
Chris Dreja: rhythm guitar
Jim McCarty: drums
Paul Samwell-Smith: bass guitar
Released: 5 December 2011
Easy Action EARS035
Mostly live recordings, including some previously unissued, and a scattering
of semi-official and bootleg tracks of dubious or undocumented origin.

CD 1 1963-1964

1. 'Honey In Your Hips (alternate studio take)' 2:24
2. 'Baby What's Wrong' 2:41
3. Eric Clapton interview 0:43
4. 'I Wish You Would' 3:32
5. 'You Can't Judge A Book By Its Cover (studio demo)' 2:41
6. Jim McCarty interview 0:26
7. 'Louise' 2:54
8. Eric Clapton interview 0:23
9. 'Someone To Love' 2:15
10. 'Too Much Monkey Business' 3:07
11. 'Got Love If You Want It' 4:16
12. 'Smokestack Lightnin'' 5:52
13. 'Good Morning Little Schoolgirl' 3:37
14. 'Respectable' 5:30
15. 'The Sky Is Crying' 6:40
16. Eric Clapton interview 0:40
17. 'I Wish You Would' 2:52
18. Chris Dreja interview 0:22
19. 'I'm A Man' 3:26
20. 'Someone To Love' 1:56
21. 'Boom Boom' 3:36
22. 'I'm A Man' 3:12
23. 'Little Queenie' 3:27
24. 'Too Much Monkey Business' 2:53
25. 'Respectable' 3:46
26. 'Carol' 2:33
27. 'Here 'Tis' 3:44
28. Jim McCarty interview 0:26

CD 2 1965

1. 'Evil Hearted You' with Keith Relf introduction, 27 September, 2:26
2. Keith Relf interview 0:25
3. 'Heart Full Of Soul' with Paul Samwell-Smith interview, 1 June, 3:15
4. Chris Dreja interview 0:38
5. 'I Ain't Done Wrong', 3 July, 2:27
6. Jim McCarty interview 0:36
7. 'Smokestack Lightnin'', full version 16 November, 4:56
8. 'You're A Better Man Than I' with 16 November interview, 3:56
9. 'Train Kept A-Rollin', 16 November, 2:39
10. Jim McCarty interview 0:44
11. 'I'm Not Talking', 16 March, 2:33
12. Keith Relf interview 0:15
13. 'I'm A Man', 9 April, 3:55

14. Keith Relf interview 0:25
15. 'Jeff's Boogie', 9 June, 2:31
16. Keith Relf interview 0:46
17. 'Steeled Blues', 1 June, 2:36
18. 'Louise', 4 June, 2:56
19. Keith Relf interview 0:21
20. 'I Wish You Would', 6 August, 2:31
21. 'Love Me Like I Love You', 9 August, 2:46
22. 'The Stumble', 27 September, 1:53
23. Paul Samwell-Smith interview 1:26
24. 'You're A Better Man Than I' 2:23
25. 'Train Kept A-Rollin'' 2:41
26. Chris Dreja interview 0:41
27. 'I've Been Trying', 9 June, 3:02
28. 'Shapes Of Things' with interview, 5:02
29. Paul Samwell-Smith interview 2:40
30. 'For Your Love' long version 2:07
31. 'My Girl Sloopy' long version 5:49
32. 'I'm A Man (live)' 3:35
33. 'I Wish You Would (live)' 1:02
34. 'McLeans' toothpaste TV advert, 'it's McLeans the toothpaste that cleans, with a new kind of taste that's wild', 0:30

CD 3 1965-1966

1. 'Happenings Ten Years Time Ago', 26 July, 20 September, 2 October 1966, 2:55
2. Keith Relf interview 0:39
3. 'Psycho Daisies' 1:48
4. 'Stroll On' with soundtrack coda, 3:31
5. Chris Dreja interview 0:11
6. 'Great Shakes' TV advert using the 'Over Under Sideways Down' riff with lyrics amended to promote a brand of powdered milkshake, 1:02
7. 'I Wish You Would' 3:18
8. 'I'm A Man' 2:37
9. 'Train Kept A-Rollin'' 2:21
10. 'Over Under Sideways Down (live)' 2:13
11. 'Shapes Of Things (live)' 2:21
12. 'He's Always There (alternate version)' 2:29
13. 'Turn Into Earth (alternate version)' 3:09
14. 'I Can't Make Your Way (alternate version)' 2:23
15. 'I'm A Man' 3:12
16. 'For Your Love' 2:12
17. 'Heart Full Of Soul' 2:23
18. 'I Wish You Would (live)' 2:27

19. Jim McCarty interview 0:12
20. 'Questa Volta (live)' 4:05
21. 'Paff… Bum (live)' 2:52
22. Chris Dreja interview 0:19
23. 'Train Kept A-Rollin' (live)' 2:30
24. 'Shapes Of Things (live)' 2:15
25. Jim McCarty interview 0:15
26. Jimmy Page interview 1:09
27 'Jeff's Boogie', 6 May 1966, 2:15
28. 'You're A Better Man Than I (live)' 3:07
29. Keith Relf and Jeff Beck in a televised interview with Ravi Shankar, 8 June 1966: 'I'm sure you must have been asked this lots of times before, but what's your opinion of – erm, sort of – English pop groups and American pop groups using the sitar and the Indian influence on their records?' asks Keith respectfully, sitting cross-legged. Ravi fears it could be a passing phase. 'How far back does the sitar date? And how was it … sort of … was it like that when it was first built?' asks Jeff. Nearly 700 years, says Ravi, and it evolved from an earlier form, 0:56
30. 'Shapes Of Things (live)' 2:18
31. Jim McCarty interview 0:30
32. Jim McCarty interview 0:27
33. Chris Dreja interview 0:17
34. 'I'm Not Talking', 4 June 1965, 2:26
35. 'Heart Full Of Soul', 9 June 1965, 2:22
36. 'Spoonful', 9 April 1965, 3:10
37. 'Bottle Up And Go', 9 April 1965, 1:57
38. 'All The Pretty Little Horses (Hushabye)', 9 April 1965, 1:56
39. Jeff Beck interview 0:08

CD 4 1967-1968

1. 'Shapes Of Things' 2:55
2. 'Happenings Ten Years Time Ago' 4:25
3. 'Over Under Sideways Down' 2:14
4. 'I'm A Man' 6:24
5. Chris Dreja interview 0:39
6. 'Shapes Of Things' 2:31
7. 'Heart Full Of Soul' 2:16
8. 'You're A Better Man Than I' 3:52
9. 'Most Likely You Go Your Way (And I'll Go Mine)' 3:15
10. 'Over Under Sideways Down' 2:32
11. 'Little Games' 2:40
12. 'My Baby' 2:43
13. 'I'm A Man' 7:07
14. Chris Dreja interview 0:49

15. 'Train Kept A-Rollin'' 3:18
16. 'Dazed And Confused' 5:46
17. 'Goodnight Sweet Josephine' 2:33
18. 'Glimpses' with sound effects, 1:22
19. 'The In Sound' 1:36
20. Chris Dreja interview 0:37
21. 'Think About It', work-in-progress, 5:33
22. Jimmy Page interview 0:22
23. 'Dazed And Confused (live)' 9:09

CD 5 BBC Radio

1. 'I Ain't Got You', 22 March 1965, 2:00
2. 'For Your Love' with Keith Relf interview, 22 March 1965, 3:17
3. 'I'm Not Talking', 22 March 1965, 1:46
4. 'I Wish You Would', 1 June 1965, 2:36
5. 'Too Much Monkey Business', 6 August 1965, 2:29
6. 'Love Me Like I Love You', 6 August 1965, 2:50
7. 'I'm A Man', 6 August 1965, 2:27
8. 'Still I'm Sad' with Paul Samwell-Smith interview, 3:44
9. 'My Girl Sloopy', full version, 27 September 1965, 3:40
10. Keith Relf interview, 28 February 1966, 1:19
11. 'Shapes Of Things', 28 February 1966, 2:17
12. 'You're A Better Man Than I', 28 February 1966, 3:03
13. 'Dust My Broom', 28 February 1966, 2:30
14. 'Baby, Scratch My Back' with Keith Relf interview, 6 May 1966, 4:01
15. 'Over Under Sideways Down', 6 May 1966, 2:11
16. 'The Sun Is Shining', full version, 6 May 1966, 3:32
17. 'Shapes Of Things', 6 May 1966, 2:24
18. 'Most Likely You Go Your Way (And I'll Go Mine)', 17 March 1967, 2:49
19. 'Little Games', 17 March 1967, 2:21
20. 'Drinking Muddy Water', 17 March 1967, 2:40
21. 'Think About It', 16 March 1968, 3:09
22. 'Goodnight Sweet Josephine' with Jimmy Page interview, 16 March 1968, 4:19
23. 'My Baby', 16 March 1968, 2:50
24. 'White Summer', 5 and 6 March 1968, 4:24
25. 'Dazed And Confused', 5 and 6 March 1968, 5:47
26. 'Think About It', 5 and 6 March 1968, 3:15

Making Tracks

Personnel:
Dave Smale: bass guitar, backing vocals
Jim McCarty: drums, backing vocals
Andy Mitchell: lead vocals, harmonica, guitar

Chris Dreja: rhythm guitar, percussion
Ben King: lead guitar
Released: 7 October 2013
Wienerworld WNRCD5069
Live recordings from the 2010-2011 American tours, at the Infinity Music Hall, Norfolk, Connecticut (2 September 2011), the Tupelo Music Hall, Londonderry, New Hampshire (4 September 2011), the Showcase Live, Foxboro, Massachusetts (28 May 2010) and the Downtown Concert, Springfield, Massachusetts (1 September 2011). A tie-in concert film – *Making Tracks* – was issued on 11 December 2012 as an MVD Visual DVD, with bonus tracks by The Jim McCarty Band.

Yardbirds '68

Personnel:
Keith Relf: lead vocals
Jimmy Page: lead guitar
Chris Dreja: rhythm guitar
Jim McCarty: drums
Released: November 2017
Live and studio recordings from New York City, March and April 1968. Although previously issued in 1971 as *The Yardbirds! Featuring Jimmy Page* and frequently bootlegged, this is the approved edition.

Yardbirds (Roger The Engineer)

Personnel:
Keith Relf: lead vocals
Jeff Beck: lead guitar
Chris Dreja: rhythm guitar
Jim McCarty: drums
Paul Samwell-Smith: bass guitar
Released: June 2021
Demon Records DEMRECBOX55X
There had been an earlier reissue in 1983 from Edsel Records (ED116M/S) in mono and stereo editions with original artwork upgraded by Chris Dreja, and liner notes, but this is an expanded Super Deluxe Edition, with both full mono and stereo albums, a 7" replica single of 'Happenings Ten Years Time Ago' b/w 'Psycho Daisies' and a '1966 Studio Recordings' outtakes CD of alternate mixes, early takes and Keith Relf's solo 'Mr Zero' and 'Knowing'.

Charles Shaar Murray selected this album as one of his 'Top Twenty Cult Albums' for a feature in *The Observer* newspaper on 21 April 1996, writing 'The Yardbirds were always odd: Stones understudies during Eric Clapton's occupancy of their guitar chair, they took a left turn into chart-crunching pop psychedelia after kamikaze special-effects merchant Jeff Beck replaced him, and never looked back. Vocalist Keith Relf had the misfortune to be a punk rock singer years before the genre was formally identified, so people thought he simply had a weedy voice and pitched relentlessly flat. The group backed his nasal whine with a distinctive blend of ethnic borrowings, revved-up blues rock and pop mysticism.' In *NME* on 25 December 1976, Murray pointed out that 'though it wouldn't be for another two years on the *Truth* album that Beck was to bring to full fruition what he got into on this album, *Yardbirds* still has such an aura of heady excitement of being on the verge of something that it eclipses much of what was to come after it.'

New Beginnings

James McCarty Solo Work – Out Of The Dark

Personnel:
Rod Demick: bass guitar
Dugard Brown: guitar, backing vocals
Matthew Fisher: keyboards
James McCarty: drums, keyboards, vocals
Jackie Rave, Mandy Bell, Jane Relf: backing vocals
Eddie Phillips: guitar (on 'Signs From An Age Gone By' and 'Home Is Where The Heart Is')
Matthew Hammond: keyboards
Don Crane: guitar, backing vocals (on 'Back To The Earth')
Released: 1994
Higher Octave Music HOMCD 7057
No chart position

This was a solo project written and produced by James 'Jim' McCarty, assisted by drop-in guests Don Crane – who had been frontman with Downliners Sect (as Don Craine), and who died on 24 February 2022 – and Eddie Phillips, who had been guitarist with the Op-Art band Creation, and was the man who inspired Jimmy Page to play guitar with a violin bow. The two had toured the US with McCarty as part of the nostalgia collective The British Invasion All-Stars (Jim sings on their 'Train Kept A Rollin'' on 1990 album *Regression* (Promised Land 82152) and 'I'm A Man', with Pretty Things' Phil May singing 'Shapes Of Things' on *United* (Promised Land 246890)). Jim was involved with Brisk Productions, who marketed such material, including *The British Invasion All-Star* video, as well as *Drumming The Yardbirds Style*, a 35-minute VHS musicians' tutorial in which Jim demonstrates how to play various Yardbirds numbers (available by mail-order from: 27 Old Gloucester St, London WC1N 3XX).

He was also joined on the *Out Of The Dark* album by friends and previous colleagues, such as Jane Relf and Matthew Fisher. The cover art shows Jim's unshaved face superimposed in red over the Stonehenge 'circles of mystery', giving a mystic slant to the smooth jazzy groove of the title track, while 'Just Breaking Through' has a slow electro pulse ornamented with cutting near-Floydian guitar. There are pattering toms on the reflective 'We're Still Dreamers', which looks back to when 'we were young, we were strong', but he reconfirms his commitment to their vision of love.

Track Listing

'Out Of The Dark' (4:30)
'We're Still Dreamers' (4:57)
'Signs From An Age Gone By' (5:22)
'Just A Breath Away' (4:30)

'Just Breaking Through' (5:01)
'What If Summer Never Came' (3:44)
'Still You Don't Believe' (3:27)
'Longing (Link)' (0:32)
'Home Is Where The Heart Is' (4:08)
'Back To The Earth' (3:43)

In many ways, Jim had become the most prolific former Yardbird, hitting his stride as writer and musician, playing a long residency at Latimer Road's 'Station Tavern' from the late 1980s, and under various flags of convenience – as The Ruthless Blues at the Brentford 'Red Lion' and 'The Black Dog' in Twickenham. McCarty had also joined with Louis 'Loui' Cennamo to form new-age ambient neo-folk outfit Stairway for albums of 'healing music' – *Aquamarine* (1987, New World Cassettes NWC143) and *Moonstone* (1988, New World Company NWC168) with Jane Relf and Clifford White – plus two albums with psychologist-healer Malcolm Stern – *Chakra Dance* (1989, New World Music NWCD179, issued in the US as *Valley Of The Sun* CD106), and the all-instrumental *Medicine Dance* (1992, New World Music NWCD217), with 11 tracks named after spirit-guide creatures: Eagle, Deer, Horse, Dolphin. A further album – *Raindreaming* (1995, Oasis OASCD1012) – was followed by a compilation called *Pearls Of The Deep* (2015, Angel Air Records SJPCD475). Stairway also subsumed the Yardbirds track 'Turn Into Earth' as part of their live set.

There was also Pilgrim. With poetic Carmen Willcox lyrics sung by John Richardson, with music by and arranged by McCarty, the band released the self-consciously arty *Gothic Dream* (1996, New World Music NWCD 425) and *Search For The Dreamchild* (1998, New World Music NWCD297).

The Yardbirds Reunited Album – Reunion Jam

Personnel:
Rod Demick: bass guitar, blues harp
Jim McCarty: drums, backing vocals, executive producer
'Detroit' John Idan: lead guitar
Chris Dreja: rhythm guitar, executive producer
Mike Bernard Ober: producer, sequencing
Released: 1 December 1999
Mooreland Street Records 70729-2
No chart position

There comes a time when members of lapsed bands get together to reminisce. After all the ego trips, the experimental art-prog projects and the solo careers have run their course, they get to thinking, 'You know, we had a really nice little thing going back then before the head-games, the management and the record label politics took over. Why don't we get the old band back together again?' It happened with The Animals. It happened with The Small Faces. Could it work for The Yardbirds? Obviously, Keith was no longer around, and his pretty fragility was always the group's visual focus. But Chris and Jim were there to constitute the necessary quorum of original members, with their induction into The Rock Hall Of Fame to provide the catalyst.

Jimmy Page had already used 'The New Yardbirds' name during the transitional phase into Led Zeppelin ... so was this to be The Newer New Yardbirds? Was this projected reunion to be an interrupted continuity, or was it to be a reversion to the most blueswailing 'factory settings'? As it turned out, it was neither.

In a chance 1988 meeting, McCarty had been reunited with a recovered Top Topham, which led to the formation of The Topham-McCarty Band, which played together until July 1990. American-born John Idan met McCarty and Topham during a London visit, and he subsequently joined the duo's band in 1988. But while Topham returned to session work, Idan seemed an obvious candidate for the lead guitar role in what was shaping up to be the new Yardbirds. The addition of Rod Demick on bass, also from the Topham-McCarty group, completed the lineup. Although born in the north Wales resort of Prestatyn, he'd grown up in Belfast, where he joined The Wheels, who recorded Van Morrison's 'Gloria' (1965, Columbia DB7682) and 'Bad Little Woman' (February 1966, Columbia DB7827), which was covered by American garage band The Shadows Of Knight. A working musician, Rod was part of Bees Make Honey, Meal Ticket and The Strawbs, as well as the reconstituted Yardbirds.

More cumbersomely re-named *Yardbirds Reunion Concert Featuring The Rock Hall Of Fame's Jim McCarty And Chris Dreja* for its UK release on Promised Land CD202020, this was a live recording at the '100 Club' from 1 January 1992, remastered at the SRT Studios. The vocals are split three ways, with Jim McCarthy and John Idan carrying seven and eight, respectively, and Rod

Demick stepping in for 'Ain't Superstitious', plus some back-up vocal support. It carries the legend 'there were no overdubs whatsoever on this album.'

'Back Where I Started (Ricky Ricardoe Rave-Up)' (Dreja, McCarty, Idan, Ober, Demick) 6:32
More accurately, this is taken from The Box Of Frogs' debut outing, but with a more prominent harmonica and guitar blizzard, with an opening that recalls the 'Rave-up' sequence from 'Smokestack Lightnin'' on *Five Live Yardbirds*. But why the misspelling of Lucille Ball's sitcom bandleader husband Desi 'Ricky Ricardo' Arnaz? 'This is from Mike Ober's live recording?' Jim McCarty tells me in answer, 'he gave it that name for some reason.' Then 'Let's Rock 'n' Roll' McCarty invites ... and delivers.

'I'm Not Talking' (Mose Allison) 3:01
Opening with a crash, this is a heavied-up version of the Mose Allison song that had first appeared on The Yardbirds' America-only *For Your Love* album, and only sneaked into the UK market as part of the *Five Yardbirds* EP. Some of the jazzier elements have been exorcised in favour of live attack.

'Heavy Weather' (Jim McCarty, Matthew Fisher, Mike Ober) 2:34
Matthew Fisher was the songwriter and producer who played the Hammond organ on Procol Harum's 'A Whiter Shade Of Pale'. Here, the band play tightly with no showcasing, although both bass and drums work together in immaculate symmetry. It seems to end too soon, just as it hits an impressive groove.

'Train Kept A-Rolling' (Howie Kay, Lois Mann, Tiny Bradshaw) 3:27
As though direct from the *Blow-Up* soundtrack, 'aboard a train, I met a dame, she was a hipster, man, a real gone dame,' with harmonica breaks that recall Keith Relf, it builds to a formidable climax. 'With a heave and a ho, I just couldn't let her go.'

'Crying Out For Love' (Jim McCarty) 4:33
The first of two original songs from Jim, plus 'Heavy Weather', on which he wrote collaboratively. The dynamics of heavy upfront guitar riff and soloing, allied to a thumping drum pattern, tend to overshadow the fact that this is a song of some melodic sensitivity. The Yardbirds will return with a corrective studio revision on the next album.

'Heart Full Of Soul' (Graham Gouldman) 2:43
With a special introductory mention for 'my old colleague' Chris Dreja, this is largely a straight run-through of the hit single, with no radical points of departure, complete with a note-perfect replication of Jeff Beck's stinging guitar work.

'Three Lane Highway' (Jim McCarty) 3:24

Driving pedal-to-the-metal on motorvating boogie-rhythms, 'moving down to Texas, breaking through the State-line, leaving my blues behind' – just feel that engine-power! As much Status Quo as it is Yardbirds, but in a good way, as it dissolves into a furious rave-up jam.

'Ain't Done Wrong' (Keith Relf) 2:11

Another storming track that looks back to the American *For Your Love* album. Dramatic power chords open for edgy harmonica and energy-rush riffing that – judging by the audience reaction – builds effectively in a satisfying way. However, I do confess to missing Keith's own vocal lead.

'Sitting On Top Of The World' (Vinson, Chatmon) 5:36

The Yardbirds had never recorded this country blues song from 1930, written by Walter Vinson & Lonnie Chatmon and originally recorded by The Mississippi Sheiks. It had been picked up and reshaped by Howlin' Wolf for a 1957 Chess single, which is probably how it was drawn into the repertoire of both The Grateful Dead ... and Cream (on the studio sessions of their 1968 *Wheels Of Fire* double-album). And Eric Clapton had been a Yardbird, hadn't he? So that made its inclusion here entirely rational.

Where Jack Bruce takes the song at a slow 44bpm crawl punched out by Clapton's soaring Gibson solo, The Yardbirds revision centres around Rod Demick's similarly-paced harmonica interpreting the ironic 'she's gone' mood.

'Ain't Got You' (Calvin Carter) 2:11

All the way back to where it had all begun, the B-side of 'God Morning Little Schoolgirl', and nothing much has changed across the intervening decades; it still sounds stroppy and dirty, with a reasonable approximation of Eric Clapton's guitar.

'Rack My Mind' (Dreja, McCarty, Beck, Relf, Samwell-Smith) 3:44

Announced as 'a song we borrowed off Slim Harpo', this was always one of the strongest blues-driven tracks from the *Roger The Engineer* album, and it stands up well to this reinterpretation.

'Ain't Superstitious' (Willie Dixon) 3:50

Howlin' Wolf recorded a slow country-blues version of this Willie Dixon song in 1961 about how he 'ain't superstitious, but a black cat just crossed my trail'. However, when Rod Demick takes it into live muscular blues-rock territory with The Yardbirds, he is probably using the model taken from Jeff Beck's 1968 album *Truth* (Columbia SX6293), where Rod Stewart takes vocals and Jeff dusts off 'Shapes Of Things' and a version of 'Beck's Bolero' using John Paul Jones' bass and Jimmy Page on guitar.

'Bad Boy' (Eric Clapton, Bonnie Bramlett) 5:26
Jim McCarty sings 'I'm just a bad boy, a long way from home' in a song of classic slow blues structure taken from the 1970 album *Eric Clapton* (Atco-Polydor), the one-time Yardbird guitarist's debut solo album.

'Dust My Broom' (Robert Johnson) 5:34
With a history taking it back to Robert Johnson – and there are probably even earlier forms than that – but reinvented into the 1960s blues repertoire by the 1951 Elmore James recording, this most iconic of all riffs became a staple of Brit-blues, particularly through Jeremy Spencer's glistening slide guitar on Fleetwood Mac's *Mr Wonderful* 1968 album. The Yardbirds did it live, to the extent that it's on *The Yardbirds: Live At The BBC* album (2016, Repertoire Records REP2304/ RVPUK1309) – from a session recorded on 28 February 1966 and broadcast on Brian Matthew's *Saturday Club* show on 5 March 1966 – with Jeff Beck vocals. This *Reunion Jam* treatment is a more rough-and-tumble effort powered by chugging rhythms, but retaining its essential raunch with some tasty guitar fills before returning to the instantly recognisable signature riff.

'You're A Better Man Than I' (Mike & Brian Hugg) 3:37
Although Civil Rights issues have travelled a long way forward since the song first appeared as the flip of 'Shapes Of Things', the lesson still needs to be repeated. And they repeat it well.

'For Your Love' (Graham Gouldman) 4:20
The tempo-switching Yardbirds' first hit single is not an easy song to replicate decades later live on stage, yet the harmonies still sound sweet, it still sounds remarkably adventurous and it closes the album with rapturous audience applause.

The Yardbirds Studio Album – Birdland

Personnel:
Jim McCarty: drums, percussion, vocals
John 'Gypie' Mayo: lead guitar
John Idan: bass guitar, lead vocals
Alan Glen: harmonica, percussion
Chris Dreja: rhythm guitar
Ken Allardyce: producer, engineer, mixing
Released: 21 April 2003
Favoured Nations FN2280-2
No chart position.

Making explicit for the first time The Yardbirds' titular connection to bebop jazz genius Charlie 'Bird' Parker, this is the debut studio album by the Dreja-McCarty Yardbirds, recorded at Maison Rouge and Sensible Music in London and 'The Mothership' Los Angeles for Steve Vai's record label, with several top-line guests who were delighted to participate. The album features seven original compositions plus eight returns to The Yardbirds of the 1960s. It was dedicated with affection to Top Topham, Eric Clapton, Jeff Beck, Jimmy Page, Paul Samwell-Smith and Keith Relf.

'I'm Not Talking' (Mose Allison) 2:44

The Yardbirds track that debuted on the American 1965 *For Your Love* album, replicated faultlessly with McCarty taking a confident blues-shouting vocal supported by Mayo's scorching guitar. Born John Philip Cawthra on 24 July 1951, Gypie replaced Wilko Johnson in Dr Feelgood in 1977. He died on 23 October 2013. Harmonica player Alan Glen had worked with Nine Below Zero.

'Crying Out For Love' (James McCarty) 4:36

Although it first appeared in concert on the *Reunion Jam* album, this is a gentler, less raucous studio take of the song, the guitarwork is more sensitively nuanced and the more thoughtful vocals allow the song's richness full rein.

'The Nazz Are Blue' (Dreja, Beck, McCarty, Relf, Samwell-Smith) 3:15

The familiar *Roger The Engineer* power-riff comes harder and louder – 'gonna get myself a car, and I think I'll paint it blue, but no matter what's done to this baby, the Nazz are always blue' – with its sound density enhanced by the addition of Jeffrey Allen 'Skunk' Baxter, formerly of Steely Dan as well as The Doobie Brothers.

'For Your Love' (Graham Gouldman) 3:20

Another track from the *Reunion Jam* album, done more cleanly and studio-precise, it features an unexpected harmonica break, plus guitarist John Rzeznik of Goo Goo Dolls. Ken Allardyce had done studio engineering work on the Goo Goo Dolls' *Gutterflower* (2002) album.

'Please Don't Tell Me 'Bout The News' (James McCarty) 4:00
Vaguely exotic rhythms underlie a lyric concerning a scandal leak in the press about the mess the world is in, and the way it's reported through the news media, then about revelations of a more personal nature leaked on the local grapevine, leading into an intense instrumental jam propelled by nifty walking bass and harmonica.

'Train Kept A-Rollin'' (Howie Kay, Lois Mann, Tiny Bradshaw) 3:38
Slide-guitar locomotive effects feed into another take on The Yardbirds' classic track, featuring Joe Satriani, the versatile American rock guitarist with a string of successful albums under his own name, who also briefly played with Deep Purple.

'Mr Saboteur' (James McCarty) 4:55
He's always there, waiting behind the door. A well-constructed guitar-driven song that allows the question to hang: is he the urban terrorist or the hunt saboteur? Or maybe it's just the dark dog-day moods deep down inside that 'stops your inspiration and all your creation'?

'Shapes Of Things' (McCarty, Relf, Samwell-Smith) 2:38
Although this track sorely misses Keith Relf's anguished Cold War vocal, there's powerful compensation in an off-script guitar excursion from guesting Steve Vai, who started out playing in Frank Zappa's band but has also toured and recorded with the likes of David Lee Roth and Whitesnake.

'My Blind Life' (Chris Dreja) 3:33
This track features grinding blues guitar and growling vocals over powerful percussion from Simon McCarty. Lines such as 'knocking over chairs' and 'gonna take a fall' are used, maybe, as a metaphor, rather than a literal reference to blindness. The track was recorded in Sussex and features Jeff Beck. Seeing as Jeff had played on all the major Yardbirds singles – except 'For Your Love' – and on *Roger The Engineer* – their only studio album of original compositions – it's entirely appropriate that he returned to strengthen the revived lineup with his distinctive contribution. When Jeff succumbed to bacterial meningitis and died on 10 January 2023, Samwell-Smith said 'Jeff was *The* Yardbirds guitarist. Since his death, especially, I've been forced to realise just what he was to us.' Jimmy Page and Eric Clapton were pallbearers at his funeral.

'Over Under Sideways Down' (Dreja, Beck, McCarty, Relf, Samwell-Smith) 3:16
A faithful reimagining of the classic single that features Slash taking an extended fade-out solo, although the Guns 'n' Roses guitarist responsible for stone killers such as 'Paradise City' and 'Sweet Child Of Mine' falls just short of his usual incandescence. It's useful to compare and contrast this version

with Jimmy Page taking the original Jeff Beck role on The Yardbirds' frantic live recording taken from the 15 March 1967 Swedish *Beat! Beat! Beat!* show (collected on *Live In Stockholm & Offenbach*, 2018, Repertoire Records), which, according to *Mojo* writer Mark Blake, adds 'extra fire and drive to the previous summer's hit.'

'Mister, You're A Better Man Than I' (B & M Hugg) 3:22
Clear production values and loud-soft dynamics are evident here, with Brian May of Queen soaring into the mix. Brian famously played guitar on the top of Buckingham Palace, but he was equally keen to write himself into the history of The Yardbirds. It was always a startling song, and this is one of its better interpretations.

'Mystery Of Being' (James McCarty) 4:08
While the album artwork cleverly takes its cue from Chris Dreja's quirky artwork for *Roger The Engineer*, especially the bird shapes on the rear, keeping things in-house, McCarty's quasi-mystical song opens with the oriental sounds that thread their way through the track, with hints of eastern philosophy about 'the journey is the learning'. It succeeds in being both novel and well within the mainstream of Yardbirds tradition.

'Dream Within A Dream' (James McCarty) 4:44
With an opening strum that deliberately recalls 'For Your Love', the track develops at a slow and reflective pace, with a scintillating guitar solo. The lyrics are lifted to James' purpose from the Edgar Allan Poe 1849 poem of the same name, about the illusory nature of being, adapting Poe's 'take this kiss upon the brow, and, in parting from you now, thus much let me avow, you are not wrong who deem, that my days have been a dream.' This song was premiered on Jim's Pilgrim album *Gothic Dream* in 1996.

'Happenings Ten Years Time Ago' (Beck, McCarty, Page, Relf) 3:22
An accurate reconfiguring of events from future's past, complete with an echo of the submerged conversation beneath American Toto guitarist Steve Lukather's nimble fretwork. When I tell Jim McCarty that this was my favourite Yardbirds single, he tells me, 'Good – I like 'Happenings', too!'

'An Original Man (A Song For Keith)' (Dreja, Gypie Mayo, McCarty, John Idan) 5:21
With distinctive Dreja trip drum patterns and oriental guitar tuning, this tribute to 'a man I knew, died too young' has an affecting acoustic guitar sequence recalling Keith Relf's pastoral phase before descending into the kind of Gregorian chant familiar from 'Still I'm Sad'. A touchingly effective way of drawing Keith's spirit into the new Yardbirds incarnation and building a continuity bridge across the years.

The Second Live Album – Reunion Jam Vol. II

Personnel:
Rod Demick: bass
Jim McCarty: drums
Chris Dreja: guitar
John Idan: guitar, vocals
Mike Ober: producer
Released: 25 June 2007
Voiceprint VP417CD (UK) and Moorland Street Records (US)
No chart position.
Less a new album, more further outtakes from the '100 Club' recorded live in
London, 1992. Total playing time 45:41.

'Shapes Of Things' (Samwell-Smith, Relf, McCarty) 2:18
When he's being interviewed for *Mojo* in June 2024, 'at the time of writing,
lone Yardbird Jim McCarty, aged 80, is about to lead his modern-day version
of the group back on the road in America. 'It's about the songs,' he says
finally, 'and they are *still* great songs.' He's correct. This is still a great song.

'Over Under Sideways Down' (Dreja, McCarty, Beck, Relf, Samwell-
Smith) 2:46
A Yardbirds 'Consumers Guide' assembled by Charles Shaar Murray with Roy
Carr in the *NME* on 7 April 1973 points out that, on its first release 'by now,
Beck's personality really dominated the band. His guitar figure was derived
from Hungarian Czardas, while other passages revealed more than a mere
passing knowledge of Arabic music.' Well, maybe. Manager Simon Napier-Bell
later claimed that Keith Relf's original lyric 'Over under sideways down, that's
the best way I have found' was switched to 'Over under sideways cown,
backwards forwards square and round', anticipating that BBC censors might
object to the vaguely suggestive line!

'Gloria' (Van Morrison) 10:59
It has been said that every American garage band starts out by rehearsing to
the raw chord structure of the Van Morrison song that had started out as the
B-side of Them's first UK hit, 'Baby, Please Don't Go' in 1964. The song took on
new life when it was covered by The Shadows Of Knight and entered the
standard repertoire of US rock, to be ultimately remade and remodelled by Patti
Smith in 1975. The Yardbirds effectively take it back to its beat-group origins.

'Going Down' (Don Nix) 3:24
A hard guitar-led blues instrumental that had been recorded as a Bobby
Tench vocal on the fourth studio album by *The Jeff Beck Group* (UK Epic EPC
40-64899, USA Epic PE 31331). The Yardbirds take it raw and rauccus. 'Wanna
bit of rock 'n' roll?' yells John Idan at the close.

'Talkin' About You' (Chuck Berry) 3:01

The Yardbirds cut a 1:56 demo of this 1961 Chuck Berry single as early as *London 1963: The First Recordings!* (1981, L+R Records LR 44.001), which was taped at The Crawdaddy Club on 7 and 8 December 1963. The Beatles had done their version of the same song live on the BBC radio *Saturday Club* on 16 March 1963. It is not to be confused with the Ray Charles song 'Talkin' 'Bout You', which was covered by The Animals.

'Route 66' (Bobby Troup) 3:53

'It winds from Chicago to LA, more than two thousand miles all the way', and it's a great place to get your kicks.

'I Just Want To/Make Love To You' 3:32

There's an argument to be made that the new incarnation of The Yardbirds had traded in their earlier taut subtlety for a more muscular Dr Feelgood brand of r&b. But bands evolve as lineups change – it's inevitable.

'Hey Joe' (Dino Valenti) 4:39

The authorship may be disputed, although usually credited to Dino Valenti aka Chet Powers, but this is another primal garage-band staple, time-tested through versions by The Leaves, Love, Tim Rose, The Byrds and definitively by The Jimi Hendrix Experience. The Yardbirds mix and match from earlier blueprints to create a new mix very much of their own.

'Back Door Man' (Willie Dixon) 3:51

Recorded by Howlin' Wolf for Chess Records in 1960, this song had already been convincingly covered by The Doors, opening side two of their debut album.

'For Your Love' (Graham Gouldman) 3:32

For a band with such a limited discography of original albums, there have been a plethora of authorised compilations, as well as swathes of barely legal anthologies of rare and live Yardbirds material. An album – *Live At BB King Blues Club* (2007, Favoured Nations Entertainment FN2580-2) – digitally recorded from an XM broadcast in New York City on 19 July 2006, catches this late Yardbirds incarnation on fine form, with a blistering 3:27 version of 'For Your Love'.

'I'm A Man' (Ellas McDaniels aka Bo Diddley) 3:55

In *NME* on 3 March 1984, Charles Shaar Murray pointed out that 'in Muddy (Waters') 'Mannish Boy' or Bo's 'I'm A Man', the unspoken punchline to the title is 'I'm a man (don't EVER call me 'boy').' It's expressed through sexual braggadocio, but the sentiment was clear to any black radio or club audience of the time. Transplanted to the Marquee Club and sung by – say, Keith Relf of The Yardbirds – the song becomes 'I'm a man (you're a woman, get 'em off)'.' Well, maybe.

Afterword

Carrying the story over into the 2000s, Top Topham guested with the McCarty-Dreja Yardbirds, and then full-circled the legend by officially replacing Dreja in the lineup, when Chris was forced to quit due to medical complications. Topham's second stint as a Yardbird lasted until May 2015, when he was replaced by the American Johnny 'A' Antonopoulos, who toured and played with the band until July 2018. More recently, Jim McCarty and John Idan have continued with New Yorker Kenny Aaronson, who played with Foghat in 1983 (bass), American-born Myke Scavone, who played with Ram Jam on their 1977 hit 'Black Betty' (harmonica and percussion), and Godfrey Townsend (lead guitar and backing vocals).

But there were other links and ongoing continuities. After a period of 'spiritual development', Louis Cennamo joined Jim McCarty's side-project band Flip Side for a one-off return to Twickenham's Eel Pie Club on 3 April 2014 for a set drawing on their shared Renaissance and Illusion albums.

The Yardbirds' back-catalogue continues to be sought-after because – as we have seen – they were cool r&b cult. They were effortless art-school class. They were a contact-high of blissful nostalgia for mod anoraks. They were there at psychedelia's first Dayglo quivers. The Yardbirds were all this ... and yet they were also more.

Sources

Carson, A., *Jeff Beck: Crazy Fingers* (Backbeat Books, 2001)

Clayson, A., *The Yardbirds* (Backbeat Books, 2002)

Dreja, C., McCarty, J., Platt, J., *The Yardbirds* (Sidgwick & Jackson, 1983)
The cover subtitle 'The band that launched Eric Clapton, Jeff Beck, Jimmy
Page' is probably there more for marketing purposes than for strict accuracy.
This is the inside story.

French, D., *Heart Full Of Soul* (McFarland, 2020)
The first full-length biography of Keith Relf, with a foreword by Alice Cooper.
David has also published *Shapes Of Things: From The Yardbirds To Yusuf
With Paul Samwell-Smith* (ISBN 978-1304606-518), an edited series of
interviews with Paul covering his time with The Yardbirds through to his
extensive production career afterwards.

Mackay, R., Ober, M., *Over Under Sideways Down: Yardbirds World 2*
(Yardbirds World Publications, 1992)
Collected from back issues of the *Yardbirds World* fanzine, which guarantees
a degree of authentic scrupulous attention to minuscule detail.

McCarty, J., with Thompson, D., *Nobody Told Me!* (Lulu.com, 2018)
Subtitled 'My Life With The Yardbirds, Renaissance And Other Stories', with an
introduction by Jimmy Page.

Mojo, Issue 367 (June 2024)
Plus a multitude of features, reviews and press-cuttings from *New Musical
Express*, *Melody Maker*, *Record Mirror*, *Disc*, *Fabulous* and other sources, with
issues, dates and writers specified in the text wherever possible. Apologies
and thanks where sources have proved impossible to trace, and thanks to
those other contributors who prefer to remain anonymous.

Russo, G., *Yardbirds: The Ultimate Rave-Up* (Crossfire Publications, 2001)
This is the third edition.

Yardbirds World (Yardbirds World Publications, 1989)

On Track series

AC/DC – Chris Sutton 978-1-78952-307-2
Allman Brothers Band – Andrew Wild 978-1-78952-252-5
Tori Amos – Lisa Torem 978-1-78952-142-9
Aphex Twin – Beau Waddell 978-1-78952-267-9
Asia – Peter Braidis 978-1-78952-099-6
Badfinger – Robert Day-Webb 978-1-878952-176-4
Barclay James Harvest – Keith and Monica Domone 978-1-78952-067-5
Beck – Arthur Lizie 978-1-78952-258-7
The Beat, General Public, Fine Young Cannibals – Steve Parry 978-1-78952-274-7
The Beatles 1962-1996 – Alberto Bravin and Andrew Wild 978-1-78952-355-3
The Beatles Solo 1969-1980 – Andrew Wild 978-1-78952-030-9
Blue Oyster Cult – Jacob Holm-Lupo 978-1-78952-007-1
Blur – Matt Bishop 978-178952-164-1
Marc Bolan and T.Rex – Peter Gallagher 978-1-78952-124-5
David Bowie 1964 to 1982 – Carl Ewens 978-1-78952-324-9
David Bowie 1963 to 2016 – Don Klees 978-1-78952-351-5
Kate Bush – Bill Thomas 978-1-78952-097-2
The Byrds – Andy McArthur 978-1-78952-280-8
Camel – Hamish Kuzminski 978-1-78952-040-8
Captain Beefheart – Opher Goodwin 978-1-78952-235-8
Caravan – Andy Boot 978-1-78952-127-6
Cardiacs – Eric Benac 978-1-78952-131-3
Wendy Carlos – Mark Marrington 978-1-78952-331-7
The Carpenters – Paul Tornbohm 978-1-78952-301-0
Nick Cave and The Bad Seeds – Dominic Sanderson 978-1-78952-240-2
Eric Clapton Solo – Andrew Wild 978-1-78952-141-2
The Clash (revised edition) – Nick Assirati 978-1-78952-325-6
Elvis Costello and The Attractions – Georg Purvis 978-1-78952-129-0
Crosby, Stills and Nash – Andrew Wild 978-1-78952-039-2
Creedence Clearwater Revival – Tony Thompson 978-1-78952-237-2
Crowded House – Jon Magidsohn 978-1-78952-292-1
The Damned – Morgan Brown 978-1-78952-136-8
David Bowie 1964 to 1982 – Carl Ewens 978-1-78952-324-9
David Bowie 1964 to 1982 – Carl Ewens 978-1-78952-324-9
Deep Purple and Rainbow 1968-79 – Steve Pilkington 978-1-78952-002-6
Deep Purple from 1984 – Phil Kafcaloudes 978-1-78952-354-6
Depeche Mode – Brian J. Robb 978-1-78952-277-8
Dire Straits – Andrew Wild 978-1-78952-044-6
The Divine Comedy – Alan Draper 978-1-78952-308-9
The Doors – Tony Thompson 978-1-78952-137-5
Dream Theater – Jordan Blum 978-1-78952-050-7
Bob Dylan 1962-1970 – Opher Goodwin 978-1-78952-275-2
Eagles – John Van der Kiste 978-1-78952-260-0
Earth, Wind and Fire – Bud Wilkins 978-1-78952-272-3
Electric Light Orchestra – Barry Delve 978-1-78952-152-8
Emerson Lake and Palmer – Mike Goode 978-1-78952-000-2
Fairport Convention – Kevan Furbank 978-1-78952-051-4
Peter Gabriel – Graeme Scarfe 978-1-78952-138-2
Genesis – Stuart MacFarlane 978-1-78952-005-7
Gentle Giant – Gary Steel 978-1-78952-058-3
Gong – Kevan Furbank 978-1-78952-082-8
Green Day – William E. Spevack 978-1-78952-261-7
Steve Hackett – Geoffrey Feakes 978-1-78952-098-9
Hall and Oates – Ian Abrahams 978-1-78952-167-2
Peter Hammill – Richard Rees Jones 978-1-78952-163-4
Roy Harper – Opher Goodwin 978-1-78952-130-6
Hawkwind (new edition) – Duncan Harris 978-1-78952-290-7
Jimi Hendrix – Emma Stott 978-1-78952-175-7
The Hollies – Andrew Darlington 978-1-78952-159-7
Horslips – Richard James 978-1-78952-263-1
The Human League and The Sheffield Scene – Andrew Darlington 978-1-78952-186-3

Humble Pie –Robert Day-Webb 978-1-78952-2761
Ian Hunter – G. Mick Smith 978-1-78952-304-1
The Incredible String Band – Tim Moon 978-1-78952-107-8
INXS – Manny Grillo 978-1-78952-302-7
Iron Maiden – Steve Pilkington 978-1-78952-061-3
Joe Jackson – Richard James 978-1-78952-189-4
The Jam – Stan Jeffries 978-1-78952-299-0
Jefferson Airplane – Richard Butterworth 978-1-78952-143-6
Jethro Tull – Jordan Blum 978-1-78952-016-3
J. Geils Band – James Romag 978-1-78952-332-4
Elton John in the 1970s – Peter Kearns 978-1-78952-034-7
Billy Joel – Lisa Torem 978-1-78952-183-2
Journey – Doug Thornton 978-1-78952-337-9
Judas Priest – John Tucker 978-1-78952-018-7
Kansas – Kevin Cummings 978-1-78952-057-6
Killing Joke – Nic Ransome 978-1-78952-273-0
The Kinks – Martin Hutchinson 978-1-78952-172-6
Korn – Matt Karpe 978-1-78952-153-5
Led Zeppelin – Steve Pilkington 978-1-78952-151-1
Level 42 – Matt Philips 978-1-78952-102-3
Little Feat – Georg Purvis – 978-1-78952-168-9
Magnum – Matthew Taylor – 978-1-78952-286-0
Aimee Mann – Jez Rowden 978-1-78952-036-1
Ralph McTell – Paul O. Jenkins 978-1-78952-294-5
Metallica – Barry Wood 978-1-78952-269-3
Joni Mitchell – Peter Kearns 978-1-78952-081-1
The Moody Blues – Geoffrey Feakes 978-1-78952-042-2
Motorhead – Duncan Harris 978-1-78952-173-3
Nektar – Scott Meze – 978-1-78952-257-0
New Order – Dennis Remmer – 978-1-78952-249-5
Nightwish – Simon McMurdo – 978-1-78952-270-9
Nirvana – William E. Spevack 978-1-78952-318-8
Laura Nyro – Philip Ward 978-1-78952-182-5
Oasis – Andrew Rooney 978-1-78952-300-3
Phil Ochs – Opher Goodwin 978-1-78952-326-3
Mike Oldfield – Ryan Yard 978-1-78952-060-6
Opeth – Jordan Blum 978-1-78-952-166-5
Pearl Jam – Ben L. Connor 978-1-78952-188-7
Tom Petty – Richard James 978-1-78952-128-3
Pink Floyd – Richard Butterworth 978-1-78952-242-6
The Police – Pete Braidis 978-1-78952-158-0
Porcupine Tree (Revised Edition) – Nick Holmes 978-1-78952-346-1
Procol Harum – Scott Meze 978-1-78952-315-7
Queen – Andrew Wild 978-1-78952-003-3
Radiohead – William Allen 978-1-78952-149-8
Gerry Rafferty – John Van der Kiste 978-1-78952-349-2
Rancid – Paul Matts 978-1-78952-187-0
Lou Reed 1972-1986 – Ethan Roy 978-1-78952-283-9
Renaissance – David Detmer 978-1-78952-062-0
REO Speedwagon – Jim Romag 978-1-78952-262-4
The Rolling Stones 1963-80 – Steve Pilkington 978-1-78952-017-0
Linda Ronstadt 1969-1989 – Daryl O. Lawrence 987-1-78952-293-8
Roxy Music – Michael Kulikowski 978-1-78952-335-5
Rush 1973 to 1982 – Richard James 978-1-78952-338-6
Sensational Alex Harvey Band – Peter Gallagher 978-1-7952-289-1
The Small Faces and The Faces – Andrew Darlington 978-1-78952-316-4
The Smashing Pumpkins – Matt Karpe 978-1-7952-291-4
The Smiths and Morrissey – Tommy Gunnarsson 978-1-78952-140-5
Soft Machine – Scott Meze 978-1078952-271-6
Sparks 1969-1979 – Chris Sutton 978-1-78952-279-2
Spirit – Rev. Keith A. Gordon – 978-1-78952- 248-8
Stackridge – Alan Draper 978-1-78952-232-7
Status Quo the Frantic Four Years – Richard James 978-1-78952-160-3
Steely Dan – Jez Rowden 978-1-78952-043-9

The Stranglers – Martin Hutchinson 978-1-78952-323-2
Talk Talk – Gary Steel 978-1-78952-284-6
Talking Heads – David Starkey 978-178952-353-9
Tears For Fears – Paul Clark – 978-178952-238-9
Thin Lizzy – Graeme Stroud 978-1-78952-064-4
Tool – Matt Karpe 978-1-78952-234-1
Toto – Jacob Holm-Lupo 978-1-78952-019-4
U2 – Eoghan Lyng 978-1-78952-078-1
UFO – Richard James 978-1-78952-073-6
Ultravox – Brian J. Robb 978-1-78952-330-0
Van Der Graaf Generator – Dan Coffey 978-1-78952-031-6
Van Halen – Morgan Brown – 9781-78952-256-3
Suzanne Vega – Lisa Torem 978-1-78952-281-5
Jack White And The White Stripes – Ben L. Connor
978-1-78952-303-4
The Who – Geoffrey Feakes 978-1-78952-076-7
Roy Wood and the Move – James R Turner 978-1-78952-008-8
Yes (new edition) – Stephen Lambe 978-1-78952-282-2
Neil Young 1963 to 1970 – Oper Goodwin 978-1-78952-298-3
Frank Zappa 1966 to 1979 – Eric Benac 978-1-78952-033-0
Warren Zevon – Peter Gallagher 978-1-78952-170-2
The Zombies – Emma Stott 978-1-78952-297-6
10CC – Peter Kearns 978-1-78952-054-5

Decades Series

The Bee Gees in the 1960s – Andrew Mon Hughes et al
978-1-78952-148-1
The Bee Gees in the 1970s – Andrew Mon Hughes et al
978-1-78952-179-5
Black Sabbath in the 1970s – Chris Sutton 978-1-78952-171-9
Britpop – Peter Richard Adams and Matt Pooler
978-1-78952-169-6
Phil Collins in the 1980s – Andrew Wild 978-1-78952-185-6
Alice Cooper in the 1970s – Chris Sutton 978-1-78952-104-7
Alice Cooper in the 1980s – Chris Sutton 978-1-78952-259-4
Curved Air in the 1970s – Laura Shenton 978-1-78952-069-9
Donovan in the 1960s – Jeff Fitzgerald 978-1-78952-233-4
Bob Dylan in the 1980s – Don Klees 978-1-78952-157-3
Brian Eno in the 1970s – Gary Parsons 978-1-78952-239-6
Faith No More in the 1990s – Matt Karpe 978-1-78952-250-1
Fleetwood Mac in the 1970s – Andrew Wild
978-1-78952-105-4
Fleetwood Mac in the 1980s – Don Klees 978-178952-254-9
Focus in the 1970s – Stephen Lambe 978-1-78952-079-8
Free and Bad Company in the 1970s – John Van der Kiste
978-1-78952-178-8
Genesis in the 1970s – Bill Thomas 978178952-146-7
George Harrison in the 1970s – Eoghan Lyng
978-1-78952-174-0
Kiss in the 1970s – Peter Gallagher 978-1-78952-246-4
Manfred Mann's Earth Band in the 1970s –
John Van der Kiste 978178952-243-3
Marillion in the 1980s – Nathaniel Webb 978-1-78952-065-1
Van Morrison in the 1970s – Peter Childs –
978-1-78952-241-9
Mott the Hoople & Ian Hunter in the 1970s –
John Van der Kiste 978-1-78-952-162-7
Pink Floyd In The 1970s – Georg Purvis 978-1-78952-072-9
Suzi Quatro in the 1970s – Darren Johnson
978-1-78952-236-5
Queen in the 1970s – James Griffiths 978-1-78952-265-5
Roxy Music in the 1970s – Dave Thompson
978-1-78952-180-1
Slade in the 1970s – Darren Johnson 978-1-78952-268-6
Status Quo in the 1980s – Greg Harper 978-1-78952-244-0
Tangerine Dream in the 1970s – Stephen Palmer
978-1-78952-161-0
The Sweet in the 1970s – Darren Johnson 978-1-78952-139-9
Uriah Heep in the 1970s – Steve Pilkington 978-1-78952-103-0
Van der Graaf Generator in the 1970s – Steve Pilkington
978-1-78952-245-7

Rick Wakeman in the 1970s – Geoffrey Feakes
978-1-78952-264-8
Yes in the 1980s – Stephen Lambe with David Watkinson
978-1-78952-125-2

Rock Classics Series

90125 by Yes – Stephen Lambe 978-1-78952-329-4
Bat Out Of Hell by Meatloaf – Geoffrey Feakes 978-1-78952-320-1
Bringing It All Back Home by Bob Dylan – Opher Goodwin
978-1-78952-314-0
Californication by Red Hot Chili Peppers - Matt Karpe
978-1-78952-348-5
Crime Of The Century by Supertramp – Steve Pilkington
978-1-78952-327-0
The Dreaming by Kate Bush – Peter Kearns
978-1-78952-341-6
Let It Bleed by The Rolling Stones – John Van der Kiste
978-1-78952-309-6
Pawn Hearts by Van Der Graaf Generator – Paolo Carnelli
978-1-78952-357-7
Purple Rain by Prince – Matt Karpe 978-1-78952-322-5
The White Album by The Beatles – Opher Goodwin
978-1-78952-333-1

Other Books

1967: A Year In Psychedelic Rock 978-1-78952-155-9
1970: A Year In Rock – John Van der Kiste 978-1-78952-147-4
1972: The Year Progressive Rock Ruled The World –
Kevan Furbank 978-1-78952-288-4
1973: The Golden Year of Progressive Rock
978-1-78952-165-8
Eric Clapton Sessions – Andrew Wild 978-1-78952-177-1
Dark Horse Records – Aaron Badgley 978 1-78952-237-7
Derek Taylor: For Your Radioactive Children –
Andrew Darlington 978-1-78952-038-5
Ghosts – Journeys To Post-Pop – Matthew Restall
978-1-78952-334-8
The Golden Age of Easy Listening – Derek Taylor
978-1-78952-285-3
The Golden Road: The Recording History of The Grateful
Dead – John Kilbride 978-1-78952-156-6
Hoggin' The Page – Groudhogs The Classic Years –
Martyn Hanson 978-1-78952-343-0
Iggy and The Stooges On Stage 1967-1974 – Per Nilsen
978-1-78952-101-6
Jon Anderson and the Warriors – the Road to Yes –
David Watkinson 978-1-78952-059-0
Magic: The David Paton Story – David Paton
978-1-78952-266-2
Misty: The Music of Johnny Mathis – Jakob Baekgaard
978-1-78952-247-1
Musical Guide To Red By King Crimson – Andrew Keeling
978-1-78952-321-8
Nu Metal: A Definitive Guide – Matt Karpe 978-1-78952-063-7
Philip Lynott – Renegade – Alan Byrne 978-1-78952-339-3
Remembering Live Aid – Andrew Wild 978-1-78952-328-7
Thank You For The Days - Fans Of The Kinks Share 60 Years
of Stories – Ed. Chris Kocher 978-1-78952-342-3
The Sonicbond On Track Sampler – 978-1-78952-190-0
The Sonicbond Progressive Rock Sampler (Ebook only) –
978-1-78952-056-9
Tommy Bolin: In and Out of Deep Purple – Laura Shenton
978-1-78952-070-5
Maximum Darkness – Deke Leonard 978-1-78952-043-4
The Twang Dynasty – Deke Leonard 978-1-78952-049-1

... and many more to come

Would you like to write for Sonicbond Publishing?

We are mainly a music publisher, but we also occasionally publish in other genres including film and television. At Sonicbond Publishing we are always on the look-out for authors, particularly for our two main series, On Track and Decades.

Mixing fact with in depth analysis, the On Track series examines the entire recorded work of a particular musical artist or group. All genres are considered from easy listening and jazz to 60s soul to 90s pop, via rock and metal.

The Decades series singles out a particular decade in an artist or group's history and focuses on that decade in more detail than may be allowed in the On Track series.

While professional writing experience would, of course, be an advantage, the most important qualification is to have real enthusiasm and knowledge of your subject. First-time authors are welcomed, but the ability to write well in English is essential.

Sonicbond Publishing has distribution throughout Europe and North America, and all our books are also published in E-book form. Authors will be paid a royalty based on sales of their book. Further details about our books are available from www.sonicbondpublishing.com. To contact us, complete the contact form there or email info@sonicbondpublishing.co.uk